Fighting the Lamb's War

Skirmishes with the American Empire

The Autobiography of Philip Berrigan

WITH

Fred A. Wilcox

Common Courage Press

MONROE, MAINE

First printing

Common Courage Press
Box 702
Monroe, Maine 04951
Phone: (207) 525-0900
Fax: (207) 525-3068

Typeset by Strong Silent Type, Madison, Wisconsin
Cover Design by Matt Wuerker

Library of Congress Cataloging-In-Publication Data

Berrigan, Philip.
    Fighting the lamb's war: skirmishes with the American Empire:
the autobiography of Philip Berrigan / with Fred A. Wilcox. -- 1st ed.
        p.   cm.
    Includes index.
    ISBN 1-56751-100-7 (alk. paper). -- ISBN 1-56751-101-5
    1. Berrigan, Philip. 2. Catholic Church--United States--Clergy--
Biography.   3. Peace movements--United States--Biography.   4. Political
activists--United States--Biography.   I. Wilcox, Fred.   II. Title.
BX4705.B3846A3   1996
322.4'4'092--dc20
[B]   96-7940
                                                                        CIP

Contents

"But I say to you, offer no violent resistance to one who is evil. When someone strikes you on the right cheek, turn the other one to him as well. If anyone wants to go to law with you over your tunic, hand him your cloak as well."

—Matthew 5:39–40

INTRODUCTION

When Common Courage Press sent me an advance copy of *Fighting the Lamb's War: Skirmishes with the American Empire*, I read it straight through with hardly a pause for dinner. And while expecting only the best from my friend and fellow non-violent activist Philip Francis Berrigan, I was amazed at the profound effect this book would have on me. Transported back to the turbulent sixties, I experienced the civil-rights movement, the struggle against the war in Vietnam, and the effort to bring an end to nuclear madness. I felt the sting of tear gas, heard the hollow thump of a policeman's club, and stood before judges who condemned anti-war resisters to jail for opposing the government's genocidal policies in Southeast Asia.

Readers will find no posturing or self-serving narcissism in this book. With modesty and at times painful self-criticism, Berrigan writes that he was an enthusiastic killer in World War II. We see him marching home as "Philip the Bold", the toughest Irish-American kid on the block, a proud participant in mass slaughter. We follow him to New Orleans where he teaches in an all-black high school and struggles with his own and his fellow Catholics' racism. We hear him accuse his brother Daniel of being a grandstander and "dime store liberal", and we applaud his extraordinary honesty when he confides that he himself has acted like a tyrant, driving people from Jonah House, the community in which he, his wife Elizabeth McAlister, and their three children have lived for more than two decades.

Fighting the Lamb's War is far more than the story of a courageous and truly great American. Philip Berrigan challenges us to probe our hearts and minds, asking not only what it means to be a Catholic, a Protestant, or a Jew, but what it means to be human. He forces us to take a hard critical look at spending more than 260 billion on the military while our schools deteriorate, our streets are crowded with homeless families, and one out of five American children lives in poverty. He challenges us to ask whether declaring war on the poor will make our streets safer; whether destroying the lives of millions of welfare recipients will provide job security for workers; whether executing men and women will teach our children respect for human life.

Philip Berrigan describes himself as a Catholic trying to become a Christian. His witness is a powerful inspiration to people throughout the world who are searching for an alternative to violence. "We must learn to love one another or die", wrote W.H. Auden. That was the message of Jesus Christ, who was among the greatest nonviolent revolutionaries the world has ever known. Philip Berrigan is a revolutionary whose weapon is nonviolent resistance, rather than guns and bullets. Without doubt, he has established his place in history. I consider it an honor and a privilege to have been his friend these many years. And I can't thank him enough for sharing his life's story. Now, more than ever before, the world needs Philip Berrigan's vision, his courage, and his commitment to peace and social justice.

—David Dellinger

Philip and Frida Berrigan, 1929.

❦

ONE

Wordsworth and a Few Good Fists

Pop is singing, one hand held over his heart, his audience crowded together on a ratty couch. One of his eyes is swollen and the cut on his lip looks rather nasty, but not to worry. Just another free-for-all with one of his sons. Now he stands there singing, and we can almost smell the turf fire, hear it bubbling on the hearth. A gale pounds over our roof, the ocean roars. Connemara mountains, their summits haloed in mist, rise out of our shabby carpet. We climb Croagh Patrick in our bare feet, dig turf from bogs, kneel before Celtic crosses, their inscriptions washed smooth by time. We have never set foot in Ireland, except in books, but we can see and feel all these things when our father commences to sing. Romantic ballads, teasing ditties, rousing calls to battle; sometimes, just plain silly tunes.

Tom Berrigan is a highly emotional man, blessed with some of the best qualities of his Gaelic ancestors, cursed with some of their fatal weaknesses. He is egotistical and melodramatic. A haughty dreamer, and a jovial tyrant. Generous to a fault, often making small "loans" to friends and fellow workers, knowing he will never be repaid. A character straight out of John Synge, James Joyce, or Brendan Behan. Tormented by the belief that he is an unrecognized heroic figure living in a world too stupid, or just too mean-spirited, to acknowledge his great gift. He likes his whiskey at social gatherings, but he's not a heavy drinker.

Pop is a great man for reciting poetry, spouting reams of Shakespeare, Wordsworth, Keats, and Shelley—all at one standing. He loves Shelley's work, and seems to identify with the drama of Percy B.'s life.

My brothers and I sit knee-to-knee in the living room, daydreaming and falling asleep, pretending to listen while he rattles on. Our father hopes that his sons will become writers, or "literati," as he calls himself, but he has no luck getting published, even when he gives his work over to priests, asking them to critique it, and to send it to editors. His poems are highly romantic, utterly incomprehensible and, for the most part, doggerel. His similes and metaphors flop and his figures of speech don't work.

After the singing I lie in bed, listening to my parents quarrel. They fight over how to raise their children—six boys, no girls. They fight over money, and over my father's family, who treat Frida Berrigan with condescension and even contempt. We wait for a truce, some resolution, but no one ever wins these battles. Frida and Tom simply retire to their corners, licking their wounds, waiting for the next round.

Tom Berrigan's mood changes are unpredictable. Sun and cheer in the morning, thunder and lightning by noon. If we are lucky, a rainbow by supper time. We never know when the next row might erupt. He creates a climate of fear, a storm beneath the surface of things. We adjust, discover ways to survive, and profit from this unhappy upbringing.

Frida stands up to our father. She shows us the meaning of courage, and she teaches us how to handle our fears.

Pop is a radical socialist and a labor organizer, an Irish-American with fire in his blood, a great love for poetry, and a quick pair of fists. His parents tried farming in Iowa, and when that didn't work they returned East, settling near Nedrow, New York, just south of Syracuse. They were upwardly mobile "lace-curtain" Irish. One of his sisters became a high school teacher, another a nurse, and still another a Catholic nun. One was secretary to a U.S. Senator. His brother was a priest. My father, and his brother John, are the only ones who failed to become professionals.

Pop's family thinks he married "down"; that Frida is beneath him. Nothing could be farther from the truth. She is far superior to him.

She is balanced, has more common sense, better judgment, and is emotionally stronger. She has few friends in Syracuse with whom she can speak German, and perhaps talk about her life. But her real support comes from her children, especially Dan who is always very close to our mother. When my brothers and I go out to the field to work with our father, Dan stays at home to help Frida. She always has an enormous amount to do—laundry, cooking, cleaning.

Tom Berrigan expects hardship. Nothing, he says, is ever given. Every gain for working people must be bought with sweat, blood, and tears. For decades, American workers have walked out, gone on strike, fought back against economic exploitation. Their families often go hungry, their children die from disease and malnutrition, militias fire on them when they are on strike. Determined to destroy labor unions, employers hire gun-toting thugs to attack and to kill organizers. Workers are forced to sign contracts, agreeing never to join a union.

Pop tells the bosses to go to hell. He isn't afraid of them, and he isn't afraid of their hired guns, who might win a bonus for killing a man like him. He is fired and blacklisted for his union activities.

Frida tries her best to protect her children from her impetuous, hot-tempered husband. He suffers from bouts of depression, and he believes that Frida is indulging his children. We have so little, yet Pop insists that we are being given too much. He accuses our mother of dressing us up like "little Lord Fauntleroys," and of not preparing us for life in the real dog-eat-dog world. In fact, she is teaching us compassion for our fellow human beings. She is *showing* us the meaning of love.

We watch our parents closely, and our mother is consistent, dependable, her behavior irreproachable. She holds their marriage together and it is rough going, mostly because of our father. Things are so bad at one point—Tom is depressed, wrathful, particularly nasty—that Frida visits his brother, a diocesan priest, to ask about a trial separation. He advises against it, urging her instead to return home and work it out. My mother is desperate enough to consider taking her children and leaving, though she has no idea where to go.

Thomas Berrigan wants his way, and often fights to get it, insisting that Frida knows little or nothing about raising children, accusing her of sheltering, spoiling, mollycoddling us. He wants to raise us according to his own uncompromising ideas, projections of himself, really. We are boys, and boys must be turned into real men. Hardened for a world in which life is nasty, brutish, and short. We must learn to work with our hands. We must be good with tools. We should develop our minds, but never be afraid to use our fists. We should work hard on our studies, play contact sports, hang tough, act macho.

My brothers and I start working when we are five years old. Hot, sweat-sticky, tiring chores like forking hay into the loft, hoeing the corn, cultivating the truck garden, picking fruit, gathering berries. Pop maps out the tasks every morning; he will raise holy hell if the work is undone when he arrives home from work. My older brothers are left in charge, and they try to coerce Dan and myself, sometimes Jerry, to help bring in the hay or cultivate the corn. But we dig in our heels. We refuse, and this starts fights.

Pop is a hard driver, can't stand excuses, and detests slackers. He works, you work, we work. The only people who can afford not to work, says Pop, are the rich. And they work real hard at making sure that they keep getting richer, while the working man stays poor. We get up at dawn, and we sweat it out together, because there simply is no other choice.

Pop plays favorites. He loves Tom, his oldest son, more than any of us. They are very much alike, and I think that will affect Tom all his life. My father is a farmer, Tom will become a farmer. My father loves the railroad, Tom loves the railroad. My father is a man's man, Tom will go off to war, storming into Normandy with the 29th Infantry, fighting his way across Europe. On the other hand, Pop rejects John, who will drink heavily, suffer from bouts of depression, and brood all his life. Pop also rejects Dan, who refuses to come to heel. He is physically weak, and to Pop that means he is weak in other ways. I think our father more or less accepts me because I am a big strong kid who helps him around the farm.

The Sisters of Charity run an orphanage on Court Street in Syracuse, and they own a small farm near Liverpool where we live rent free as caretakers, struggling to put food on the table, and to keep a roof over our heads. My father grew up on a farm, and he decides to plow and plant the sisters' acreage so that his own sons will learn to work the land. The plowing must be done in the spring, and just at the right time or the clay soil will fuse into huge unwieldy clumps. Rain or shine we are out there together, smashing our shovels into those sticky clumps, breaking them, and our backs, at the same time. We keep two or three milk cows, raise hay for them, and corn for our hogs. We are lucky, because living in the country and rais- ing our own food helps us get through some of the hungriest years of the Great Depression.

We are taught a rather simple code of morality and honor and ethics. No one helps me reason that people shouldn't strike or beat or kill others. We live near a Sicilian neighborhood, and those Ital- ian kids are tough, but John doesn't care. He will fight them after school, then come home and fight with our father. When Pop gets too abrasive with our mother, John jumps between them, threaten- ing to knock Pop down.

I am getting ready to go to school when Pop comes downstairs. His face is covered with cuts and bruises, and I ask him what hap- pened. "Well," he says, and he is perfectly balanced, not angry at all, "I had a fight with one of your older brothers, and he punched me." That is the end of it. He is almost decent to live with for a week.

I won't get struck by a bolt of nonviolent lightning. I won't fall off my donkey, or my bicycle, only to rise in a cloud of light. After I go to prison for the first time I will read Henry David Thoreau, and study Gandhi's nonviolent campaign to drive the British out of India. In time, I will become a great admirer of Martin Luther King, meet and become close friends with Dorothy Day, David Dellinger, A.J. Muste, and other pacifists. I will also be inspired by Thomas Merton, a man who struggled with, and managed to work through, many of his own demons.

Frida and Tom Berrigan care nothing about wealth or material things, and these qualities deeply impress their children. Tom and Frida read the rather traditional Catholic magazines, *America* and *Commonweal,* but they also subscribe to the *Catholic Worker,* which critiques capitalism, racism, materialism, and offers a radical vision of Catholicism. My parents and their friends discuss these ideas. Week after week, Frida brings great bags of books home from the library. Like lion cubs waiting for the kill, we devour those books, then call for more. There are no couch potatoes in Tom and Frida's home. We are encouraged to read and to read. During the worst years of the Great Depression, when our family has little or nothing, we share that *virtual nothing* with the homeless, with our poor neighbors, and with other friends and their children. At times, we have only cornmeal to eat; if we are lucky we eat it three times a day. We don't go hungry, though we aren't very well fed. We share berries, milk, fruit, and vegetables, even giving slabs of pork from our slaughtered hogs.

Our mother just can't turn those itinerant men away when they come to our door looking for a handout.

There is no unemployment insurance, no aid to dependent children, no public assistance. People lose their homes or farms, go hungry, get sick, and die. Millions of unemployed men and women hop freight trains, criss-crossing the country trying to find work, willing to take any kind of job no matter how low-paying, dangerous, or degrading. They live in "Hoovervilles," clusters of tarpaper shacks named after the original proponent of "trickle-down" economics. Herbert Hoover's motto: "What's good for business is good for America." Helping the poor, said Hoover, would destroy America's "get-up-and-go."

When hungry men and women come to our door, my mother invites them in, sits them at the table, makes them welcome. It doesn't matter how little we might have, everyone at the table is served the same amount.

Christ divided a few loaves of bread to feed the multitudes. He instructed His followers to feed, not starve, the hungry. He told us to clothe, not to abuse the naked. To house, not to persecute, the homeless. My mother doesn't preach the gospels, she practices their meaning—even if that means her own children might have less to eat, even if that means that we break bread with ragged, dirty, sometimes smelly, strangers.

Frida Berrigan shields people from the law, giving the authorities false information, deliberately leading them away from their prey. She knows that the only crime these men have committed is standing up for their rights as workers, or stealing a little food for their families. My mother, a devout Catholic, understands that poverty is a misfortune, not a genetic weakness, and not a crime.

Now and again the police come to our door. They don't really frighten me, because I have no idea what they stand for, or why they come. I respect authority, overwhelmingly. At the same time, I have no idea of how the police undermine democracy and justice. Nor do I know, yet, that the state is the enemy, not the champion, of ordinary people. Much later I will learn through hard experience that laws are written to protect power and privilege; not to make life more secure for people like Thomas and Frida Berrigan.

Everyone knows my parents are hardworking people and devout Catholics who do their best to support our parish. So the nuns never treat us unkindly, or unfairly, just because we are a little ragged. There are kids at St. John's school who are in worse straits than we. And, further in our favor, there is no movement (organized by neo-fascists masquerading as patriotic budget balancers) to blame poor people for our nation's social, political, and economic crisis. No one looks down on me in school because I am poor. My mother is very skilled with a sewing machine. She buys cloth from a downtown department store, and creates good, warm, well-made clothes, even overcoats. These clothes will be handed down from child to child, a great source of shame for my brothers and me. Sometimes I rebel, refusing to wear clothes that had belonged to older brothers.

My brothers go to work for a dollar a day, pulling weeds and digging vegetables on truck-garden farms. Tom Jr. hires out to farmers all over the Central New York area, always reserving a portion of his monthly wage for the family. After Roosevelt's election in 1932, Jim and John join the Civilian Conservation Corps (CCC). They live in barracks and go out to work building roads, parks, and golf courses. They never fail to share their salaries with our family. Jerry, too, is diligent and generous; he works for Niagara Mohawk Power Company. When the the United States declares war on Japan, he joins the Air Force.

The nuns who befriend and teach us have a profound and nurturing influence on my brothers and myself. One Italian-American nun is quick to slap us in the face, but there are others, like the nearly blind Sister Mary Lua. She is a kind and wonderful 7th-grade teacher, and a great influence on myself, Daniel, and Jerry.

Years later, Pop will support us when we go to prison. He knows that American workers have been beaten, jailed, and murdered for demanding better working conditions. He knows who rules America, and it is definitely not the people. He is proud of his sons when they fight against the Nazis; proud of them, years later, when they are sentenced to spend years in the penitentiary.

Our parish in Syracuse is St. John the Baptist. We go to school there and all except Tom graduate. Tom drops out after the tenth grade. Jim and I play basketball in high school, and I also play baseball, making the Parochial League all-star team in senior year. I love sports and am not afraid to fight, particularly when someone rides hard on Daniel, who is small for his age. I am also a rather quiet, very inward-looking teenager, quite shy, and slow to speak up, more inclined to listening. Not because I am altruistic or because I understand that it's sometimes better to listen than to speak. Not at all. I am just afraid someone will laugh at me, or mock what I have to say. I am afraid of being misunderstood. Around women, I am positively tongue-tied, hardly able to utter so much as a squeak. In this ethical climate, boys learn to fear women.

I do have a couple of crushes in high school, one on a very pretty cheerleader; but it just never occurs to me to fall in love. Other students talk about getting married, settling down, having a family. I'm not sure why I don't think that way. Nor will I ever consider becoming a priest until after I return from the war.

My outlook as a student is just very limited. I have no great "ear" for the world around me. Pop is business agent for the first Electrical Workers Union in Syracuse, and he lobbies for the rights of African-Americans long before there is a civil rights movement, but I am not especially interested in his union activities. He is too erratic in his views, loving Franklin Roosevelt when he is first elected, hating him with a passion just a few years later. We never derive much clarity from him, and we are neutral, indifferent, or perhaps unconsciously solid advocates of the system. I go to school every day, do my homework, do what I am told. Like most students, I learn by rote, swallowing propaganda, and in examinations regurgitating nonsense and half-truths. Our textbooks reflect the grandeur and glory of our country's past, thrilling us with stories of our forefathers' conquests over savage peoples, with tales of their heroism in battle, their triumphs over a hundred enemies. A world where good (white European males) always triumphs over evil (anyone else). Our teachers don't talk about the Robber Barons—John D. Rockefeller, J.P. Morgan, Andrew Mellon, Billy Vanderbilt, et al. They don't tell us how they lied, cheated, and pillaged, building their empires on the backs of immigrant labor. We don't learn about the stock manipulation and scam-artist money deals that sent the stock market crashing in 1929, destroying the lives of farmers and factory workers, driving millions into poverty, hunger, and early death. We are never told that 50 to 100 million Africans perished in the holds of slave ships, or that George Washington, Thomas Jefferson, and other American heroes owned slaves. No one tells us how our Native American brothers and sisters were massacred, starved, and poisoned into submission. We aren't told why our country went to war in 1917, or why we have been fighting someone, somewhere, for something, ever since the War of Independence.

I cannot blame those priests and nuns, because they are passing down to us what they learned; what they believe to be true; what they think everyone has always known. Only after I come home from the war will I learn that we were firing on Japanese shipping *before* the attack on Pearl Harbor, and that American tycoons were worried about the expanding Japanese Empire, which was threatening our hegemony in the Pacific. It was inevitable that we would go to war against Japan.

Only much later, after I have killed other human beings, will I find out that World War II was not about saving Jews from Nazi extermination, any more than the Civil War was about liberating slaves. Hitler invaded Austria, stomped through Czechoslovakia, slaughtered his way across Poland. We watched. His brownshirts killed Jews, socialists, homosexuals, and communists. We stood by. I know none of this when I am drafted in 1943. I just accept that the insidious Japanese and Germans have stabbed Uncle Sam in the back, and need to be defeated, even destroyed.

Soon after I start college my draft notice arrives. I am 19 years old, and excited to be following my older brothers into battle, anxious to slaughter infidels and to return home bearing the standard of peace and justice. It never occurs to me to remain in Canada where

I'm attending St. Michael's college. Not for a moment do I consider resisting the draft, or offering to do alternative service. (It doesn't occur to me that anyone would object to going to war.) Long ago, my brain, my heart, and my soul have been scrubbed clean of all doubt. My decision is a simple one. I return to Syracuse where I become a proud, enthusiastic soldier in the United States army.

I DELIVERED THIS HOMILY AT FRIDA BERRIGAN'S FUNERAL, DECEMBER 24, 1976.

Sisters and Brothers,

I judge this an occasion to share our joy and gratitude with you. For God has released our mother from the quiet battle which distinguishes life. And for this, we have nothing but thanks.

I sense my incapacity—or the incapacity of anyone—to appraise a life like Frida's. In such a life, one can only explore the mystery of themes, of meanings and markings. And then strive to remember, to learn and grow up.

Jerry and I were privileged to witness her death at 6:20 p.m. on Thursday. It was a death woven from her life; she struggled to breathe quietly and steadfastly, as she had lived for nearly 91 years, quietly and steadfastly. And when she could struggle no longer, when her exhaustion became final, she stopped breathing, giving herself over to that "King for whom all live," as the Office for All Souls calls God—then to begin in Him, resurrection and life.

Since witnessing the peace which attended her death, and the credentials of struggle marking her wasted body, I have thought of Christ's appearance to the disciples on the first Easter: "Jesus came and stood in their midst and said to them, Peace be to you! and when He said this, He showed them his hands and his side." (John 20:19). Which is to say, He traced the connection between peace and the cross; between peace, and suffering endured for others. I began to understand the old biblical axiom that there is no reconciliation without bloodshed—no reconciliation without an offering for others. His peace was indistinguishable from his wounds. In fact, He could only offer peace because He first gave himself as ransom for all.

A central Old Testament theme has it that no one knows God until one knows injustice. And—the prophets were careful to stress—one knows nothing about injustice until one struggles against it. Today, knowledge of God means struggling against the bombing of the innocent, against victimizing the weak, against the put-down of women and blacks, against the imperilment of everyone by atomic wrath. Struggle against these and you will know injustice; struggle against these and you will know God. So would prophecy remind us today.

It seemed that Frida knew God. The signs of struggle were striking at that last vigil. Emaciated and depleted, she literally had nothing left to give at death—as though work, life, service, vocation, were all complete. I remembered the way she mysteriously controlled and paced her life during these last years—staying alive because she sensed we needed her. Needed her certainly during the Indochina war, but even more since, when Americans grew silent before the humiliation of their country at the hands of politicians, generals, and arms hucksters. Needed her spirit of prayer, her humility before encroaching weakness; needed the resistance which had revolutionized her own spirit and life.

She was, I conclude, a sister and mother to us all—and teacher as well. And as the nuclear weapons race, led by our country, mounts to insane heights; as nuclear proliferation careens out of control; as humanity arms for a convulsion of mass suicide—she reminds us of the Child at Bethlehem, of his Cross at Calvary, of Him who offered us peace at the price of wounded hands and side.

We will remember her as Elizabeth, Jerry, Dan, and I go back to the War Department (the Pentagon) for the nth resistance, the nth arrest, the nth brush with federal courts and jails. For without remembering her, we would tend to forget the victims—which under the declared policy of our government's "counterforce," are all of us. And forgetting the victims would be to forget God, his Christ, whether at Bethlehem or in the Upper Room.

We of the family wish you her memory—which is to say, her peace and her life. We wish you the same breath—the Lord's last gift to us— His peace and His wounds. Have a blessed Christmas!

Philip in uniform, Camp Gordon, Georgia, June 1943.

TWO

Worlds On Fire:
Fighting in World War II

"There is no religion, no god in war. No leader, shaman, priest, philosopher, poet, or prophet who can stand up in the middle of withering enemy fire, raise his hand and give meaning or heal the slaughter. He will go down. He will go down screaming 'Corpsman! Corpsman!' just like everybody else. There are no masks you can wear in war."

WILLIAM CRAPSER
Remains

Before I left for basic training, my brother invited me to visit the Jesuit Novitiate in Poughkeepsie. Daniel wanted me to think a little harder about going to war, and he arranged for me to take a four-day retreat at St. Andrews. The rector provided me the exercises of St. Ignatius, and I walked alone, praying for guidance, trying to decide what to do. Should I ask for a deferment from military service? Should I agree to enter the seminary, and begin to study for the priesthood? What did God have in mind for me? I didn't really want to be a priest, and I longed to join my older brothers at the battlefront. I wanted to join the hunt for Adolf Hitler, to hack him into pieces, and to count the demons as they flew out of his wounds. I wanted to charge pillboxes, blow up machine gun nests, and fight hand-to-hand with my country's enemies. I was 19 years old. Willing, and most able, to be a warrior.

I hugged Dan goodbye, thanked the Jesuit fathers for their kindness, and saw my parents one more time before boarding a train for Camp Gordon. There were no bands or cheering crowds. No rousing speeches or rhetorical binges. Our parting was quiet, loving, gracious, and altogether devoid of drama. As young men had been doing for centuries, I rode off to slay the enemy. A tough and rather cocky kid, striding toward the valley of death. Never imagining, for one moment, that I might come home like the soldier in Dalton Trumbo's novel, *Johnny Got His Gun.* A limbless torso. Blind, unable to speak, yet fully alive. Capable of feeling love and loneliness and despair. Abandoned to a miserable hospital bed, knowing that the nurses and doctors considered me little more than a cooked carrot.

The train chugged through the afternoon. Woods flew by, mountains, swamps. Small towns bobbing in the night, like buoys guiding us through rough waters. War didn't haunt my dreams. I didn't see its bloody face in the mirror when, rocking through north Georgia, I struggled to shave. War was an abstraction. Pictures in a book. Words on the radio. Flourishes good to hear, and good to feel running up and down my spine.

We got off the train. Tall, strong, hard-muscled Americans. Our drill instructors taught us how to march, and how to crawl through machine-gun fire. They taught us how to rip out the enemy's throat, and how to fire bullets into his brain. Some of these trainees would actually come home like Trumbo's Johnny. Others would die crying for their girlfriends or mothers, mouths clogging with blood and snow, eyes frozen open. All of us would change. Not for just awhile, but for the rest of our lives. War does that. Gets inside. Doesn't want to leave. I carry it. A discovery, a wound, a challenge. A face that cries for mercy in a world where more than forty armed conflicts are raging.

At Camp Gordon, Georgia, we lived in oversize chicken coops, and that winter was cold, damp, and very dreary. The coops, which the army called barracks, were heated by coal stoves that went out rather often, leaving us to shiver during stand-up inspections. I was a tall, lanky kid, run down by playing too much basketball in college, and I soon wound up in the infirmary with bronchitis and a touch of pneumonia. I was frightened, not because I might die in some crummy army hospital, but because I might be sent home instead of off to war. Although most of those recruits were college kids, or just out of high school, the government was starting to scrape the bottom of the barrel, drafting beer-guzzling steel workers from the Buffalo-Erie region, pot-bellied cab drivers from New York City, worn-out salesmen from the Midwest. The training was hard on these older guys, and when some of them just couldn't hack it, they were told to pack up their bags and go home. I felt sorry for them, because they were going to miss out on going to war.

We marched and drilled and went to the firing range with our 1903 Enfields, killing thousands of cardboard German and Japanese soldiers. The cadre were tough-talking boys from the hills of Kentucky, racist crackers from the swamps of Mississippi, rednecks from small towns in east Texas. Poor boys trying to escape a lifetime of hunger by serving in the military. Our commander was a Lt. Colonel in the National Guard, a real Prussian who sneered at us, constantly ridiculing our stupidity and ineptitude. He served in World War I, was very proud of that, and wanted us to know that war sorts the mice from the men. We were mice, he was a man.

War is a necessary *rite of passage* for turning boys into warriors. We were boys, he was a warrior. Some day, if we listened closely, trained hard, and got real smart, we too might become real men. Before that happened, we could play at being soldiers, killing the enemy during war games. I became an expert marksman with the .37 millimeter anti-tank gun, an obsolete weapon, but the best we had for our training. We fired at our targets from a three or four-hundred yards range and I was very good, knocking enemy tanks off like clay pigeons, parboiling Nazi soldiers inside their steel ovens. I received a promotion to corporal for being the best at headquarters battery with this weapon.

Week after week we maneuvered through that strange, time-warped Georgia landscape, marching past little tarpaper shacks, flapping in the wind, smoke coughing out of metal chimneys sprouting from their roofs. The blacks who lived in those hovels were share-croppers. They didn't own their shacks, and they didn't own the land they worked sunup to sundown. They rented these plots from white men, bought seed and other necessities from white men, borrowed money at usurious rates from white men. Seventy-five years after their emancipation from slavery, southern blacks were still living in brutal poverty, kept down by Jim Crow laws and racist violence, working like mules, and dying without hope.

We passed by those tumbledown shacks, determined to liberate the world from Nazi domination. Sometimes the tenants threw us a wave, sometimes they didn't. The military was giving us only three candy bars a day for meals. One for breakfast, one for lunch, and one for dinner. And we were always hungry. Practically starving. So when we saw this little stand selling barbecued chickens, we bought several. They looked scrawny, but tasted great, and we chewed them right down to the bones, patting our guts, counting our good fortune. Later, we found out that those birds were buzzards, not chickens, and I never did get a chance to ask those entrepreneurs what they thought about Pearl Harbor. Nor did I ask those sharecroppers how they felt about our war to liberate Europe from Nazi supremacists.

We sailed for Scotland on the *Queen Mary*, crossing the Atlantic in winter, the white troops sleeping in warm staterooms with bunk beds and blankets, the blacks huddling together on the deck. We went out to exercise every day and there they sat, shivering under blankets, stocking caps pulled down over their ears. Most of them were Southern blacks, and they weren't used to the cold at all. Just freezing in the rain and snow.

No one protested on their behalf. Nor did it seem particularly odd that the troops were segregated, since that's the way it was outside the military. North or south, it didn't really make much difference. In 1943, the United States was two separate and entirely unequal nations.

The ship chopped through great waves, taking us closer every hour to the killing zone. We played cards, told stories, crawled into our warm beds at night, while our black brothers-in-arms shivered on the ice-slick deck of the *Queen Mary*.

From Scotland we made our way to Wales, preparing to head for Brittany. My job was to travel about Great Britain picking up ammunition, clothes, weapons, vehicles, everything our outfit needed. We were far from the front lines, but I began to see, to smell, and to feel the horrors of war. I drove, and also walked, through Bristol, London, and Sheffield, cities the Luftwaffe had attacked without mercy. And I was shocked because I could see that civilian casualties were very heavy. Children suffocated in the rubble. Old people burned to death in the firestorms. Survivors were crippled for life. Those raids were so deliberate, such a massive, prolonged, all-out air war against civilian populations. Watching waves of British bombers moving toward Germany, and the sky turning dark with them, I waved and cheered. The Krauts were evil, the Krauts deserved to die. I was hoping the Brits would bomb Germany off the face of the earth.

I did know, because I had seen the results of indiscriminate bombing in Britain, that now it was our turn to burn German children alive. Now we were burying mothers in concrete, making tombs out of German houses and hospitals and schools. I knew what was happening to the German people, but I couldn't dwell on this. I was an ordinary soldier, not a politician or philosopher. I wasn't thinking about St. Augustine's criteria for a "Just War." Ending the war was all that mattered. The noble end would justify our savage means. That's all I knew, all I cared to know at the time.

I saw the results of blanket bombing in Münster, a German city completely leveled, utterly destroyed, by allied planes. Our bulldozers scraped roads through the ruins, shoving rubble and rotting civilians into great, putrid-smelling heaps. Miraculously, a Catholic hospital was still standing, and one afternoon I happened to be talking to an officer who claimed that something strange was going on in the cellar of this building. He said that the the place was stacked floor-to-ceiling with bodies and, even stranger, that German doctors were conducting experiments on these corpses.

So down we went into this frightful charnel house where forty or fifty civilians were bobbing up and down in huge vats of formaldehyde. Some were decapitated. Others appeared to be untouched. A teenage boy floated in one vat. His head was missing, but the rest of his body was perfect. Not a mark on that poor boy. The captain had been right. In the middle of all that carnage, those doctors were conducting research, trying to learn better ways to save the lives of people who were ripped to pieces in bombing raids or blown apart in artillery strikes. Preparing for the next war, even though this one was still a long way from being over.

I was blasé and cynical about the dead. The Germans had been terrorizing Europe for years, and now it was payback time. I didn't really regard the civilians in those vats as innocent bystanders. They were the enemy. Just part of the rubble of the Third Reich. I felt neither pride in what we had done, nor remorse for the victims of our bombing. I did what soldiers must do in order to justify their actions. I demonized the German people.

In Catholic church and parochial schools, I had learned that God created man in His own image and that all human beings carry the divine within us. In order to kill other men and women, I needed to make them less than human. I needed to become anesthetized; more, I had to believe that I would never become one of those mutilated things. Unlike them, God was on my side. Unlike them, I was blessed, surrounded with the armor of pure goodness.

We had gone overseas with 105 howitzers, but someone got the bright idea that, because of our marksmanship, we should be outfitted with new guns. So they got us 8-inch weapons, which were actually naval guns fitted for field artillery use, and our battalion went into Brittany armed with these guns, which could reach targets twenty miles away. We fired on Germans hunkered down in submarine pens in Brest, until the pockets of Nazi soldiers were either killed, or the stragglers crawled out and surrendered. The Germans were heavily fortified, and they were resisting, even though the sub pens were no longer operating. They just wanted to hold on, and we kept firing and firing.

I was a vertical control operator, receiving information from forward observers and then adjusting the length of trajectory for our guns, making sure that we weren't firing short or long, but right on target. We used our 8-inch guns on the city of Lorient too, before moving across Northern France and on into the Netherlands, stopping near the Ruhr valley.

We were there in 1944 when the Battle of the Bulge erupted. Everyone thought the Germans were finished, down for the count. They had slaughtered their way across Poland and attacked Russia, only to stall outside Stalingrad, their troops starving, the oil freezing in their tanks and trucks, thousands of soldiers dying in great snow-covered heaps, far short of the glorious victory Adolf Hitler had predicted. Hitler's boast that his Third Reich would last a thousand years was falling about 990 years short, but megalomania drove him on. He rounded up a half million older men, adolescents, kids, and survivors of the Eastern front, and ordered them to drive the allies back into the sea, fight to the death, reclaim the fatherland's glory. Heil to the Fuehrer.

Then he went off to his bunker to await certain victory. Until the push began, we had no idea that the Germans were capable of mounting another big attack, or that, under the command of Von Rundstedt, they would actually break through our lines.

My brother Tom was a first lieutenant in the 29th infantry, and he began noticing our unit's trucks, so he ordered his driver to catch up with one, found out where we were located, and drove into our camp one day. I hadn't seen him in two-and-a-half years, but I knew that he had been through hell, fighting all the way from the beaches of Normandy into Belgium. We shook hands and hugged, nearly in tears, trying to catch up on all the news, knowing that this might be the last time we would see one another alive.

I went with him to the front where American troops were dug in on a very wide arc, fully expecting to be overrun because they didn't have enough men. Two regiments were spread over a twenty mile front; they were very sparse. It wouldn't have taken much for the Germans to break through those lines, and then come for us. Our unit had been under mortar fire. We lived through bombing attacks, and were pounded by the Germans' terrifying 88-millimeter anti-tank gun, an excellent, highly accurate weapon. We took some casualties, but I was still a reckless kid who thought he could stroll, unscathed, through the valley of death. I had come to Europe to do a job that, I thought, would involve great danger. The more death I faced, the better off the world would be. I needed to keep proving that I wasn't just an ordinary soldier. I was Philip the Bold, son of Thomas the Brave, toughest Irish-American kid on the block. More ignorant, I know now, than brave.

The Luftwaffe's back was broken, but they still sent planes over to raise hell, dropping a few bombs, then fleeing back into Germany. While I was at the front with Tom, one of Goering's planes came over with a load of hundred-pound bombs and they were exploding about a block away. But I stood there, excited by the whole thing, slow to move. And all the while Tom was screaming, "Hit the deck!" He was absolutely furious at me for being so stupid. He had no patience with hero-types.

Just push your face in the mud, pull your butt down tight, and start praying. Don't try to be cute, because some poor bastard will have to pick up your pieces, chop a hole in the ground, and drop you in. The Germans were breaking through our lines. There was no time for idiots like me, time only to fight back, hoping our bombers would stop the Nazis' ferocious assault.

I went to infantry OCS—Officer Candidate School—at Fountainbleau. Then I was assigned to the Eighth Infantry Division, a hard-core combat unit that had already fought its way across Northern France and on into Germany, stopping close to the Danish border.

When I graduated from OCS, I was a skilled killer, trained in the use of all small arms, clever with the bayonet, good with a submachine gun and the Browning automatic rifle. That is exactly what I was: a highly skilled young killer.

Northern France was in ruins, Germany fared even worse. Visions from hell, pure madness, towns, cities, villages smashed to pieces. Bloated horses, rotting corpses, dead hope in the eyes of survivors. Cities like Dresden and Düsseldorf and Münster were smoldering crypts, stacked high with charcoal logs that didn't look at all like human beings. Eye for an eye, tooth for a tooth, and the whole world was being driven blind and toothless.

I started training in Denmark with an anti-tank platoon, using .57 millimeter rifles. We went through maneuvers, but the war in Europe ended in May 1945, and we were were ordered back to the States to begin training for a massive invasion of Japan, an island of cliffs and high bluffs. No good place to land an assault force. It seemed like a great and very tragic irony that men who fought their way across Europe were going to die scaling the cliffs of Japan.

We didn't know, of course, that Oppenheimer and friends were working on a new, science-fiction, weapon. Of this there was not even the hint of a rumor. We went home for thirty days, happy to be alive, thrilled to see our families again, wondering if this would be our last visit, our last meeting with our loved ones here on earth.

And then, on August 6, 1945, the Enola Gay dropped "Little Boy" on Hiroshima, killing a hundred thousand Japanese. Three days later, the United States Air Force dropped "Fat Man" on Nagasaki. The Japanese capitulated, the war ended, and President Truman proclaimed to a grateful nation that the United States of America had discovered the secret of the universe.

We cheered. We danced. We celebrated. We were sick of war, and we thanked God that it was finally over. I was twenty-one years old, a survivor of fifteen months in Europe, happy to be back in the states, grateful to Harry Truman for dropping the atomic bomb. I had no idea that the Japanese were talking about surrender *before* the bomb was dropped, that they only wanted to be assured that their Emperor would not be tried as a war criminal, or harmed in any way. I didn't know that General Douglas MacArthur had given the Japanese his word that the United States government would not put the Emperor of Japan on trial. I didn't know that General Eisenhower was opposed to dropping the bomb, or that the Japanese code had been broken and President Truman knew Japan wanted to surrender *before* the bomb was dropped.

Like most Americans, I believed that a million U.S. soldiers would die in the invasion of Japan. "Little Boy" vaporized Japanese women and children, incinerated the elderly, poisoned the survivors, but it saved American lives. It saved my life, and that was good enough for me.

Returning from Europe on a troop ship, I won four or five hundred dollars in a poker game, so I had plenty of money in my pockets when I got home. I met old friends, told a few war stories, started dating. It seemed to me that I had been spared, because my war experiences could have been much worse. I didn't lose any limbs, and I didn't feel particularly traumatized, even though I had seen some pretty ugly things: a concentration camp with its crematoria still intact and the stench of death permeating the ground, the air, the buildings; bombed-out cities piled high with decaying bodies; headless torsos floating in formaldehyde.

I helped free the world from Hitler's reign of terror. I served my country in wartime because I thought that's what patriots do. God may tell us not to kill, but when the state calls, we must obey. We must become skilled, remorseless killers, willing to use any means to defeat the enemy.

Daniel was at the Jesuit seminary in Woodstock, Maryland, outside Baltimore, and I wanted very much to see him. In another era, I might have ridden a great white horse, decorated with my coat of arms, into a swarm of merry revelers; but it was 1945 and I couldn't so much as catch a cab. So I put on my uniform and started hitching my way to Maryland. The welcome was warm, very enthusiastic. We sang, toasting the war's end, patting ourselves on the back. There were many men in uniform, but I was the only officer so I carried the flag as we marched around the main building—a couple of platoons of soldiers, two hundred Jesuits, friends, family, kids— all cheering our country's victory, congratulating ourselves.

Philip the Bold headed the procession, warm shivers of patriotism rushing up and down my spine. I had done the right thing. Harry Truman had done the right thing. The crew of the Enola Gay had done the right thing. We marched, that day, for God and country, cheerful victors, celebrating the end of the war, and the use of the most barbaric weapon the world had ever seen. Years later, I learned that eight or nine thousand Americans refused to serve in the war, but I knew nothing about these people then. I think, now, that this was part of the government's genius. No one knew about these resisters. They were stowed away in detention camps or federal prisons, and the whole affair—that anyone would dare to oppose killing—was kept secret. The American people must not be allowed to know about patriots like David Dellinger, Robert Lowell, and Ammon Hennacy. We must never know that, in a warrior society, it takes real courage to refuse to kill.

Once upon a time I rode off to a crusade, and rode home again the proud victor. I killed in order to prove the immorality of killing. I massacred in order to demonstrate the illegality of mass murder. I laid waste to show that laying waste is unjust. Strange and rather bewildering contradictions.

Years later, my friend Thomas Merton would write "A Devout Meditation in Memory of Adolf Eichmann," a beautiful and provocative essay which explores the meaning of sanity in a world where sane men and women systematically slaughter their fellow human beings. Eichmann was a faithful servant of the Third Reich, doing his part to help kill six million Jews, escaping to South America after the war and living a very ordinary life until Nazi hunters found his hiding place and extradited him to Israel where he was executed for war crimes.

Adolf Eichmann didn't wake screaming in the night, the horrors of Auschwitz burning his brain. When he looked at food, he didn't see the bonewracked faces of starving Jewish children. Eichmann had a very good appetite, he slept well, he spoke clearly, and he wore clean clothes. Merton tells us that Eichmann "had a profound respect for system, for law and order. He was obedient, loyal, a faithful officer of a great state. He served his government very well." By all accounts, Adolf Eichmann was sane.

I, too, was sane when I marched through Georgia on my way to liberate Europe, instead of fighting to free those sharecroppers from racist terror and oppression. Sane, when I slept in my warm room while black soldiers huddled in the snow. When I calibrated those long-range guns, determined to kill men I had never met, never talked to, would never see until their bodies were scattered about the bunkers. When I toured those German towns and cities, my nostrils contracting from the stench of death, my heart unmoved by all that misery.

I came home from the war, feeling that I had done my best. I hadn't played it safe, volunteering for the infantry after serving with an artillery battalion, receiving my commission, fully expecting to keep slugging it out with the Germans or Japanese. I was just another cog in the killing machine of the United States government and the allied powers, but I didn't understand that yet.

I slipped back into the civilian world almost as quietly as I had left, never expecting that one day I would have to confront my ghost-filled past; never knowing that I would come face-to-face with that 19-year-old warrior who, like his German and Japanese adversaries, was "sane enough" to go to war. Thomas Merton concluded that if sane men could orchestrate the Holocaust, if sane men could build nuclear weapons, and if sane men could prepare to annihilate not only their enemies but the world community, then "The 'sanity' of modern man is about as useful to him as the huge bulk and muscles of the dinosaur."

Years after my return from the killing fields, I looked into the mirror of my own violence. What I saw there forced me to rethink and redefine the meaning of sanity. I realized that while I considered Adolf Eichmann a war criminal and despised him for participating in the Holocaust, we actually had a few things in common. Like him, I had only been following orders. Like him, I was sane enough to do my duty, and to do it well. Like him, I believed that wars are fought for noble reasons. We were both true believers, one a mass murderer, the other a killer on a smaller scale.

When I first started to think about these things, my heart turned to stone, my head swam with clouds of confusion. Examining my own responsibility for the death of 70 million people in World War II, it occurred to me that the United States government, and I as a soldier, had adopted some of the worst aspects of Nazism. The Luftwaffe bombed London, so we had the right to firebomb Dresden. The Germans murdered civilians en masse, so we were entitled to slaughter their women and children. Our actions were not crimes against humanity, they were retaliating for *their* crimes. Their actions were barbaric, our reactions were just. I vacillated between feeling betrayed, and the sense that I was betraying some sacred trust, some sacrosanct ideal.

My world began to shift, rather slowly at first, more dramatically as I read and thought and prayed, seeking for answers in a nation that condemned its warriors to the silence of agreement. Seventy million dead. Hundreds of billions of dollars in damage. Physical and psychological and spiritual wounds that would never heal. And after the war, my country helping high-ranking Nazis find safe haven from justice, protecting the very people against whom I and my brothers fought.

No, such things were not compatible with reason or sanity.

Then what, I wondered, did it all mean? Eventually, but not until the early sixties, I would conclude that war is the big lie, subordinated to, and entrenched by, lots of little lies.

In his great novel, *War and Peace,* Tolstoy writes that during the resistance to Napoleon's invasion of Russia, everybody had a job. From the stable boy to the general, to the politician, all had their little or their large lies to live out.

For many years I clung to my own set of lies, hiding within the shell of collective agreement. In time, that shell began to crack. Light streamed in, forcing me to re-examine killing, making me take a hard, non-rhetorical, look at war. I saw a boy standing on the field of battle, bristling with weapons, preparing to shed his blood, and spill the blood of his enemies, for *his* king, *his* emperor, *his* state, some grand, everlasting, ideal. An ancient figure, stooped with the knowledge that the killing had gone on for centuries, and could well continue until the end of time. The boy took off his helmet, and I could see the pain in his eyes, see that he wanted to lay down his sword and shield, but that he feared the consequences. It was one thing to die on the field of battle, quite another to be banished to the realm of cowards. I reached out to him, and found myself. We walked together, this ancient young warrior and I, knowing that the road we were taking would be lonely, even more dangerous than the battlefield had been. No one would recognize us when we returned home. There would be no welcome for traitors who break their swords into pieces, leaving their armor and their weapons "down by the riverside."

THREE

God and Ordinary People

I am not yet born; O fill me
With strength against those who would freeze humanity, would
dragoon me into a lethal automaton . . .
LOUIS MacNEICE

When the war ended, everyone I served with in the military wanted to be reunited with their families, to start working again, and to heal their physical and spiritual wounds. Rotation was based on a point system, and I didn't have quite enough—less than sixty after the army added up my overseas duty, battle stars, and other things. I was rotated to Fort Campbell, Kentucky, to await demobilization.

We had virtually nothing to do except play softball, march, and run through a few lazy training exercises. No real sweat. Just get through the day, shower, chow down, and head for the officers' club at night. Drink a little, or drink too much, which I often did, dance with civilian employees, tell a few war stories.

I had nothing to complain about. The country was locked in an orgy of self-congratulation, and I was a hero. Pat me on the back. I deserve all the thanks you want to give. I was up for first lieutenant in the military, and could have stayed in, made the army a career, had my family not urged me to do otherwise.

I had walked through the valley of death and emerged in one piece. Now, I just wanted to float in a sea of ennui, to wash away the sights and sounds of World War II.

We were treated like heroes, and we were alone with our memories, some too horrible to acknowledge. Parades, medals, and promotions wouldn't fix us. Ernest Hemingway believed that time heals everything, but I've seen too many old men, weeping over battles a half-century past. There are no panaceas for the wounds of war.

Not that I felt remorse, guilt, or regret. I was just grateful that the killing was over, and wanted to get on with my life. I returned to Syracuse with a fair amount of money (separation allowances from the military were quite generous), and started looking for work. The city of Syracuse was building a convention center and I got a job pushing a wheelbarrow. Hard physical work, but it was pleasant, I enjoyed it, and the pay was quite good.

At night, I went drinking and chasing women with my friends, all veterans of the war. My life was pointless, but I really didn't care. I had no plans, no purpose. Like Krebs in Hemingway's great short story, "Soldiers Home," I was content to sit on the front porch, read the newspaper, watch the girls go by. No one ever questioned what I had done in the war, or how I behaved when I came home. I was alone with my ghosts.

Outside of some vague feeling that I ought to be in college, I enjoyed being home. My parents treated me with genuine kindness, accepting my experience and respecting my taciturnity. Frida and Tom Berrigan were grateful to God that I was home, and uninjured, and as my brothers arrived home from the war, they showed them the same love and gratitude. My mother's prayers had been answered. Her sons, four of whom had served in the military, had survived. We had done our duty and had been honorably discharged. The future looked bright.

I didn't go to John Wayne or Audie Murphy films, never read books on the war, and wasn't interested in assessing what the United States and its allies had done in Europe or the Far East. I didn't care how this monumental tragedy, which killed 70 million people and culminated in the dropping of two atomic bombs, had come about.

I sought out other veterans, drinking and talking until "last call," then hoping to find a party. Some were good athletes, playing baseball again on weekends, happy that no artillery shells were dropping on home plate. I was dating the sister of a close friend who had been shot in the throat in Germany. He made a miraculous recovery, returned home, and joined us on our nightly prowls. His sister was an immensely attractive and intelligent young woman. We got along well, went steady for a while, and even talked about marriage, but I wasn't ready to make that kind of commitment.

The average age of a combat soldier in World War II was twenty-six. I was 19 when I went to war, still a boy in many ways. Now, home from the killing fields, I had no direction. The sun rose, the sun set. Days turned into weeks. I worked, went drinking, slept. Weeks turned into months. My friends and I seemed to be waiting for something, but we didn't know what it might be.

In the summer of 1946, mostly under pressure from my brothers Daniel and Jerry, and also from my mother, I returned to college. They had to work, gently and always with love, to break through my apathy. And I can't stress enough that, without my family's urging, I might never have gotten out of my postwar torpor.

I chose Holy Cross because it was a Jesuit school, Daniel was a Jesuit priest, and Jerry had just completed his freshman year there. Jerry liked Holy Cross a great deal, had made many friends, and he strongly advised me to attend, providing the college would accept me. My marks in high school and at St. Michael's were average or below, and it was not at all certain I would be accepted at Holy Cross, where standards were quite high.

The campus is called Mount St. James, and sits on a high rise of ground just off the thruway to Boston. Some of the buildings are more than a hundred years old, and the grounds are really quite beautiful. Our class numbered well over 400, half of them World War II veterans, so I never felt awkward or out of place because of my age.

I remember only one interesting or exciting professor at Holy Cross, a Jesuit who taught Shakespeare. Professor Brennan wasn't a great student of the bard, but he knew how to make his students see, and understand, the moral content of Shakespeare's plays. Instead of talking down to his students from some pedagogical height, Brennan inspired us to critique Shakespeare's plays in terms of our own lives. We didn't just read about deranged kings, murderous queens, and lovers driven to the brink of despair. We *became* these characters, trapped by our own ambitions, torn by our own conflicting loyalties and human frailties. We lived through Shakespeare's tragedies and comedies because, though written three centuries earlier, these works reflected our own hopes and fears, our individual and collective humanity.

I waited tables on campus to help pay my way through college. On holiday breaks, I labored on the railroad, and during the summer I worked for a line construction company, putting up telephone and electric light lines outside of Syracuse. In my senior year, I started painting houses with my brother Jerry. We were young and strong, had done a good deal of painting around our family's house, and we did quite well at this work.

At Holy Cross, as I'm sure was the case at most American colleges and universities, we didn't engage in any kind of systematic study of World War II. America's post-war euphoria might have diminished, but Hollywood was busy transforming a great human tragedy into patriotic soap operas. The next generation of warriors waited, popcorn in hand, for their chance to march off to war.

The veterans at Holy Cross were an open-minded bunch of guys, many of whom had seen combat, some of it quite heavy, in Europe and the South Pacific. They would have been receptive to any truthful analysis of the war, but the country and the college weren't ready to do that.

I made a lot of friends at Holy Cross, where we lived three-to-a-room in dormitories, graduating from one dorm to another as we advanced toward graduation. As a freshman, I lived in Wheeler Hall, advancing to Carlin when I became a senior. All four years, I had the same roommates—Frank Dermody from Needham, Massachusetts, and Richard Cusack, who lives in Chicago and is the father of John and Joan Cusack, both very prominent actors. Richard himself is an excellent playwright and a fine actor.

I was by no means an outstanding college student. Quite the contrary, I was average, or even somewhat less. Not because I lacked the intelligence to excel at Holy Cross, but because the material didn't make much sense to me. On some subconscious level, I was looking for meaning that wasn't there. I had little patience with abstract discussions that, so often, ended in linguistic *cul de sac*s.

The great Brazilian educator-activist, Paulo Freire, writes that if people are isolated from the world, their consciousness can't be liberated. Genuine learning takes place not in some contrived, academic setting, but in the context of the real world, with all of its pain, suffering, and injustice. Perhaps that explains my difficulty at Holy Cross. Seared by war, I found the cloistered calm of academic dialogue uninspiring, even meaningless.

Holy Cross had the reputation of being a small-scale Catholic Harvard. It proposed to turn out the outstanding Catholic laymen, which meant people who were outstanding in professional life—doctors, lawyers, college professors. But also, people who would make significant contributions to the church, people who were active in parishes, and in Catholic organizations. It turned out a kind of Catholic mafia.

I entered college as a wandering G.I., trying to return but not entirely home from the war. During the first three years at Holy Cross, students were required to go to mass and holy communion every day. During the senior year, this was optional, but by that time daily mass and holy communion were so habitual that most of us continued with that habit. In addition, during the first three years we were expected to be in by 11:00 or 11:30, and if we didn't show up on campus or make bed check, there was hell to pay. We were given a blue slip, and had to be interviewed by the Dean of Discipline. All of this benefited me. After the military, I needed this kind of discipline in order to find direction, and I am very indebted to Holy Cross for helping me do that.

I've returned to Holy Cross several times to speak. Not because the faculty is enamored with me, or considers me a luminary graduate, but because I have friends in Worcester, Massachusetts, who lobby to have me speak, and make all the arrangements to get me on campus. It makes me sad to return to Holy Cross, because I see the loss of a very stringent, disciplined, moral life there. Instead, it appears to be a Catholic rich kids school, lacking the kind of rigorous training that once turned out graduates who, in spite of their narrow vision, were highly trained and disciplined Holy Cross men.

My brother Jerry was in the seminary, studying to be a Josephite priest, and Daniel was a Jesuit. Though I greatly admired and respected my brothers, I just couldn't imagine following in Dan's footsteps. He studied for twelve years to become a Jesuit, and that was too much for me. I was in my mid-twenties, a veteran, and a graduate of Holy Cross. I couldn't imagine spending more than a decade sequestered from all the world's torments and temptations. I wanted something short and sweet, not long and painful.

On the deck of the *Queen Mary*, and again on the European front, I had seen black soldiers treated with contempt. Blacks were given the most menial jobs, scrubbing dishes, cleaning out latrines, polishing shoes. They were forced to sleep in the suffocating bowels, or out on the snow-covered decks, of troop ships. They were not allowed to go into battle with white units, and their bravery went unrecognized. Blacks were drafted from a racist society into a segregated army, which treated them like pariahs.

Witnessing this injustice may help explain my decision to join the Josephite order, whose primary mission was with African-Americans. I entered the seminary in 1950, for a year of novitiate or spiritual training. I went to Newburgh, New York, where the Josephites not only had the novitiate, but a minor seminary including two years of high school and four years of college. After completing two years of college, seminarians went to Washington, D.C., to a seminary near Catholic University. There, they completed two years of philosophy and four years of theology.

This year of novitiate was pivotal and, I think, largely beneficial. We were given a lot of experience in prayer, self-denial, and preparation for our ministry, whatever that might turn out to be. I was a member of a large class of about twelve very serious young men. Many had undergone seminary college, and they were highly ascetic, doing their best to deny themselves, to fast, and to pray regularly, tempering their spirits for the many struggles ahead.

In addition to our intellectual and spiritual training, we did hard physical labor at the seminary, mowing, planting, pruning, gardening. In the late fall of that first year, a hurricane struck, knocking down many of the great old pines and oaks on our grounds. We had to clear these wonderful trees away, and that kept us busy for quite some time.

We were all in fine physical shape, and then at Lent we fasted, losing more weight. Our denial was largely a joyous experience, a shared discipline that would help us serve God and community. This was my first attempt to discipline myself, to concentrate on improving my spirit and my mind, to do a great deal of spiritual reading, to fast, pray, and relish the sacraments.

I read the *Lives of the Saints*, and the work of many prominent theologians, but we weren't allowed newspapers or radio. We were to be guarded from any worldly influence, and to live cut off from the world, just as though we were in the desert. Even visits from family were restricted to once a month. The rest of the time, we saw no one. Toward the end of the novitiate, we did have more freedom, and sometimes we went to a nearby ice cream parlor and ogled the waitresses.

I didn't have any teachers during the novitiate year, only the novice master who was our spiritual director. He was a fairly well-balanced priest, a moderate fellow who did his best to temper our excesses. A couple of seminarians fasted quite rigorously, and he would advise them to reduce their fasting and to pay more attention to their health.

I completed the novitiate, and went on to study theology at St. Joseph's Seminary in Washington, D.C. The professors were competent, in a theoretical way. The course I remember relishing was scripture. We loved the professor, a native Iowan who had studied in Rome, and received his doctorate from a Biblical institute in Jerusalem. He knew Greek, Hebrew, and Latin, and was a very competent teacher; but we were never encouraged to apply the Gospel to everyday life, and no connection was drawn between the teachings of Jesus and the here and now. His fellow professors called him a liberal, which they didn't mean as a compliment.

Ironically, as I attended lectures on theology and pored through religious texts, an inquisition was in progress just a mile away. Reinvigorated by Senator Joseph McCarthy's actions, the House Un-American Activities Committee (HUAC) was excoriating people it suspected of harboring communist sympathies. A priest at our seminary was a friend of Joe McCarthy's, had been given tickets to the HUAC hearings, and attended them every day. We were not only impressed, but absolutely thrilled that Senator McCarthy would invite one of our teachers to witness this theater of cruelty.

My fellow seminarians and I didn't understand that all real hope for a constitutional democracy in the United States ended when Harry Truman signed the National Security Act in 1947. We had no idea that while we prayed for justice, the newly established Central Intelligence Agency was plotting to overthrow popular governments in Iraq and Guatemala. We weren't aware that the Cold War was escalating, not because the Russians were ahead in the doomsday race, but because right-wing ideologues like J. Edgar Hoover, John Foster Dulles, and Joseph McCarthy had mesmerized, and terrified, the American people.

I still believed in the Just War theory, and had learned absolutely nothing in college or at the seminary about pacifism. To me, and to my fellow seminarians, people who resisted the government's policies were screwballs or communists. Three cheers for Senator McCarthy. He was keeping the country, and our seminary, safe for democracy.

I should mention one rather amusing incident of these years. We broke a rule which was strictly enforced in our training. One provision was that we walk over to Congress on Wednesday afternoon to witness the inspired debate there. I did that a few times, but couldn't bear watching the triviality and self-serving egotism of our elected representatives. We could also visit one of the art galleries, or take a walk in a park.

That's what we were supposed to do. But we broke the rule by going to see "High Noon," with Gary Cooper and Grace Kelly. How risqué it felt, to be sitting there in the dark, munching popcorn, waiting for the big shootout. We didn't know that just a couple of rows back sat the rector. He kept his silence during the film, only to call us on the carpet later that evening, threatening us with expulsion. We were given another chance, but only if we agreed never to break another rule. We could watch the clowns in Congress, but no cowboys on the silver screen.

My graduation in 1955 coincided with the reception of the sacrament of holy orders at Catholic University, the Shrine of the Immaculate Conception. This was the culmination of five years of intense study. I was anxious to be among the people, to minister to them, and to help them in any way I could.

Prior to my ordination, I had taught catechism to young people in Josephite parishes in Washington, D.C. This gave me exposure to African-Americans; in addition I was privileged to study for the priesthood with several black seminarians. For the most part, they were from the deep South, and we were good friends.

It was rather odd, really, that one day we were seminarians, and the next day priests. After we were ordained, that is, once we officially became priests, people treated us quite differently. I remember one fellow with whom I went through training, who is now a priest in a black parish in Los Angeles. He had been taken prisoner by the Germans in World War II, and was in a camp for a long time before being liberated by our military. The Germans couldn't feed their POWs, and this poor man used to forage for potato peels in garbage heaps, seriously undermining his health.

The former POW did badly in the oral examinations, which were a two-hour ordeal, covering all of our philosophical and theological training, before a panel of three priests. He failed his orals, and was forced to study intensely before he could take them again. Some faculty questioned whether he should even be ordained; but once he became a priest, he was treated with respect.

The war in Korea was over, and no one seemed to know the real reasons for this conflict. World War I, and then World War II, were supposed to have been wars to end all war. Yet there, in all the papers, were photographs of young men with ancient faces sculpted out of pain. Rivers of refugees, scorched villages, heaps and heaps of bodies. Familiar sights, but who could explain the carnage this time?

While I was living and teaching in New Orleans (1955-62), I was in contact with the Fellowship of Reconciliation (FOR), and when one of the staff members from the national office came to town, I was asked to organize his speaking tour. I set up lectures for this fellow, who spoke candidly and with great conviction about civil rights and racism.

Albert Camus wrote that "beginning to think is beginning to be undermined." The worm begins to turn. As I listened to this speaker, my own bearings loosened. Doubt churned where confidence had once rested, secured to the bedrock of ignorance. I was 37 years old and, I thought, highly educated. Yet I knew nothing about the Cold War—how it began, why it continued, its devastating effects on our country, and the world. I knew nothing about peacemaking from the gospel standpoint. I had been educated to accept my own stupidity.

The longer I listened to the speaker from FOR, the deeper Camus's worm burrowed. I was lightheaded with wonder; undermined and, simultaneously, enlightened.

The speaker, Brewster Kneen, sent me material from the Fellowship for Reconciliation, suggesting that I read certain books and articles. I began by reading William Appleman Williams from the University of Wisconsin, D.F. Fleming from Vanderbilt University in Nashville, and other scholars who were writing about the tragic debacle—the Cold War, arms race, and fanatic anti-communism—into which our leaders had drawn us. I also subscribed to a number of magazines like *Ramparts, The Nation,* and *The Progressive,* reading them with a great deal of excitement and deep appreciation.

Writing on the role of the intellectual in American society, Thomas Merton claimed that we stand in the middle of the power pyramid. Intellectuals keep the people under control by *interpreting* the government's policies of power to them. College and university teachers do this, the clergy likewise, members of the business and military communities also. We accept, and we use, the language of power, which in turn creates the illusion of good taste, reason, rational dialogue.

To do otherwise is to step outside the pyramid, which means becoming vulnerable. One might be passed over for promotion, turned down for publication, denied tenure. One might be marginalized, tagged with some pejorative "ism." Standing in the middle of the power pyramid, we can pretend to challenge the status quo, while accepting its rules and rewards.

I began to see that there is no separation of church and state in America. There is merely a collective articulation of power, by individuals and groups who claim to be critical thinkers. As a priest, I stood square in the middle of the power pyramid, interpreting positions of power to my parishioners and students. Though I didn't realize it at the time, my job was to interpret the capitalist, expansionist, war-driven paradigm of America's military-industrial complex, making it appear rational when, in fact, it is destructively irrational.

My brother Jerry and I were not only supported by the government in college, but all through the seminary as well. In my case, the G.I. bill extended through nine years of education. In a fundamental sense, we paid for our education through our ignorance and our silence. We questioned neither the government nor the church. We were striving to be middle men in the pyramid of power, and for awhile we even achieved our goal.

I became a priest, someone my parishioners could depend on and trust, a representative of the Roman Catholic church. But what, really, did I know? I had spent fifteen months in Europe, participating in the horrors of modern warfare, and knew nothing about war. I was determined to help men and women live together in holy matrimony, and knew nothing about marriage. I wanted to help people be good citizens, even though I didn't know how our government functions. I had committed my life to helping others, yet I didn't have the slightest idea why millions of Americans live in poverty. I was going to be a friend to working men and women, without understanding the labor movement's struggle for safe working conditions and fair pay.

Looking back, I marvel at how little we learned in the seminary. Would I study for the priesthood again? Yes, but only under certain conditions. We, the novices, would have to be assured that we would be free to develop, and to act upon, our conscience. We would have to be guaranteed the freedom to express our political views, whatever these might be. We would learn, in our classrooms and through interaction with people, about the Gospel as it applies to the world.

Most important, we would be encouraged to enter into an active, experiential dialogue concerning justice. I would insist on experience with the peace movement, with the poor, with African-Americans, Latinos, and Native Americans.

When I studied in the seminary, priests were mass-produced to be silent, to be conformists, and to be patrons of the government. We weren't allowed to read the whole range of political thought, and its applicability to the marketplace. Like most of our counterparts in colleges, universities, public schools, and seminaries, we were taught to believe in the capitalist system, never questioning how a system that poisons the environment, imprisons and executes the poor, and thrives on war, could be compatible with the teachings of Christ.

I doubt if the Catholic hierarchy will ever ask me to reform the seminary; however, in the ideal setting, I would want prospective priests to think about service to the poor, about resistance to power, especially state power, about nonviolence, and how they might dedicate their lives to nonviolence as a way of living, rather than merely a tactic. I would invite guest speakers like David Dellinger, Daniel Ellsberg, Rosalie Bertell, George Wald, Mairead Corrigan Maguire, Robert J. Lifton, Elizabeth McAlister, Richard Falk, and, of course,

Daniel Berrigan. Men and women who would inspire seminarians not only to think critically, but to act upon and *live* what they learn.

Thoughtful religious people are beginning to view the church as increasingly irrelevant. They are seeing the church as an institution, rather than a community of belief. Many people long to see women treated, inside and outside of the church, on an equal basis with men. Others are tired of the war game, sickened by the terrible toll it takes, every day, on the poor. The United States government (using taxpayers' money) spends $5 billion every week, $700 million a day, $500,000 a minute, and $8,000 a second on the military. Worldwide, 50,000 people die each day from hunger. At home, 27 children die from poverty *every single day.* In 1994, we spent $7 billion on child nutrition.

The church is a major, worldwide institution, and it is even more conservative, perhaps, than our government. Not conservative in the sense of "conserving" the gospel, but in maintaining useless rituals and policies that are designed to protect, and perpetuate, the institution. Pope John Paul will never allow priests and nuns to marry, or permit women to become priests. I doubt whether his successor will change that. The institution is dominated by men, who apparently are unwilling, or unable, to acknowledge our world's desperate environmental, economic, and spiritual crisis.

The church is a major bureaucracy, and major bureaucracies are disobedient to the gospel. They seek primarily to control their members, and others. And so the priority of the Catholic church, which is central to the major institutional establishments, is survival. To guarantee this, control of the clergy and Catholic laypeople is essential. Mandatory celibacy, for example, has little to do with the purity of the clergy, and everything to do with control. Nonviolence, which is the spirit of the gospels, is about truth and justice, rather than control. Nonviolence is about reflecting and acting upon God's nonviolence toward us.

If the church wanted to come to grips with the gospel, it would have to give up its property and its exemptions from the state, and involve itself with resistance on a major scale. It would have to resist the violence against our poor, and stop pretending that one political party is more humane than the other.

Politicians from both parties have conspired, together, to cut cash assistance programs to poor children. Republicans *and* Democrats have refused to show compassion for the approximately five million adults, mostly women, who receive Aid to Families with Dependent Children (AFDC). Both parties have chosen to use poor people as scapegoats for the nation's economic, social, and political problems. Republicans *and* Democrats are on a binge of hatred, choosing to blame the victims of a system that is designed to destroy human beings.

I never had the slightest temptation to leave the Catholic church, and I am extremely grateful for everything the church has done for me, not only in the early years of my life, but also in later years. After I was excommunicated in 1973, several other Christian bodies asked me to join them, and to minister under their aegis. I refused, because I have never considered myself anything but a Roman Catholic, trying to become a Christian. My roots are in the church, and in spite of all the prostitutions and betrayals of the institutional church, these roots are life-giving.

My brother Daniel has often said that many priests and nuns learned their (our) politics by confronting the church and resisting it, through calling it to the accountability of the gospel. The transfer to resisting the state from that experience was automatic.

NOTES FROM A TALK GIVEN TO THE N.O. COUNCIL ON PEACEFUL ALTERNATIVES, MAY 1963

I have been asked to present a few concepts on Papal thought relevant to peace, beginning with Pope Pius XII during World War II, in the postwar years, and then John XXIII, particularly in reference to his two great social encyclicals, *Mater et Magistra,* and *Pacem in Terris.* I think it only fair to add at this time, that the Popes were and are far more than mere theorists, and that to counterbalance their condemnation of modern war, they offered explicit and highly pragmatic programs for peace. So perhaps it may be apropos for me to add at the end of this, a brief and inadequate outline of the Papal directives for peace, through the medium of social justice.

Before giving a bit of the mind of Pius XII on modern war, it must be remembered that here was a man, one of the greatest intellectuals of the Church's history, and without question, one of the saints of his time, who was an observer of the greatest war of history, a war which degenerated

into senseless and unbelievable savagery, ranging from the simple shooting of prisoners to the rape of Coventry and Rotterdam by the Luftwaffe;
to the great Gomorrah raids by the Royal Air Force on Hamburg in July,
1943 which left 70,000 cooked or suffocated in the firestorms that swept
the doomed city; to Dresden, swollen with refugees from the Russian
advance, and left with 250,000 dead after round-the-clock bombings; to
Tokyo, which, with its 100,000 dead after napalm bombings, meant to condition the Japanese people for Nagasaki and Hiroshima. World War II
demonstrated to Pius XII, and much more clearly to him than to most men,
that inevitably, military expediency pushes aside moral restraint when war
waxes hot, and it becomes all too easy for the so-called Christian com-
batants to equal and even eclipse their adversaries in barbarism. After all,
we were the first to use the Bomb, and it was we who demanded unconditional surrender and *everything* demanded to gain it.

Perhaps one of the earliest expressions of the horror of Pius at the course
that World War II was taking came in 1943, and it shows a painful realization of what had already happened and what was to come. He said then,
"In every nation there grows a hatred for the brutality of modern war which
passes every bound of morality and every rule of right, divine and human.
More painful than ever this doubt pierces the spirit and the heart of the
nations and gnaws them, namely, is the continuation of such a war still
justifiable before the human and Christian conscience? Elsewhere, it will
say of this war: One would call it an apocalyptic monster, born of a civilization in which the ever-growing progress of technical science is accompanied by an ever-deeper decline in morals. The present generation has
passed through an ocean of blood and tears, such as perhaps has never
been known in times past; it has lived through unspeakable atrocities, that
the remembrance of so many horrors ought to remain impregnate in its
memory and to the very depth of the soul, as the very images of hell, so
that anyone, who keeps in his heart any sentiment of humanity, could never
have any more ardent desire than to shut the doors against it forever."
Notice his conviction that the war, already descended to incredible depths
of brutality, is already "total," the vehicle of a technology running berserk
over its only controlling force, "an ever declining morality." And in another
address in 1943, he says about the same thing, "Monstrous means of strife!
No one can deny that the progress of man's inventions, which ought to
proclaim the coming increase of well-being to the whole of humanity, has
been turned aside from its end to be used to destroy that which the centuries had built up. But by that, too, is shown in a way always more clear,
the wickedness of this war of aggression." To his view at this time, with
the end of the war still two years away, and with still more unimaginable

violence to bloody its course, the conflict was beyond the point of reason, that there was no question any longer of justice for either side, and that it was now purely a "war of aggression," i.e., that the participants on both sides could no longer resort to postures of morality. Summarily, the war had become an arena of runaway nationalism, economic exploitation, and unbridled human passion.

In 1944, more profoundly convinced than ever of the uselessness and madness of modern war, Pius stated in his Christmas message, "If ever a generation ought to hear the cry: 'War on war!' rise from the depth of its conscience, it is certainly the present generation. . . . The theory of war as a proportionate means to resolve international conflicts is already out of date." Obviously, from what he says here, the Christian has an imperative obligation to make war on war. In another part of the message, he maintains that it is a moral obligation "to ban all wars of aggression," a duty which is binding on all, and one that "brooks no delay, no procrastination, no hesitation, no subterfuge." It may be worthwhile to ask if the present nuclear impasse would be possible if Christians had a sense of morality in this regard, or if they had paid serious heed to his words.

In 1954, in an address to the World Medical Association, observing the power blocs of the West and the East in the arms buildup of even more serious nature than the one supposedly terminated by peace in 1945, he said, "Aggressive Atomic, Bacteriological and Chemical warfare is a sin, an offense and an outrage against the majesty of God." And he went on to maintain that "Should the evil consequences of adopting this method of warfare ever become so extensive as to pass utterly beyond the control of man, then its use must be rejected as immoral." It seems to me, if this statement is taken at face value, our preparations for this type of warfare could be considered immoral, as in the process of passing beyond the point of control. Concentrations of strontium-90 in Alaskans are four times that found in Americans—Swedish Lapps were found to have thirty to forty times the concentrations of cesium-137 than their southern countrymen. The International Commission of Radiological Protection tells us in a report that units of strontium-90 per liter of milk is now daily averaging 20 picocuries in New York and 25 in Boston. A region of Louisiana, Mississippi, and Arkansas averaged 30–40 picocuries of strontium-90 per liter in a recent test, exceeding the maximum levels recommended. It is the opinion of many meteorologists that the continuous testing of the last years has accomplished, among other things, a disturbance of the atmosphere which is largely causative of the harsh winters of recent times. What would happen to the atmosphere if the full arsenal of present weapons were used, even presupposing that life still survived?

Perhaps the anguish that this great man felt at the arms buildup is best expressed by the following quote, which, in my opinion, sums up his attitude toward modern war. Previous to it, he had made statements which could be viewed as a justification of just war theory, envisioning military encroachments by international Communism, even to the extent of first strike. Here, however, he emphatically denounced the applicability of the theory of just war. He said, "Wars are waged in defiance of all international laws, with bestial ferocity. It is seen that following war crimes, there is a great irreparable damage to morals which comes from this school of hatred and misery called war. Secret arms foil plans of governments which thought it would be possible to wage war justly in the hope of gaining victory. All this and many other things show that today it is impossible in waging war to fulfill the conditions which in theory make a war lawful and just. Nowhere can there be a cause proportionate or of such importance as to justify so much evil, slaughter and destruction, and moral and religious ruin. In practice, then, it will never be lawful to declare war."

Before turning to Pope John, two statements are deserving of attention. The first is by Cardinal Saliege in 1949, the second by the French Bishops at their annual convocation in 1950. The Cardinal makes this powerful statement: "From now on, we can destroy all life on the earth, and even shatter this planet. We can apply fearful new instruments to inflict suffering; we have not neglected them and doubtless will not neglect them. Are we drunk, or are we insane? We are using our power in order to destroy. Ten million men were killed in the first world war, forty million in the second; if a third war comes, there is every indication that far more than a hundred million will die. You can truthfully say that the devil is calling the tune. . . . God did not create the world in order that it might be made into a hell. God did not create man to be a permanent murderer. . . ." The Bishops in turn, when asked about the lawfulness of nuclear weapons, replied that such a question did not even need to be asked, since nuclear war was already condemned by the elementary sense of humanity. And they said unequivocally, "We condemn nuclear weapons with all our strength."

It is undoubtedly part of the genius of Pope John that his approach to the Cold War and the issues of peace is supranational and worldwide. In neither *Mater et Magistra* nor *Pacem in Terris* does he identify Communism by name, nor does he accuse it of being the total cause of international tensions. Communism, I suspect, he recognizes as being the rank fruit of a misinterpretation and malpractice of Christianity, and therefore, by a relevant treatment of the doctrine of Christ in reference to the social order, he hopes to strip it slowly of both its reason for being and its *modus operandi.* And so he builds upon the more particularized views of Leo XIII and Pius XI, and suggests a reconstruction of the social order along the following lines (very briefly): Foreign aid as essential to alleviate nationalism, to redistribute the balance of power through responsibility to the "have-not" nations; Second, peace conferences as useful to banish suspicion and to serve as an alternative to violent, ill-timed action; Third, technology as meant to serve man's interests by creating a climate wherein he can enhance his spiritual welfare; Fourth, industry, to be interpreted more and more as the vehicle which will provide initiative, a sense of belonging to one's work, and above all, the "human family wage"; Fifth, private property, recognized simultaneously as a natural right with a social function, i.e., meant also for the common good; Sixth, agriculture, as needing improvement through government to establish a more equitable balance between urban-rural rewards; Seventh, socialism, which calls for a strong introduction of individual responsibility in terms of overall good of the community, the nation or the world. And to further illustrate this, he advances his famous principle of subsidiarity, wherein government has the obligation to supply to lower structures and groups of the community those things which they need, and yet cannot provide for themselves.

To make the above practical, the Pope suggests a series of eminently sound procedures. Society must be known, man must become a student of his world—otherwise, he cannot judge it and act upon it. Organizations, essential to the complexities of modern society, are necessary for social justice, because very simply, they have become the dynamic principle of modern life. In payment for the greater freedom and greater control over matter that man has gained in today's industrialized society, he must assume more responsibility in organizations. And here morality plays a salient part, for without it, organizations become an arena for vicious group-interests, for demagoguery and class exploitation. The Pope recognizes very well that the great catalyst of change in our society is natural science, with the focus of scientific change being man's control over matter. Science can only be harnessed to genuine human needs by anticipating the consequence of science, i.e., knowing the philosophy and psychology of man's use of material things in an industrial society. The organization, then, becomes the necessary framework in which man's control of creatures is learned and made responsible through free, mature action.

I suggest that the incisive treatment of issues that came as a sequel to *Mater et Magistra* in the Pope's next encyclical, *Pacem in Terris,* caused widespread doubt and in some cases, vehement denial. The dignity of the person stood as the cornerstone of the whole message, racism was condemned ("Racial discrimination can in no way be justified, at least doc-trinally or in theory"), and the nuclear impasse attacked as being contrary to justice, right reason and humanity. The Pope states that "justice, right reason and humanity therefore urgently demand that the arms race should cease; that the stockpiles which exist in various countries should be reduced equally and simultaneously by the parties concerned; that nuclear weapons should be banned; and that a general agreement should eventu-ally be reached about progressive disarmament and an effective method of control." No one is about to quarrel with these proposals who has any elements of humanity about him. But his view of Communism in the Encyclical is another thing, and it has caused sort of a "crisis of confi-dence" in the Pope. This is mostly because the Church's stand against Communism has been unequivocal from the time of Pius XI's encyclical. The Church has suffered mightily at the hands of the Communists, and continues to do so today. Mass agreement by Catholics of all shades of states and conviction against Communism has been very much a part of the Church's public image. But the Pope suggests, with vision and logic, that the Church's stand on Communism is not an absolute, and what we are living with today in the world under the form of Communism, might well demand an entirely new approach. The problems of the present gen-eration are not going to be solved with the solutions of the past; some middle ground must be found between submission to Communism and nuclear annihilation. The Communist is still a person; as he puts it, "the person who errs is always a human being." And so he draws a sharp and realistic distinction between "false philosophical teachings regarding the nature, origin and destiny of the universe and man," and historical move-ments that have economic, social, cultural or political ends. Or to put it another way, ideological Communism as a philosophical system, and the historic movement that we observe today are not one and the same thing, for the latter, we cannot deny, and as he puts it "cannot avoid change, being subject to change, even of a profound nature." In the course of time also the historic movement will deeply alter the philosophy of Communism— it is well on its way to doing that just now. Finally, he implies in the encyclical that the intransigence and lack of imagination shown by the Church in regard to Communism, characteristics which have been more than matched by the West in the Cold War, have gotten us precisely nowhere, unless one were to regard the nuclear brinksmanship of the last 15 years as somewhere.

I received word recently of a priest I know in the North who was con-tacted by Communists from New York City—they wished to set up some communication with him and others of like convictions—probably with an end to doing some common work in social programs. He was not able to do this, as he put it—"We are still some years from this." Yet both the possibility and the need are there—and obviously, if Pope John has anything to say about this, it will come quickly. Pius XII was explicit on several occasions concerning the need for joint action with those whose beliefs are foreign to our own, when a common humanitarian ground has been reached. I have lay missionary friends who have worked with considerable harmony with Communists in Latin America. As one of them explained, "It is the only situation in which they can be led to question their system, i.e., when our dedication equals or exceeds their own." Pope John's reception of Khrushchev's son-in-law accomplished more than at first view might be concluded, and among the effects was favorable comment on *Pacem in Terris* by the Communist world press. Furthermore, his effort to remove Cardinal Mindszenty from Budapest has already initiated positive measures on the part of the Kadar regime to relax its strictures on religious freedom in Hungary, and there has also come the expression of desire to resume diplomatic relations with the west. Finally, if the Pope is successful in setting up diplomatic connections with the Kremlin, with Warsaw and Budapest, this cannot help but ease present tensions, and might well have the effect of causing a progressive reevaluation of Cold War diplomacy. To my mind, this man is the largest hope of the world—and our prayers for his health should be unflagging and fervent.

Finally, I venture that the Papal recommendations for peace are strikingly coincident with the objectives of the Ecumenical Council, i.e., the reform of the person with an eye to the renewal of social structures—or to make it more applicable in regard to the Church, its renewal so that it may be more pertinent to man. Whatever facet of John's proposals that are explored, reductively, they come to the same thing—an emphasis upon fellowship in the unity of humankind, and a consequent feeling of responsibility for the loftiest interests of men anywhere, of whatever condition, race or creed. And in dictating what seems to me to be the only course to lasting and Christian peace, he is also dictating the erection of a social order that will take man into an era which is radically new, staggering in its potential, sobering in its responsibility, a challenge which nonetheless must be met, since the alternative is fast becoming simple and one—the destruction of civilization as we know it, or the possible extinction of the race. May God help us in our effort to grow up to the thinking and example of both Pius XII and John XXIII.

Father Philip Berrigan with friends. Anacostia, Washington, DC,
October 1955. Photo courtesy of Cornell University, Carl A. Kroch
Library, Division of Rare and Manuscript Collections.

FOUR

Auction Blocks
and Lynching Posts

On a steamy August day in 1955, a team of lawmen pulled the body of a fourteen-year-old boy from the Tallahatchie River, just outside Money, Mississippi. The boy's killers had forced him to lug a seventy-five-pound cotton gin fan to the river. They told him to strip, and when he obeyed they shot him in the head, gouged out one of his eyes, and smashed in his forehead. They lashed the fan around his neck with barbed wire, and tossed his naked body into the river. Emmett Till was from Chicago, and he was murdered, apparently, for looking at a white woman in the wrong way. His killers said they just wanted to teach the boy some respect.

Emmett's mother held an open-casket funeral for her son, and gave a photograph of his mutilated body to *Jet* magazine. She wanted the world to see what racists had done to her child, and to the children of countless other African-American mothers. On September 23, 1955, the 166th anniversary of the signing of the Bill of Rights, an all-white jury deliberated less than seventy-five minutes before finding Emmett Till's amused killers not guilty.

These were the happy day fifties. A five-star general sat in the White House. He spoke to the nation in bacon and eggs English, played golf, and acted as our rhetorical mirror; looking at him we gazed at ourselves. When cracks appeared at the mirror's edges, we covered them, skillfully, with hubris. After all, Emmett Till's killers weren't like the rest of us. They lived in the Deep South. Chewed

tobacco. Talked slow and stupid. They were aberrations, not genuine fissures, in our narcissistic mirror.

Hollywood created our reality. We had won the great war
against evil, killed the Axis beasts, and we would conquer the
communist hordes. Fixated by our mythical beauty, we ignored all
contradictions.

My parishioners in Washington, D. C.'s Anacostia section were
surviving America's post-war euphoria in dilapidated, dangerous,
destitute public housing. They lived in poverty, and suffered discrimination. When they looked into the magic mirror, it didn't smile back.

For them, the road of sorrow was paved with stories about slave
auctions, licentious masters, and cruel overseers. Their past was inextricably woven into the present. Nevertheless, they were always willing to share what little they had with a young, idealistic priest. I loved
those people, and valued their friendship greatly, even though I realized that I could never *become* one of them. My grandparents hadn't
been slaves. I wasn't shipped to the back of the bus every day of my
life. The Ku Klux Klan didn't burn crosses in my yard, or threaten
to hang my friends from lampposts. People didn't refuse to rent apartments to me, banks didn't deny my loan applications, and cops didn't
break my head, simply because of the color of my skin.

I knew little about African history, and less about the folkways
and mores of African people, Jim Crow laws, and the evils of segregation. Like most Americans, I grew up in a predominately white
neighborhood, went to white schools, attended white churches, had
white friends. A few black families lived in Syracuse when I was
growing up, but we didn't mingle. My community didn't denounce
them, or preach hatred toward them. We just assumed that blacks
resided over *there,* and whites lived *here.* After high school I met a
few blacks at the roundhouse where I worked cleaning engines, but
no friendships developed. We did our jobs, got paid, and went home.
I never knew them, they never knew me.

During the twelve months I lived and worked in Washington's
Anacostia district, my parishioners were educating me as a novice
of the scripture. I didn't reflect on this, it just happened. I taught them
catechism and scripture; they taught me the real meaning of hate,
fear, and discrimination. Postwar Washington resembled (and still
resembles) a huge plantation. Blacks lived in battered neighbor-

hoods, went to rundown schools, and worked at rotten jobs. They were expected to be thankful for small favors, to grin and shuffle before their masters. Whites sat in Congress and the Senate; blacks collected their garbage. Whites owned the banks and businesses; blacks mopped the floors. It was a systematic oppression of African-Americans, not the collective failure of a people.

Some blacks did manage to beat the odds: Dr. Ralph J. Bunche, the first black official in the State Department and winner of the Nobel Prize for peace in 1950; Langston Hughes, a talented and courageous poet; Mahalia Jackson, a great (some say the greatest) gospel singer; Charles Mitchell, winner of the NAACP's "Spingarn Medal" in 1969 for his lobbying efforts on behalf of civil rights; Paul Robeson, a great singer, crusader for human rights, and the first black actor to play "Othello" on the American stage. Beautiful, intelligent, talented, determined, courageous individuals.

Still, for every African-American who gained success, a million others were trapped inside a racist nightmare.

After a year in Washington, I headed into the Deep South to begin teaching at St. Augustine's, an all-black high school in New Orleans. My students were a cross section of the city's best young people, though most of them lived in segregated, terribly violent projects. Two-story brick buildings, which made them a little more livable than high rises, yet filled with despair, frequent killings, and other forms of violence. Some students came from professional families, some were Creole, a very handsome people of French, Spanish, and American descent. They were simply great kids, and I loved them unconditionally. They trusted me. I trusted them. And in the seven years I taught there, I don't remember one serious breach of trust on their part.

The Josephites had been in New Orleans for some time, ministering to the poor, to black children and adolescents. Of course from time to time we had disciplinary problems in our classroom, and I was not reluctant to paddle a student in front of the class, or whack them on the back of the head. The parents wanted us to do this, though they asked us not to strike their sons in the face. We never did. Sometimes, we sent a student to the principal's office for a paddling, and I have seen a marvelous clearing of the air with a simple whack on the butt. The offending student realized, without resorting to guilt or subterfuge, the seriousness of his transgression. Most often, he was led to conversion, and the problem ceased.

The school was highly subsidized by the Josephites, and well equipped with books, desks, and whatever else we might need. Tuition was about fifty dollars a year; if this became a strain on the parents, then we offered scholarships. At times, we had an equal number of scholarship and tuition-paying students.

I was quite happy at St. Augustine's, even though I resented teaching at a segregated school. No matter our love for the students, they still felt the sting of being ostracized, and of living and learning in a ghetto. In 1957-8, Archbishop Romell ordered integration of the Catholic institutions of the Archdiocese of New Orleans, a move which gave us great hope. The Deep South might be determined to remain segregated, but in the Archdiocese of New Orleans, there were more students in Catholic high schools conducted by the Redemptorist Fathers, the Jesuits, the Josephites, and the Sisters of the Blessed Sacrament, than there were in public high schools. This gave us opportunities to subvert the racist paradigm, which we often did.

At Holy Cross College and in the seminary, I learned that we should love our neighbors as we love ourselves. But no one ever encouraged me to examine my own racism. I was a racist when I arrived at St. Augustine's, because to live in America is to be a racist, either by commission or omission. Our government's domestic and foreign policies are determined, to a large extent, by racist assumptions. Racism influences where we live, whom we choose to have for friends, whom we marry, where our children go to school, where we work and worship. Racism fills our morgues, every day, with murdered black children. It jams our prisons with black men and women, crowds our death rows, and keeps the executioners busy. It poisons the hopes and kills the dreams of poor, disempowered Americans. I didn't know these things when my superiors transferred me to New Orleans. I just wanted to be a good priest and a good teacher, to serve God, and to help where and when I could.

The students of St. Augustine continued my education. Gently, but firmly, healing my blindness. And the more I learned from my black friends and students, the more outrage I felt. Outrage and a deep sense of betrayal. I was brought up to respect authority. When my country told me to go to war, I went. When the army ordered me to kill, I killed. After the war, I worked, paid taxes, entered the seminary, took vows, joined the Josephite order and agreed to live by its rules.

My black parishioners educated me, not just *telling* but *showing* me what it means to be an African-American in a racist society. They weren't vindictive. They didn't want to kill their tormentors. Three hundred years earlier, slave traders kidnapped their ancestors from Africa, chained them head to foot, starved them, beat them, raped them, and threw their broken bodies to the sharks. And still, my parishioners sang about love, not revenge. My skin is white, the color of oppression, and they accepted me. Through terrible and relentless suffering, they had discovered the meaning of charity. Their hearts refused to turn to stone. They kept their spirits miraculously and vibrantly alive.

In retrospect, I know that much of what I thought we Josephites had to offer our black students was an illusion. I did believe (out of a sense of justice, I think) that we could offer them something. We could offer them good literature, the opportunity to discuss ideas, and a theology that transcended the nonsense they were learning in some parishes. During the seven years I spent at St. Augustine's High School, I taught a theology of contribution and of involvement. These kids came from very very poor families, but they brought canned goods, packaged foods, and even money to people who were worse off than themselves. My kids had so little, so very little, and yet they were willing to help. The food and money we collected was brought directly to the projects. We did have something special to offer students at St. Augustine's. Not prizes for the best theological essay, but practical ways to make a difference.

Years before coming to New Orleans, I had passed by Georgia sharecroppers, standing quiet as horses in their humble yards. I was training to be a soldier in the United States Army, and would soon be sailing for the killing fields in Europe, so I tucked those sharecroppers' faces and plight into some mental file drawer. I had always assumed that the Emancipation Proclamation put an end to slavery; I always thought there were laws against buying and selling human beings, state and federal laws, God's laws. According to the law, the people in those Georgia shacks, and the poor people in my New

Orleans parish, were free to move into the future. Yet violence and discrimination chained them to the past. Jim Crow, their zealous and sadistic overseer, whipped them every day. Economic Servitude, their sweet-talking master, grinned and tightened their shackles.

St. Augustine's had a very good library; there I began my sojourn into black history. I wandered through bookstores, digging into dusty recesses for answers to my questions. I borrowed material from other priests, scrutinized newspapers for book reviews, wrote to friends and family, asking for their help. The Josephites subscribed to all the black magazines, and I studied the writings of Lerone Bennett, who was doing a lot of writing for *Ebony*. Later on, when I started giving talks on the struggle for racial equality, I gave him credit for his fine work.

During my second year at St. Augustine's, I was also in contact with Jesuits at Loyola University who were struggling to articulate their own response to the growing racial crisis in America. We talked, exchanged views, debated our ideas. I also took courses at Loyola so that I could be licensed to teach in the state of Louisiana. Gene McManus, a Josephite who is now superior general of the order, helped me out a great deal. He was a very bright, well-informed sociologist, and he not only suggested readings to me, but took the time to read and edit articles I was writing.

I set out to discover why my black parishioners lived in ghettos, why their children attended all-black schools, why hospitals refused black patients, why the police routinely beat and even killed black citizens. I read everything I could acquire on social commentary, searching for answers to these questions. And the quest always returned to the same poisonous tree, the roots of which were strangling our nation's soul.

We (the United States of America) had never really chopped down the slavery tree; we just pretended, now and again, to trim its limbs. The roots grew into our own back yards, wound through our homes, undermined our schools, strangled our sense of reason and fair play. I discovered that the roots of this poisonous tree are inextricable from our economic system. Greed waters these roots, keeps them healthy, enables them to keep expanding their power and influence. Avarice transplants the tree when it isn't flourishing. Exploitation supplies the tree with nutrients and fertilizer. I was also engaged in a dialogue with my brother Daniel, whose first book of poems, *Time Without Number*, had won the Lamont Poetry Prize, and had also been nominated for the National Book Award. Dan spent 1954 in Europe where he met French priests who were articulating a unique, activist theology. These "worker priests" hauled nets on fishing boats, helped farmers harvest their crops, and worked on assembly lines. They walked picket lines and participated in strikes. They took to the streets with angry workers, and they chose to live among the poor. France's bishops accused the workers of collaborating with socialists and communists, and Pope Pius XII first warned against the "spirit of innovation," then ordered the priests to return to more traditional parish work, or face excommunication.

Dan and I were intrigued by the worker priests' ideas, and inspired by their commitment to ordinary men and women. Would we, as priests, take these kinds of risks? Where should we draw the line between social activism and our more traditional religious duties? Was there really a line to draw? Christ drove the usurers from the temple. He didn't write a dissertation on the devious practices of moneychangers. He didn't conduct a psychological study of their childhoods, hoping to find out why they devoted their lives to cheating. He stopped talking, and started walking. He lost his temper. He shouted. He set aside good manners.

The worker priests, we came to realize, had not abandoned their religion. Quite the contrary, they were acting out the message of the gospels. Dan and I read, re-read, and studied the worker priests' writings, many of which were published in the *Catholic Worker*, and it seemed to us that these priests were *living* the witness so many of us knew well, but didn't want to understand. Dan was a Professor of Religion at Le Moyne College in Syracuse, New York, but much of his teaching went on outside the classroom. He established an off-campus house where students and teachers met to discuss, and to debate, the meaning of being a Christian. He worked with his students to organize rent strikes, and to picket businesses that practiced discrimination. Dan and I had spent years studying for the priesthood, sequestered from the secular world, learning the intricacies of Catholic theology. Now we were being forced to articulate how we, as representatives of the church, should conduct our lives. The church had vested us with a certain moral authority, but who would blame us if we chose to stay inside a rectory, comfortable and quietly pious, feeding our flock, and ourselves, on a diet of benign passivity?

During his year abroad, Dan substituted for priests who had gone on leave from military bases. Germany was divided between the good West and the evil East. Young soldiers stood at snow-bound borders, peering at one another through binoculars, waiting to be attacked. Young airmen swooped over the countryside in practice bombing raids. The United States and the Soviet Union built bigger and increasingly deadly weapons, rattling their atomic swords at one another, and at the world. Dan left the arms race out of his liturgy. I left the Cold War out of my sermons. German novelist Thomas Mann would call anti-communism the greatest stupidity of the twentieth century, but my brother and I were still fledgling liberals. Young, working-class, Irish-American priests. There were still lines—psychological, intellectual, emotional, spiritual, theological—that we weren't ready to cross. Concepts and connections we still couldn't quite grasp, dues we weren't ready to pay.

I started putting some of my ideas down on paper, challenging myself (and, as I hoped, the church) to think critically about the racial crisis in America. In "The Challenge of Segregation," published in *Worship,* a magazine devoted to liturgical reform, I wrote that "No current social problem tests the vocation of the Christian as fiercely as does segregation. . . . Nothing, moreover is so contrary to his vocation of unity, nothing so inimical to the mission of his Church, nothing so violates the essential unity of the men he serves." I went on to question how Christians could be so vehemently anti-communist, while accepting the evils of segregation in our own nation. I criticized the moral detachment of so-called white moderates, and challenged their willingness to translate racism into an abstract concept, something that didn't impede their religious lives, or weaken their devotion to God and state. Finally, I argued that racism is a white, not a black, problem. After three centuries of brutal experience, blacks knew what needed to be done. It was not up to them to *understand* us. They didn't need to ask for guidance. It was up to us to *start* loving them, before it was too late.

We were doing everything in our power to crush the black man's spirit, while setting impossible standards for him if he wanted to join our self-righteous club. The government was failing our black brothers and sisters. The schools were failing them. And, sadly, the churches were failing them as well. Not just other religions, but the church I served and loved with all my heart and soul.

I was sent on occasion to offer the Eucharist to the all-white parishes that ringed New Orleans. There, acting as a substitute for one of the FBI priests (Foreign Born Irish who were taking their vacations in Ireland), I would offer homilies on racial justice. Some people listened in silence, their eyes, and I assume their minds, fixed on some distant spot. Others seemed to nod, if ever so imperceptibly, their appreciation. Still others shouted from their pews, telling me I knew nothing about the south, nothing about race relations, nothing about anything. Occasionally, someone would leap to his feet during mass and leave, quietly muttering insults. I was never threatened physically, never assaulted. The parishioners who shouted at me or stormed out during mass were good people. They just didn't want to admit their complicity in our collective oppression of African-Americans. They saw nothing odd about bringing their children to Mass on Sunday, and sending them to segregated schools on Monday. They saw nothing wrong with rejoicing in an all-loving God on Sunday, and refusing to hire a "nigger" on Tuesday. In many respects, they were no different from their counterparts in the North who looked down, from their moral precipice, on people in the south.

My troubles with religious superiors began when one of my articles appeared in the *Catholic Worker,* which circulated to about 100,000 readers. I had been trying to sort out what Christ might say about all-black schools, all-black churches, all-black neighborhoods; what He might say about Christians who believed in "loving thy neighbor," but only if our neighbors are white.

In the epistles of St. Paul, the question of slavery arises, and Paul gives no answer. This issue was just too overwhelming, too much a part of the culture in which he lived, and he wasn't willing to confront it directly. Fifteen hundred years later, the Catholic church seemed to be following Paul's lead, preferring to remain silent on one of the greatest tragedies in the history of the human race.

The article was quite long. It analyzed the psychology and pathology of racism, and it included a survey of so-called religious attitudes toward African-Americans. I wrote this piece because I was scheduled to give a talk at Cornell University. I came north, spoke at Cornell and, that very evening, gave the same talk to a large audience in Syracuse. I had worked on the article for months, researching it carefully, and asking Gene McManus to critique it before I submitted it for publication. As always, Gene made some very worthwhile suggestions. I had written rather extensively for *Priest* magazine; the full text of this piece can be found in my first book, *No More Strangers.*

I hadn't meant to be critical of my religious order; the Josephites were good people, doing good work. We truly identified with the plight of African-Americans, and we prided ourselves on being more militant on civil rights than other orders or various diocesan groups who worked with African-Americans. Yet, overall, our ethos spoke of the salvation of souls; and here we fell into a dichotomy, because we were separating our parishioners' suffering from their eternal destiny. After thinking about this a great deal, I concluded that we were downgrading, or cheapening, the lives of African-Americans. Given this context, or this approach, it is inevitable that the struggle to achieve equality—good schools, decent housing, integrated neighborhoods—would be less important than saving souls.

I got into trouble, and I'm sure others did as well, when I refused to censor myself and began criticizing the racist hierarchy of the Deep South. It seemed to me that we (well-meaning Christians) could spin our intellectual wheels endlessly, but if we failed to examine the institutional nature of racism we were missing the point. It would have been easy enough, as it is now, to dismiss racists as "rednecks," or to correlate racist attitudes with low levels of education or sophistication.

What I was trying to say then, and am still saying, is that racism is found at all levels of government, at all levels of the church, deep within every institution of higher learning, inside the military, inside the White House. I was treading beyond the liberal idea that racism is primarily an attitude problem, fixable with some intensive soul searching, a little more education, perhaps a few training sessions or town meetings.

My superiors didn't find my ideas offensive merely because I argued for black equality. They, too, believed deeply in equality. They respected the Josephites' commitment to African-Americans, and they supported our work with the poor. They just did not want me, or anyone else, to castigate the racist hierarchy in the South. Most of the bishops in Mississippi, Alabama, Georgia, Florida, and elsewhere in the Deep South, were reluctant to integrate Catholic schools.The bishops didn't want to upset whites, because they had money. Nor would the bishops speak clearly and forcefully about race. Instead, they made absurd, adolescent statements about a growing crisis. Their moral ambiguity inspired me to write an article, which appeared in the *Catholic Worker.*

My superiors received letters from the bishops, demanding to know why they were putting up with this upstart priest. Get Berrigan out of the South, said the bishops. Send him to the North where he can shoot off his mouth. I was called on the carpet. Would I like to lose my teaching job? No, I would not like that. Would I like to be sent off, ignominiously, to the boondocks? No, that didn't sound like much fun either.

Summoned to our headquarters in Baltimore, I stood before our superior. He was watching a championship high school football game on television. I explained my position. His eyes were glued to the tube. The sportscaster shouted. Kids in gladiator costumes slammed into one another. Back off, warned my superior. One of the kids made a spectacular catch. Just leave the bishops of the south alone. I listened politely, agreeing to nothing. One of the kids dashed across the goal line. Wild cheering. The superior didn't shout, but he seemed quite pleased. We exchanged amenities, shook hands, and I left for my return flight to New Orleans. The whole thing was little more than a tempest in a teapot.

Regardless of what anyone in America—racists inside or outside the church—wanted to happen, history was moving inexorably forward. From the very beginnings of slavery, blacks had resisted oppression in many covert, and sometimes overt, ways. They ran away from the plantation, destroyed crops, faked illness, broke tools, and rose up in revolt, sometimes killing slave owners. A century before Rosa Parks refused to give up her seat on a Montgomery bus to a white man, Frederick Douglass declared that "without struggle there is no progress . . . the struggle may be a moral one; or it may be a physical one; or it may be both moral and physical, but it must be a struggle."

Now, the struggle that began when the first African refused to be chained to a slave ship was accelerating. Night riders rode into the fray, shooting, burning, killing civil rights workers, burning homes, lynching blacks. They were fighting a rear-guard action. History, and the courage of those who sat-in and rode-in for freedom, would wash over the segregationists. Jim Crow would die hard, taking some beautiful people down, but Mrs. Parks and so many brave men, women, and children were fanning a fire that had always burned in the hearts and minds of African-Americans. As the civil rights movement spread, it was clear that beatings, arrests, threats, bombs, and assassinations would never extinguish this fire.

Dan and I were working on a project to send students from New Orleans to study at Le Moyne, and to bring students from Le Moyne to New Orleans. Dan had set up "International House," where he and a group of students intended to live, study, and worship together. The idea was to discover, or re-discover, what Catholics could do, and should do, to enact the social teachings of the church. Meanwhile, I continued writing articles, and joined all the well-known civil rights groups—the NAACP, the Urban League, the Southern Christian Leadership Conference, the Student Nonviolent Coordinating Committee, and others.

On May 4, 1961, a group of Freedom Riders boarded a bus in Washington, D.C. They planned to travel through Virginia, North Carolina, and South Carolina, arriving in New Orleans on May 17, the anniversary of the 1954 Supreme Court decision in *Brown vs. Board of Education.* The Freedom Riders had been warned that racists were prepared to attack, and to kill them, in order to keep interstate buses segregated. At Anniston, Alabama, two hundred angry segregationists stoned one of the Greyhound buses carrying Freedom Riders. The driver raced away, stopping six miles outside of town to repair a slit tire. A firebomb tossed through the rear door of the bus exploded shortly after the Riders jumped to safety. In Birmingham, a mob attacked the Trailways bus carrying more Freedom Riders, beating William Barbee so badly he would be paralyzed for life. An informant had warned the FBI that the Freedom Riders would be attacked in Birmingham, but the bureau's agents failed to appear. Bull Connor's police also stayed away from the bus station, leaving the mob to attack the Freedom Riders.

Photographs of burning buses, and news of the savage beatings in Birmingham, quickly spread around the world. President Kennedy summoned Justice Department staff to an early-morning meeting in the White House. Attorney General Bobby Kennedy was there as well. The President discussed the possibility of sending federal troops to Alabama, and he and Bobby were ready to order federal marshals to that state. When President Kennedy called Alabama governor John Patterson (the man who had dismissed the Freedom Riders with "When you go somewhere looking for trouble, you usually find it"), Patterson's aides said their boss had gone fishing.

Later, after the furor over the Freedom Riders had died down a bit, James Farmer, director of the Congress of Racial Equality (CORE), put out a call for priests, ministers, and rabbis to fly into Jackson, Mississippi, in order to integrate facilities at the airport. I heard about this, responded immediately, and got permission from my superior in Baltimore to go. Dan heard the call as well, but his provincial in Buffalo refused to grant him permission to travel to Jackson. Richard Wagner, a Josephite and fellow staff member at St. Augustine's, was also anxious to go. We met with James Farmer in New York City, and he went over the action very carefully, telling us that we might well be beaten, and even killed, in the Jackson airport. Officials in Jackson, Mississippi, and at the airport, would be alerted that we were coming. Members of CORE would be on hand to help us. Farmer assured us that there would be no leaks to the press. So the world would not be watching until after we had been beaten, and possibly jailed, in Jackson.

We boarded a plane early in the morning, landing in Atlanta where we were to pick up a flight to Jackson, Mississippi. I had barely disembarked from the plane when airport officials surrounded me, insisting that I accompany them to answer an "urgent phone call." The receiver thrust into my hand, I heard my superior general say that Bishop Gerow of Jackson, Mississippi, was extremely upset over the pending action. Bishop Gerow wanted to know why these Josephites were coming into his diocese, said he wasn't going to tolerate having us there, and demanded that my superior withdraw permission for our visit. We were ordered to drop our plans, and hop the first flight back to Baltimore, which we did.

In April 1963, Martin Luther King released his "Letters from Birmingham City Jail," which was first published by the American Friends Service Committee (a Quaker group) in pamphlet form. In that eloquent, moving, and angry letter Dr. King challenged his fellow clergymen to agree to the necessity for direct, nonviolent action if African-Americans were to be freed from the evils of segregation. Responding to those who urged him to be patient, to avoid confrontation, and not to alienate his liberal supporters, King wrote:

> We know through painful experience that freedom is never given by the oppressor; it must be demanded by the oppressed . . . Frankly, I have yet to engage in a direct-action campaign that was "well timed" in view of those who have not suffered unduly from the disease of segregation. For years now I have heard the word "Wait!" It rings in the ear of every Negro with piercing familiarity. This "Wait" has almost always meant "Never."

In many respects, my Josephite brothers and I were still well-meaning liberals, believing that the system would eventually bend to our good will. We hadn't traveled the bitter, hate-strewn road that had brought Dr. King to Birmingham jail. But we were deeply moved by Reverend King's letter, and by his willingness to risk jail, and even his life, for the civil rights struggle. Martin Luther King's witness, and his powerful words, would draw some of us beyond sentiment, into the world of dogs and clubs, tear gas and jail cells.

Millions of people throughout the world have seen the film clips: Civil rights demonstrators approaching the Edmund Pettus Bridge in Selma, Alabama. Alabama state troopers, clubs and tear gas guns ready. Mounted troopers holding clubs and bullwhips. Major John Cloud giving the order for the troopers to charge into the crowd, beating, whipping, cursing the demonstrators. Screams for help. The thump of breaking bones. Screams of anger. The whump of tear gas. ABC interrupting *Judgment at Nuremberg* to show the brutality in Selma.

Martin Luther King responded to the attack on his followers ("Bloody Sunday," March 7, 1965) by sending out telegrams to prominent American clergymen, asking them to join him on Tuesday morning, March 9, 1965, for a march from Selma to Montgomery, Alabama. Dr. King had been awarded the Nobel Peace Prize in 1964, and the world was watching to see if America would honor, or murder, this great man. Dan and I, along with several friends from New York City, headed for Selma where we gathered in Brown's Chapel, a center of anti-racist activity in Alabama. The march, said speakers from the Southern Christian Leadership Conference, would be difficult, perhaps even dangerous, but there was no turning back. Once again, innocent people had been blinded with tear gas, beaten into the pavement, and thrown into jail. People had been hurt in Selma, but no one had been killed. We would keep marching. Keep singing. Keep going until justice prevailed. We intended to march from Brown's Chapel to the courthouse, in order to continue the voter registration drive. But before we could move out, the SCLC warned us that the police would not allow us to leave the chapel. We were shut in. Unable to move.

I'll admit that I felt a rush of panic. The windows were closed, the doors were shut, the air was stale, and we were packed in together, friends and strangers, on uncomfortable pews. This was not World War II. I was not in the field with my heavily armed unit. We couldn't maneuver around our enemy, hoping to trap and kill him. This war had to be fought without guns. We had to return love for clubs and tear gas and bullets. We waited. Time crawled through sand. The doors didn't open.

Suddenly, after perhaps an hour, we were standing on the sidewalk outside that stifling chapel, filling our lungs with fresh air, our arms flapping like wings. But we weren't about to fly to the courthouse, because deputies hemmed us in on all sides, forming a tight cage against our march. We looked at the deputies, they looked at us, and we went to our knees in silent prayer.

Our witness didn't move Sheriff Jim Clark. We would not march that day, he said. We would disperse, he demanded. We continued praying, our backs and knees growing sore and wobbly. The deputies looked more bored than angry and they didn't join our prayer group. Jim Clark ordered them to back off, leaving us for another day. We couldn't march, but at least we could return to where we were staying.

Dan and I went to Selma to support Dr. King and the people who were daily risking their lives in the civil rights struggle. We were not tear-gassed, clubbed, or arrested. Nevertheless, we crossed more than a symbolic line that day. We stepped out of rhetoric, into the reality of action, and the realm of consequence. Inside Brown's Chapel, I felt the menace of men carrying guns and clubs in their hands, intolerance and bigotry in their hearts; men who dismissed my sentiments as just so much trash strewn across Dixie by "outside agitators." I sweated for awhile, as blacks have done for centuries, inside the claustrophobic hole of fear. Feeling outrage, yet experiencing something much deeper than ordinary anger.

I didn't know what might happen once we were inside some Alabama jail, though I had heard stories about black men and women being beaten, and killed, behind bars. I was feeling rage. Not just fear, and not just righteous anger, but a deep fire. A burning at the edges of my soul which would turn into a driving force, sustaining me over the long haul, keeping me alive and operating for years to come.

The Josephites and other priests and nuns who were working in the South weren't sequestered. We walked the streets, we visited our poor parishioners' homes, we saw the scars racism carved into the hearts and minds of African-Americans. We heard Jim Crow explain the necessity for segregation, and we were called yankee carpetbaggers, told we would never understand the complexities of race relations south of the Mason-Dixon line, urged to go back home before we got ourselves killed.

Our racist critics were right about some things. We couldn't understand their peculiar ideas. We failed to see, for example, how discrimination against blacks was compatible with being a good American or Christian. We couldn't quite grasp how someone could claim to love a man one day, and lynch him the next.

John F. Kennedy was Irish Catholic, two big strikes against him when he ran for president. He was handsome and tough, liked a good joke, and wouldn't turn down a drink. All of which endeared him to millions of Irish-Americans like my own family. After the election, my brother Dan even sent President and Mrs. Kennedy copies of his books, with a lovely inscription that read: "They go to you with the prayer that your courage, cheerfulness, and moral and cultural leadership continue to hearten our country and our world." We believed in Kennedy's Peace Corps, supported the Alliance for

Progress, and when the President was assassinated I broke down and cried. I had no idea that he sent CIA assassins to kill Fidel Castro, that he was escalating the arms race, that his macho posing brought us to the brink of nuclear war, or that he was sinking the nation, inextricably, into the Vietnam quagmire. I just bought the image, instead of looking at the man, and what he was really doing here and abroad. The media wove the wool tight over my eyes, though soon enough the veil would lift, never to fall again.

I was living in New Orleans in 1962 when President Kennedy took the country to the edge of the nuclear abyss. Terrified people fled north, hoping to survive World War III. The roads and highways leading out of Louisiana and Mississippi were lined with tarpaper shacks, and the black families living in those hovels could not escape. If atomic warfare broke out, the grandsons and granddaughters of slaves would be the first to die. The Russians blinked, JFK proved his manhood, the Cuban missile crisis ended, and I commenced a lifelong study of the connections between militarism, racism, and poverty.

In the early sixties, poor folk in Mississippi were digging pine stumps from the ground. Inside the stumps was a concentration of turpentine, and they would chop away for hours, then hook up a team of mules to the stump and drag it to a mill for processing. In Louisiana, blacks worked on sugar plantations, hacking at the snake-infested cane for wages that barely kept them alive. This was a Third World setting, where workers made $600 a year.

I saw destitution throughout the South, and I began asking why so many Americans, black and white, lived in poverty. The people I knew in Washington, D.C., and Louisiana weren't lazy. They wanted a better life for their children, but the odds were against them. They couldn't save money, because they didn't make enough to save. They couldn't send their children to college, because they could barely pay their rent. I began to wonder how the government spent taxpayers' money. If Congress spent little or nothing to help the poor, what did it do with the billions it collected?

My research led to one conclusion: Congress was giving the Pentagon vast sums of taxpayers' dollars to manufacture, test, and deploy weapons of mass destruction. The government was building thousands of nuclear weapons in order to protect the American people from communism. Blacks had to live in shacks, and their children had to die from hunger and disease, so that the military could build bombs.

It wasn't difficult to make the connections between racism, poverty, and militarism. I concluded that war is the overarching evil in this country. Every other social lesion is related to our willingness to blow up the planet. We're willing to do that; otherwise, we wouldn't have these weapons. We built them with a very definite intention, which is that under certain circumstances we will use them. Racism, discrimination against women, poverty, domestic violence, are connected to this intention.

Paradoxically, the military is one of the few places where African-Americans are treated fairly. In recent years, the military has very quietly made provision for blacks to attend the Air Force Academy, Annapolis, and West Point. The military has enabled blacks to rise through the ranks, and made a genuine effort to help them break out of the cycle of poverty, despair, and street violence.

In 1964, Lyndon Baines Johnson declared war on poverty in America, giving new hope to advocates of the poor, and raising the expectations of the poor themselves. Commissions were set up, studies initiated, new visions discussed and debated. Political rhetoric swelled from the White House. Congress funded a variety of programs for "disadvantaged" inner-city residents. There was talk of full employment, of model cities, of well-fed children and garden communities instead of slums.

And then, on August 2, 1964, the captain of the *U.S.S. Maddox,* a destroyer patrolling in the Gulf of Tonkin, radioed that his ship had been attacked by North Vietnamese patrol boats. The *Maddox* was no ordinary destroyer; it was a spy ship, mapping North Vietnamese coastal and air defenses. Two days later another ship in the Seventh Fleet, the *C. Turner Joy,* claimed it too had been attacked by North Vietnamese PT boats. Before the Pentagon could confirm that this really happened, Secretary of Defense McNamara advised retaliatory air strikes on the North. The *Maddox* may have been attacked once, but not twice, by the North Vietnamese, and there is no evidence that the *Turner Joy* was ever attacked. Congress reacted to these reports by passing the Gulf of Tonkin Resolution, giving the President power to wage a full-scale, undeclared war on the

Vietnamese people. Mr. Johnson's much ballyhooed "Great Society" died in the first bombing raids against the Vietnamese people.

On July 2, 1964, President Johnson signed the Civil Rights Act, outlawing racial discrimination in all public and private facilities open to the public, but not really addressing African-Americans' right to vote. Dan and I stood across the street in Lafayette Park with Joan Baez, A.J. Muste, David Dellinger, and other anti-war activists, waving our signs and trying to speak out against the escalating violence in Vietnam. We weren't there to denigrate the courage and commitment of the people who had worked so hard, and in some cases given their lives, to secure passage of this law. We admired them, and we applauded their efforts, yet even as President Johnson lifted his pen to sign the most important piece of anti-discrimination legislation since Reconstruction, the war in Vietnam was expanding. We stood in Lafayette Park as an act of resistance, and a plea for common sense. Justice would never come from the bomb bay doors of a B 52. The war in Vietnam would never lead to peace in America. Destroying others would ultimately destroy us.

During the civil rights struggle, racists killed Medgar Evers, Viola Liuzzo, Jimmy Lee Jackson, Reverend James Reeb, and others. A KKK posse, led by the local deputy sheriff, murdered Michael Schwerner, Andrew Goodman, and James Chaney. So many good men and women died to give African-Americans the chance to vote, to attend integrated schools, to move forward from the back of the bus. I admired their courage and respected their dedication. Their work, their lives, their deaths mattered then, and they matter now. The civil rights movement didn't fail. But racism is a hydra. Cut off one head, another sprouts in its place. Malcolm X recognized this when he spoke about the chains being taken off African-Americans' ankles, only to be placed on their minds. Instead of the whip and the auction block, the white man resorts to political, legal, and social tricks to control blacks. "Never," said Malcolm, "do they change our condition or the slavery. They only change the tricks."

Tragically, more than three decades after Dr. King's great speech, the KKK doesn't have to resort to terrorizing African-Americans. Guns, drugs, and poverty are lynching thousands of African-American men every year. The courts are packing our prisons—do misery pits like Attica differ that much from concentration camps?—with black, Latino, Native American, and poor white Americans. Chain gangs are breaking the spirits of inmates who dare to question, or who attempt to resist, racist oppression. Armed with decisions from a racist Supreme Court, the executioners are busy exterminating the 3,000 inmates on death row, 40% of whom are black. In the state of Pennsylvania, 9% of the population is African-American, while 60% of the men on death row are black. Three quarters of the new admissions to prison in the United States are black or Hispanic and, at this rate, the absolute majority of black men between age eighteen and forty will be in prison by the year 2010. Cheered on by a frightened nation, the police are free to beat, torture, and murder people of color. At the great 1963 march in Washington, D.C., Martin Luther King spoke to 250,000 demonstrators about having a dream "that one day down in Alabama—with its vicious racists, with its governor having his lips dripping with the words of interposition and nullification—one day right there in Alabama, little black boys and black girls will be able to join hands with little white boys and white girls as sisters and brothers."

What might Reverend King say if he could visit our country's death cages, crowded with African-Americans waiting to die? If he could walk our inner-city streets again and see the legacy of crack cocaine, the gangs, and hopeless poverty? I imagine him weeping, his tears drowned out by sirens and the sound of automatic gunfire, his message of love and reconciliation smothered by fascist ideologues.

Black mayors. Black Congressmen. Black police chiefs. Black generals. Black rock stars. Black film stars. Black sports stars. Some commentators argue that the glass is half empty, others that it is half full. The analogy hardly matters. We lurch toward the year 2000, dragging our bloody chains, our crimes, behind us. Millions of African-Americans are still living in poverty, captive to the "tricks" of institutional racism, police brutality, white fear, and capitalist manipulation.

And then, of course, there's Colin Powell, a black man who is admired, even revered, by many whites. But what does that prove except that we suffer from a deep, and rather pathological, hypocrisy? In the morning we cheer the right wing's assault on impoverished African-Americans. In the afternoon we wait in line to buy

General Powell's book. We love black people who succeed—Bill Cosby, Magic Johnson, Maya Angelou—and hate those who fail. Colin Powell represents power, stability, and discipline. He's a soldier, a heroic figure like Dwight Eisenhower. If he convinces us that he's the nation's savior, we just might overlook the color of his skin and one day make him president of the United States.

Malcolm X intended to present his case before the United Nations. He was determined to tell the world that the United States government was systematically violating the human rights of its own black citizens. Would the white community believe him, then or now? When the police fracture a welfare mother's skull, or kill her son in the hallway of a housing project, the crime hardly makes the news. When the bullet-riddled body of another black teenager is taken to the morgue, the event is of no importance. What we don't see, we don't believe. What we don't know, doesn't happen. The mirror we looked into in the fifties has become the vicious magic show of the nineties:

- Ending affirmative action means *creating* meritocracy.

- Cutting people off welfare means *giving* people hope.

- Putting people to death means *respecting* life.

- Building atomic submarines, instead of schools, means *protecting* democracy.

- Destroying our children means *saving* them.

Before he was assassinated on April 4, 1968, Martin Luther King was still urging the oppressed to turn the other cheek; still trying to warn us that violence is always circular. It wraps around both victim and victimizer, holding them in a deadly embrace. In his letter from Birmingham jail, King warned that "There comes a time when the cup of endurance runs over, and men are no longer willing to be plunged into the abyss of despair." Malcolm X tried to tell us that the cup wasn't just running over, the brew was ready to explode.

Walking the streets of Baltimore, New York City, Washington, D.C., I see how close poor people are to the abyss, and I can't help but wonder how much longer they will wait for justice. The rioting that followed the trial of the police officers accused of beating

Rodney King should be a warning to America. Sleights of hand and magic tricks are no substitute for justice. Malcolm X argued that African-Americans should secure their rights "by any means necessary." I do not advocate violence, but I live in Baltimore, I live in the American war zone, I can see and feel and hear the apocalypse.

"And God gave Noah the rainbow sign. No more water. The fire next time." A fire that police brutality, prisons, hate radio, right-wing challenges to social justice, and racist judicial decisions are fanning.

FELLOWSHIP OF RECONCILIATION CONVOCATION. WEST COAST. OCTOBER, 1965

Perhaps we could begin with a story which is true, tragic, and somewhat illustrative of our concerns in this conference. There is a Negro family in our parish in Baltimore—a family large, poor, and Christian. Mr. and Mrs. Harris, we might call them, had fifteen children, fourteen of them living, one boy having died under surgery as a teenager. The girls, four in number, are all married and with families of their own—so it is with two of the older boys. This family is remarkable in many respects: for instance, the father is a collector of old Bibles and consequently, the Scriptures have always held a place of honor in that home. Moreover, the parents would gather their children several times weekly to discuss and reflect upon the Word of God. The children were all named for scriptural figures: Isaiah, Ishmael, Jeremiah, John, Ruth, Samuel, and so on. In these circumstances, it is perhaps no accident that profound poverty never really injured the sense of dignity and decency in that home.

Now Mr. Harris is old and sick, while his wife carries the burdens of family, gathering years and sorrows. The older children have, in a sense, "broken through"—their education is better than that of their parents, their earning power is tolerable if not completely adequate, life is no longer that of a Baltimore slum, and they will never return to it. Yet tragedy has invaded the substance of all their lives, and I would like to tell you about it.

The fifth son the parents called Jeremiah Paul, and though he was an average child, his mother noticed one unusual trait in him. In the course of the most ordinary play, Jeremiah would break apart from his companions to weep and moan in some secluded place—his room, a corner of the alley, the back yard. Mrs. Harris used to ask him what was the matter repeatedly, but the boy could never answer. In desperation, she brought him to her minister and after reflecting on the youngster's names, the good man said, "Mrs. Harris, Jeremiah was called the 'weeping prophet,' and Paul put up with more tribulation than any of the apostles. That's why this boy is what he is. He's gonna weep and he's gonna know tribulation." And so it seemed.

At fourteen, the weeping had ceased, but as Jeremiah grew older, he gave his parents other cause for worry. In his mother's words, he was "impressionable," and somewhat led by the young toughs of the neighborhood. After dropping out of high school, he had a job delivering newspapers from a tiny stand in downtown Baltimore. The proprietor was a little old white lady who lived in the rear of the store with her son—she was wizened, alert, and seemingly satisfied with her newsboy. One day, Jeremiah appeared for his papers. He knocked and waited. When the old lady came to the door, some obscure sense told her that something was wrong—the boy's face was contorted and threatening. She attempted to close the door but he caught it with his foot; and when she resisted, he swung it open, knocking her to the floor. Terribly frightened and hurt by the fall, the old lady began to scream, and at this, her son raced from the rear of the house where he had been shaving. There was his mother on the floor in obvious terror and pain, and a frightened Negro boy standing over her. Automatically responding, the man began to beat Jeremiah, demanding as he did the reason for what seemed to him a sexual assault. The lad claimed innocence, and when this only angered the man further, he broke away and ran. In due course, the police picked him up and charged him with attempted rape.

As the case developed, it became obvious to the police that the charge was a weak one. The prisoner had confessed to attempted robbery, but the only evidence of intent to rape was a physician's report of shock and a bruised hip. Accordingly, they began to inquire further. Jeremiah was grilled incessantly about his associations with white women, and finally, under promise of a light sentence, he admitted visiting a young married woman of such and such an address.

The police brought the woman in for questioning and learned that she lived alone, that her husband was a serviceman stationed overseas, and that any revelation of her liaison with the young Negro would wreck her reputation, and probably her marriage. They began to suggest to the girl that she protect herself by accusing the lad of rape under threat of violence. Fearfully, she agreed to do so, though in reality, she had provoked the friendship, had liked Jeremiah, submitted to him, had him visit her weekly, and even paid him to continue the relationship.

The prosecution now had its case. To strengthen it further, the old lady conveniently died, of course somewhat remotely in time from the alleged violence. Yet the prosecution used her death to strengthen its charges, which were substantially this: the prisoner had already raped one white woman repeatedly, had threatened her with death if she sought help, and was well on the way to doing the same thing to his employer when her son beat him away. Moreover, it was claimed by them that the old lady had died from injuries connected with the attack.

Jeremiah's lawyer was a young Negro supplied by the state, since his parents could not afford one. Whether this man was merely incompetent, or whether he was intimidated by the efforts of the state to obtain a heavy conviction never became clear, but his defense was feeble, desultory, and unconvincing. The trial was short and the conviction never in doubt—the lad was sentenced to life in prison.

He is now a man 26 years old, having served seven years of a term destined to end only with his death. Since his imprisonment, the family has made unsuccessful attempts to reopen the case, but they have neither the money nor the voice to do so. Yet one opportunist lawyer told Mrs. Harris that for $3,000, he would have her son a free man in two months.

So much for our brand of justice for many Negroes. I occupy your time with this story because the theme of Pope John's letter, *Peace on Earth*, is human dignity, and the rights that flow from that dignity, rights which are an inseparable part of human nature, rights which are inalienable, inviolable, and universal. The letter pointedly asserts that freedom from war and peace without fear are impossible without the recognition of human rights, and their possession by all men. Let us investigate briefly some of the main provisions of the encyclical, and then see them in light of Watts, Vietnam, and the arms race.

II

Peace on Earth carries a repetitious theme expressed by these words: "Peace among all people requires: Truth as its foundation, justice as its rule, love as its driving force, liberty as its atmosphere." The letter expounds this theme in its four main divisions: peace rests upon accord between individuals; between individuals and their political communities; between nations themselves; between nations and the whole community of man. It is worth noting, as the encyclical does, that the root and platform of peace is respect for the individual. Thus it is that the immense complexities of achieving world order begin at the seat of the person with the elimination of personal conflict, from which can spring the great reaches of justice needed to remove conflicts among men. "Habeas corpus," lawyers maintain, is the most basic of human rights, and the thoughtful among them who see a demand for world law as the beginning of world government, insist that every individual is an international personality, whose rights must be internationally guaranteed.

Though initiatives in areas of world law and government might be presently beyond us, the Pope strongly implies that we must be creative and nonviolent agents of peace, through which the strife and perplexity of others is faced with compassionate concern. Indeed, we must become more aware that the occasions of peacemaking are both commonplace and priceless, being found wherever injustice creates varieties of hopelessness, anonymity, or unbalanced individuality.

People who are alienated from one another have little impact upon the political community, or they use it as an arena for self-interest. Consequently, the political order often becomes a mirror of collective myopia and selfishness, reflecting the partisanship and nationalism of its people. In contrast, *Peace on Earth* tells us that "these political communities must harmonize their relations according to truth and justice, and in the spirit of active solidarity in liberty." The truth referred to demands that we admit "the natural equality of all political communities in dignity and human nobility." Truth demands that we look upon all people with objectivity springing from a realization of common nature, common rights, and common interest. Truth demands that we be truthful, and honest because we are truthful, and that we require from our church, our government, and our news media the same substance of truth that we require from ourselves. Justice, in turn, implies "the recognition of mutual rights and the fulfillment of their corresponding duties." Justice demands that "when political communities advance opposing interests, the conflicts must be settled neither by force of arms nor by fraud or deceit, but by mutual understanding, by an objective appraisal of the facts and by an equitable compromise." The sense of solidarity of which the encyclical speaks requires that both individuals and nations are obligated to develop what has been called a species-wide identity, which is at once the common denominator of mankind and the most important reality of its existence. Pope Paul clarified this point in last year's Christmas message, in which he said that brotherhood is impossible until men confront the ideology of nationalism, the division of racism, the fear of arms. Finally, the sense of liberty requires that men set up goals which are good, fulfilling, and possible, and that both people and their nations assess their freedom against the obligations of initiative and responsibility.

What can be said of the arms race in the considered light of truth, justice, the spirit of solidarity, and responsible liberty? The encyclical speaks of this contemporary curse in restrained and solemn speech: "The production of arms is allegedly justified on the grounds that in present-day conditions peace cannot be preserved without the equal balance of armaments. And so, if one country increases armaments, others feel the need to do the same; and if one country is equipped with nuclear weapons, other countries must produce their own, equally destructive. Consequently, people live in constant fear lest the storm that every moment threatens should break upon them with dreadful violence. And with good reason, for the arms of war are ready at hand. Even though it is difficult to believe that anyone would deliberately take the responsibility for the appalling destruction and sorrow that war would bring in its train, it cannot be denied that the conflagration may be set off by some uncontrollable and unexpected chance... Justice, then, right reason, and humanity urgently demand that the arms race should cease, that the stockpiles which exist in various countries should be reduced equally and simultaneously by the parties concerned; that nuclear weapons should be banned; and that finally a general agreement should be reached about progressive disarmament and an effective means of control."

Because of the arms race, and the combination of fear and social selfishness which produces it, two-thirds of mankind languishes in hunger, ignorance, and hopelessness. Against this collective and public crime, the encyclical warns that "misery does not wait," and that time cannot be otherwise than short. "In a world which counts an additional man every second, one has not the right to be an hour behind... Every year, of 60 million deaths, hunger and its consequences cause 30 to 40 million, that is to say as much as the last war in five years, with all its resources and destruction." It is necessary that this "unmerited misery" of peoples cease, for it is just another reason why the swords of which the Prophet Isaiah spoke must become plowshares. One might well be appalled by such quiet brutality, particularly in face of the world's arms budget, conservatively estimated at $140 billion annually. Unavoidably, the very existence of such arms, and the deprivation that follows their maintenance and spread, does unmerited and severe violence to the very ideal of human equality and dignity.

The encyclical next appeals for a supranational power or world government, and here the document reaches a summit of natural development. In fact, one sees within it the logical contention that individual egoism, partisan politics, and jealous nationalism must be confronted on every level, to reach culmination in an effort which secures the rights of all people and nations. "Today, the universal common good poses problems of worldwide dimensions which cannot be adequately tackled or solved except by the efforts of public authorities endowed with a wideness of powers, structure, and means of the same proportions, that is, of public authorities which are in a position to operate in an effective manner on a worldwide basis. The moral order therefore demands that such a form of public authority be established." And the Pope goes on: "A public authority having world-wide power and endowed with the proper means for the efficacious pursuit of its objective, which is the universal common good in a concrete form, must be set up by common accord and not imposed by force. The reason is that such an authority must be in a position to operate effectively; yet at the same time an action must be inspired by sincere and real impartiality. In other words, it must be an action aimed at satisfying the objective requirements of the universal common good." The United Nations, he hoped, will "become more equal to the magnitude and nobility of its tasks." Here the Pope goes on record in behalf of the U.N. as a hopeful and praiseworthy beginning toward supranational government—obviously he did not say, however, that it is world government, or that it even approaches what mankind needs in world law and government.

Pope John concludes his letter on peace with a section that might seem anticlimactic, but which is, in reality, a positive attack upon the ideologies that so rankle and divide men. Once again, he stresses the things held in common by man, at the expense of those which separate, and he implies that unless the common heritage of humanity comes alive in economic, social, political, and cultural exchange, ideologies will become frozen, becoming the theoretical basis for division to the point of war. Distinctions, therefore, must be made between those who err and their error, between philosophical systems and their evolution in history. "One must never confuse error and the person who errs. It must be borne in mind, furthermore, that neither can false philosophical teaching regarding the nature, origin, and destiny of the universe and of man, be identified with historical movements that have economic, social, cultural, or political ends, not even when these movements have originated from those teachings and have drawn and still draw inspiration therefrom. For these teachings, once drawn up and defined, remain always the same, while the movements, working on historical situations in constant evolution, cannot but be influenced by these latter and cannot avoid, therefore, being subject to changes, even of a profound nature." What he says here is of vast significance especially to many Americans who are obsessed with a naive and unhistorical fear of Communism. People just cannot be identified with the ideology they profess, nor dismissed with it, individually or collectively. The Communist is first a human being, just as our humanity is prior to our democracy. And in reversing the order of primacy between the two, we demean the person and absolutize the ideology, believing that opposing beliefs can only be confronted by arming ourselves against those who hold them. In this way, and history bears ample proof, historical evolution of ideologies is inhibited or checked completely—China still adheres to Stalinism because to a great extent, we and others like us will not give her cause to allow a relaxation.

Our century has produced marvels in engineering, in medical research, in nuclear physics. Now we are experimenting with the biology of life itself, and with interplanetary travel. Restlessness and curiosity consume us. We continue to plunge into the mysteries of nature. Yet we have not learned to understand and to love one another even to the minimal degree demanded by our survival. And so our crisis is not that caused by the atom, or cybernetics, or Cold War—it is rather one of faith and love. And so we must learn to resolve this crisis, or science fiction may become true in our regard, as we leave to inhabit another planet, while we leave this one in flames.

Pope John tells us that it is for wise and dedicated statesmen to determine the stages, the means, and the extent of reconciliation among people —while it is for us to create the atmosphere which will allow their efforts, and offer some hope of achievement. The creation of co-existence with the Communist world is not enough—what is needed is a movement as broad as revolution which will encourage men to confront their fears, to speak to one another, and to insist on their own humanity through respect and reverence for others.

WATTS

Against the calm and reasoned hope for man's potential to abolish war and to secure peace that Pope John gives us; against, too, the unthinking assumption of many Americans that there is not even need for such a document, came the debacle of Watts like a prolonged peek into Hell. Thirty-seven people died, nearly 900 were injured, 209 buildings were totally destroyed and another 1000 seriously damaged, over 3,900 people were arrested. Watts cost the country and the Los Angeles community about a half billion dollars in damage, police costs, and disaster relief, plus the incalculable price of life. And it is becoming clear now that what happened was not riot, not unrest nor strict protest. It was war, interracial war.

And as usual, many whites insisted on misinterpreting its causes and its meaning. Billy Graham maintained that Watts was the beginning of a national insurrection against the established structures of society; former President Eisenhower called the riot evidence of a widespread and growing disruption of law and order. "If we like the law," he said, "we obey it; if you don't, we are told, you can disobey it." Chief Parker linked the causes of Watts to the civil disobedience of the civil rights movement. Even the President shared the dishonesty, for though he would acknowledge something deeper at work in a ghetto like Watts, he reminded Negroes that repetitions of similar nature would only hurt the civil rights movement. Which is like advising patience to the starving while others feast around them.

More to the point would be the realization by the white community that the structures of the country must change if the Negro is to be accommodated as an equal—and if change does not come peacefully and quickly, it will come violently and quickly, and with all the character of mass insurrection prophesied by Rev. Graham. More to the point would be education to an awareness that the law to the Negro is very often an enemy, since it is part of the status quo. And in this context, the law is in fact a club used to silence those for whom the status quo has no meaning. More to the point would be the admission that the people of Watts, and hundreds of ghettos like it, neither know the civil rights movement nor care about it, simply because the movement has been able to do nothing for them. Such spokesmen, then, as they speculate from their ignorance and vested interests, are very far from understanding that this country has no serious intent to accept the Negro as a fellow human being, with the rights and security that follow that acceptance.

Adam Clayton Powell, some will claim, is the most adroit at having his cake and eating it—his people have never accused him of sellout to the white man, and yet he has publicly relished all of the embellishments of an absolutely secure political position. When, however, he ventures to speak on the causes of racism, which is often, he can usually be counted on for accuracy. He said this of Watts: "Los Angeles, and to a lesser extent, Chicago and Springfield, are only the visible sparks of the volcano of discontent and hatred which lie quietly beneath the surface now in Black communities all over America. Every black ghetto in this country is a potential Los Angeles. Until a comprehensive and massive attack on northern racial hatred is undertaken, Los Angeles is only the beginning of a long series of rioting and lawlessness not only this summer, but in many summers to come."

Powell's observations seem well taken. Far from being completely indifferent to the tragedy of Watts (and most whites are this), or indulging in furious denunciations of lawless Negroes, the white community would be far more honest to wonder why we have not had more of a display of Negro desperation and fury. The Summer of '64 had its Harlem, Bedford-Stuyvesant, Rochester, and Jersey City; last summer produced Watts, Chicago, and Springfield. Yet against all reasonable norms, we still look for reasons that are other than human, still look for the evidence that Negroes are irrational, brutal, irresponsive to opportunity, and simply incapable of appeals to decency and duty. When Watts occurred, its sheer uproar and ruin was made to fit the myths and stereotypes of white prejudice. more than that, Watts became evidence which reinforced the myths, making them more irrationally reasonable in white minds. And there existed little perception that the sickness and disorder of the myths had begotten a concrete counterpart in the sickness and disorder in the streets of Los Angeles. The chickens had indeed come home to roost. Which is to say that the unreal illness of the myths was made real in other lives beyond the point of human endurance. And when that point came, the Negroes of Watts rebelled, because life fragmented and coerced by a myth had become unendurable.

How long will Negroes, particularly the Negro masses, be content with the violence that comes with being forced to live by white myths? At what point does such existence so rob people of hope that the only possible means of self-assertion are the brick and the Molotov cocktail? At what point are Negroes forced to say No! and with such pent-up violence that they are quite indifferent to whatever form the Yes! might take? At what point will Negroes be so convinced of the sterility and despair of their lives that to die in a welter of assault and blood is a more honorable thing than to live in shame and degradation? At what point do we make the last phase of our own Civil War an inescapable contingency, since in this age, a condition of colonialism is hardly better than slavery was a hundred years ago?

We do not know the answers to these questions. We do know, however, that because they are questions and because they have gone so largely unanswered, they constitute a very heavy judgment on what we are and what we have done. We do know that Watts does not approach Harlem, Bedford-Stuyvesant, and many other Negro ghettoes in concentration of people, in alcoholism, dope addiction, unemployment, and sheer hopelessness. And yet none of them, even those that have exhibited racial unrest, can compare with Watts in furious and ferocious reprisal. What does this say to us? Certainly more than we need about the crucial urgency of the question, more than we need about the utter poverty of our national conscience, and what this poverty has done to keep the Negro disenfranchised, socially and politically.

The evil genius of American segregation is to keep the Negro poor. The dollar has always been so intimately associated with power in this country, that the ethos has been simple and profoundly effective—monopolize the wealth and one can control the power. So it is that the Negro has been tolerated in both slavery and native colonialism as an economic asset. Consciously or unconsciously, as part of prejudice or an effect of it, the Negro has been restricted in poverty as a prop to the nation's private economy. He did not cease to be Black Gold with the Emancipation Proclamation—

as cheap labor, as victim of exorbitant rents, real estate, and food prices, as customer of alcohol, narcotics, and numbers, as barter in prostitution, as one whom white law suppressed that his value might continue—the Negro has been very profitable to us indeed, as a necessary asset to private enterprise.

The benefits of segregation to the public domain are something different. The country at large pays conservatively 50 billion dollars a year for the luxury of rejecting the Negro; we spent almost 5 billion in welfare, most of which goes to the inner-city ghetto; we invest astronomical amounts in added police and fire protection; we lose thirty billion a year alone because of employment bias; we accept educational costs, which under segregation in the South and comparable devices in the North, hover one-quarter to one-third above needs, producing in turn, an educational system inadequate for both whites and Negroes.

We are very loath, however, to allow considerations of public interest to invade the private world of income or investment. This would be, in our opinion, an infringement of the sacred American rights to one's property, whether it be home, business, savings, or labor. And so we can be relatively unmoved by what the President said at Howard University, that Negroes earn but half of what whites do. We can be no more than slightly restless with the Vice President's assertion that with unemployment the lowest in ten years, Negro unemployment is constantly rising, forcing a major economic crisis among Negroes. We can continue to rot morally while the Negro deteriorates physically, and we can face the certain eventuality of a series of Watts because we firmly believe that it is cheaper to hire more police, or to call out the National Guard, than it is to remove discrimination. For we firmly believe, without daring to admit it, that police power is our only resource against the growth of Negro unrest.

The ugly face of the Vietnam War: Above, the bombed-out Vi Luong pagoda (Nam Trung village, Nam Truc district, Nam Ha province). Below, a 25-year-old mother and her year-old baby, killed in a U.S. air attack on April 19, 1966. Photos courtesy of Cornell University, Carl A. Kroch Library, Division of Rare and Manuscript Collections.

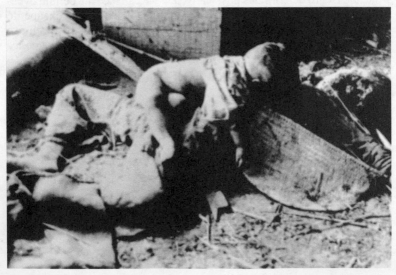

꧁꧂

FIVE

Just Wars and Genocide

Dissent without resistance is consent.
HENRY DAVID THOREAU

May 24, 1968. Judge Northrop cocks his head to one side, as though he is listening to celestial music. He shuffles his notes, sighs heavily, and pounds his gavel. "Six years," he announces.

Two thousand days away from friends and family. Two thousand nights in a steel cage. Time enough to break even the most recalcitrant spirit on the wheel of solitude, rotten food, and permanent disgrace. Sooner or later, I will be forced to accept a life of quiet desperation. I will agree to shuffle, silent, obedient, head bowed to the imperial state. Time enough to shut this crazy priest down, for good.

I listen to the judge with intense disinterest, his words falling like dead leaves. I am neither depressed nor frightened. Judge Northrop's sentence hardly matters. I feel exalted.

No hiding the facts. Our act was premeditated, and our intent was absolutely clear. On October 17, 1967, Tom Lewis, David Eberhardt, Jim Mengel, and I did walk into the Baltimore Customs House. We did attempt to destroy draft records, pouring our own blood over licenses to kill human beings. Our first trial ended in conviction and we were released on bail pending sentencing. Vietnam was burning. Watts, Newark, Detroit were burning.

On May 17, 1968, eight friends and I struck again, this time at a draft board in Catonsville, Maryland, where we carried hundreds of draft records into the parking lot and doused them with homemade napalm—soap chips and gasoline from a recipe we found in a Green Beret handbook. We watched the records burn, we prayed, and waited to be arrested.

Were we sorry? No, we most certainly were not. Would we do it again? Yes, we surely would. We understood that when the prosecutor got through denouncing us and the judge instructed the jurors, federal marshals would wrap chains around our waists, manacle our wrists to chains, shackle our ankles. The 3-H treatment: Hobble. Humiliate. Hurt. Our guards would order us to strip naked, force us to squat over mirrors, to bend forward and spread our cheeks.

When this ordeal ended, doors would crash shut, squeezing us into a few square feet of concrete and metal.

We just wanted the judge and jury to see that our government was dousing Vietnamese children with the same terrible stuff we poured over those draft files. Our government was blasting plastic pellets (X-rays could detect metal, but not plastic) into children's flesh. We were cooking Vietnamese in white phosphorus, poisoning their food and water with herbicides, burning down their homes, violating international treaties, showing contempt for God's law. Compared to the suffering of the Vietnamese, a few years in prison seemed a very small price to pay.

In 1963, I was transferred to the Josephite Seminary in Newburgh, where I taught English and theology for two years. While I liked teaching at the seminary very much, and really enjoyed my students, Newburgh itself was a racial twilight zone. According to the prevailing mystique, the North fought to free the slaves; the North believed in equal opportunity; the North didn't practice segregation. Point the moral finger toward Alabama or Mississippi, and pretend not to see the northern sweatshops where blacks worked long hours in dark, dirty, dangerous conditions, and for low pay. Pin the tail on the nasty Dixie donkey and ignore the landlords who rented squalid apartments to blacks, charged tenants usurious rents, and seldom made repairs.

I felt called to offer more than homilies about social justice, and I wanted to witness for the poor, even if this meant upsetting some profit-hungry people in Newburgh. We started out, some seminarians and myself, by opening a community center based on the *Catholic Worker*'s ideas of hospitality. We hoped to create a space where poor people could get together and rap about their problems, offer one another support, and organize around issues like hazardous working conditions, racial discrimination, and poor housing.

We distributed food and clothing to the poor, and stood in front of City Hall with our picket signs, demanding an end to racism. City officials ignored us, so we divided into investigative teams and walked through the ghetto, recording code violations in run-down buildings. This enraged the city's slumlords, who felt they had every right to exploit their tenants.

Lyndon Baines Johnson was inaugurated on January 20, 1965. In his campaign against Barry Goldwater, the conservative presidential candidate, LBJ promised the American people that "We are not about to send American boys nine or ten thousand miles away from home to do what Asian boys ought to be doing themselves." One month after he was sworn in as president, Johnson launched Operation Rolling Thunder, a bombing campaign against North Vietnam that would continue, with occasional breaks, for eight years. As the fighting escalated, I tried to ascertain who was being sent into the most dangerous front-line areas, who was being wounded, and who was dying in battle. I discovered that blacks represented ten per cent of the American population, but made up one-third of the combat troops in Vietnam. Poor young kids from the bayous and ghettos of America were joining combat units for the extra pay, which they sent home to their poverty-stricken families. Black men who couldn't vote, couldn't get an education, and couldn't get a job in America, were being sent to fight, they thought, for peace and social justice in Vietnam. This was more than cruel irony. The United States government wasn't lynching African-Americans; it was convincing them to lynch themselves.

I began working with local people to build grassroots resistance to the war. We weren't exclusive. Anyone could attend our meetings. Everyone was welcome to speak their mind, though speaking out against the war did not endear us to the Newburgh establishment, which was generally conservative and pro-war.

One late-winter night in 1965 (I think it was raining, though I can't be sure), I was giving a talk to a gathering in Newburgh, when a man leaped to his feet, demanding that I stop attacking the United States government. A short time later, the local newspaper wrote that our anti-war group harbored communist sympathies. Hardly a new refrain, and one that anti-war activists would be tarred and feathered with in the years to come.

In the fifties, Wisconsin's Senator Joe McCarthy had burned through his fifteen minutes of fame, dragging artists, writers, teachers, politicians, and even scientists into his anti-communist flames. McCarthy's power faded, but his intolerance and paranoia lingered, poisoning the debate over the Vietnam war, and branding the war's opponents communist subversives, or worse.

Newburgh was within the archdiocese of New York City and the Ordinary was Cardinal Spellman, acting military chaplain of all U.S. armed forces, and openly pro-war in a dim-bulb sort of way. He visited the troops in Indochina every Christmas, exhorting them to keep fighting and helping them celebrate the birth of the Prince of Peace. Needless to say, I wasn't invited to any cocktail parties at the archdiocese. Nor did I receive any fan mail from my society in Baltimore.

The fatal blow for me was a talk I gave at some fraternal organization in Newburgh (it might have been the Elks or the Chamber of Commerce). I tore into U.S. involvement in Vietnam, telling my listeners that Vietnam was not a just war. I asked why we were sending poor African-American kids from the Mississippi Delta to kill poor Vietnamese kids in the Mekong Delta. I said the war was a racist attack on poor people of color. The military, integrated in 1948, was racist. Congress passed the Voting Rights Act in 1964, and Congress was *still* dominated by racists. No black man should ever risk his life in Vietnam, when his own government refused to guarantee his civil rights in this country.

My Superior General, George O'Dea, had often attempted to silence me on the Vietnam war, ordering me not to demonstrate, not to speak out, and not to organize. The church resorted to this technique to prevent clergy from taking controversial stands on social, religious, and political issues, and I had already been silenced at St. Augustine's in New Orleans for some of my views on the civil rights question. I knew that the church expected me to honor this tradition. I was told, quite literally, to shut my mouth.

The archdiocese was outraged by my talk and a firestorm of protest poured in to my superiors, who ordered me to pack up and leave at once for Saint Peter Claver, a poor black parish in Baltimore. In the mid-sixties, most Catholics still supported the war in Vietnam; however, the *National Catholic Reporter* criticized my superiors, and I received many letters urging me to keep speaking out against the war. I was rather bitter, but managed to obey O'Dea's dictum for a few months.

Blinded by hubris, and ignoring Vietnamese history, President Johnson and his advisors were sending more 18-year-old Americans to Vietnam. B-52's rained bombs on North Vietnam, hoping to accomplish what the Chinese, the French, the Japanese had failed to achieve—to defeat the Vietnamese, make them welcome a foreign invader, subdue their ferocious nationalism.

I broke my silence by addressing a major conference in Baltimore. My love for the Catholic church, and for the Josephite order, had not diminished, but I kept thinking about how Jesus might respond to seeing children trapped in a sea of napalm. Would He agonize over questions of loyalty to church and state? Would He warn his followers not to question Caesar's right to incinerate the state's enemies? Would He order his disciples to keep their views to themselves?

I had sworn fidelity to the church, and I had never violated my vows, yet my conscience dictated that I speak openly, clearly, and honestly about the war in Vietnam.

While I was serving at Saint Peter Claver, I met several key doves in Congress, among them John Dow, from the Newburgh-Beacon area, and Senator Fulbright, who had championed the Gulf of Tonkin Resolution (only Senators Ernest Gruening of Alaska, and Wayne Morse of Oregon, had voted against it). Later, Fulbright broke with LBJ over Vietnam. He wanted to repeal the Gulf of Tonkin resolution, and he attempted to use his Foreign Relations Committee to find ways to end the war. Furious, President Johnson ridiculed his former supporter, calling him "Senator Halfbright."

The military believed its technological superiority would defeat the Vietnamese, and when this didn't work, the government threatened to use tactical nuclear weapons in Southeast Asia. Casualties would have been astronomical, Indochina would have been razed, perhaps permanently damaged. The entire world would have turned against us. Our arsenal of atomic warheads was useless, so we resorted to the greatest concentration of firepower in history. Yet even this failed to defeat a peasant army.

The war in Vietnam, like the war on Iraq, was a violation of international law, which supersedes and takes precedence over constitutional law. Congress didn't object when the imperial presidency declared war, the American people didn't revolt when their chief executive violated the Constitution. The Geneva Conventions, the United Nations Charter, the Nuremberg statutes, and our own Constitution, were set aside. The ends justified the means. Machiavelli outsmarted Jefferson, shredding democratic principles in the war machine.

Dan had returned home from Europe, and was living in New York City where he edited *Jesuit Missions*, a magazine that published articles on the work of Jesuit missionaries. He volunteered at the *Catholic Worker* on Crystie Street, ladling soup and handing out free clothes to street people. He saw headlines proclaiming that the Marines had landed at Danang, and on the evening news he watched B-52s raining bombs on North Vietnam. Reporters rushed to the White House to hear President Johnson announce that we were going to destroy our enemies. We were going to prevail in Vietnam because we were rich, our adversaries were poor. We were mighty, they were weak.

The President didn't talk about flag-draped coffins which were beginning to arrive home, alone or in small heart-breaking clusters. Newscasters didn't announce that American mothers, and mothers in Vietnam, would never stop mourning their dead children. Mr. Johnson didn't call press conferences to talk about young American and Vietnamese men who would never fall in love, never marry and father children, never write a poem, paint a picture, or just lie in bed listening to the rain on a summer's night. *Death. Mutilation. Madness*. Not the words governments use to inspire young men to march off to war.

Dan became co-chair of Clergy and Laymen Concerned About Vietnam (CALCAV), and was soon working nearly full-time to educate people about the war in Vietnam. American warplanes continued to pound North Vietnam, and American troops fanned out through Vietnam's jungles. More flag-draped coffins came home. More lies spun from the White House and Pentagon. Every night on the evening news, Walter Cronkite gave the body count, a grisly score card proving our side was winning the war.

On October 15, 1965, a young man stood in front of the Armed Forces Induction Center in downtown Manhattan. He was wearing a suit and tie, his hair was neatly combed, and when he lighted his draft card and held it aloft, passersby were stunned. David Miller had been one of Dan's students at Le Moyne College. Now he was the first American to publicly burn his draft card, an act of resistance for which he received a three-year prison sentence.

When reporters asked Dan and me how we felt about David Miller's action, we tried to place it in the context of American history, pointing out that people like Harriet Tubman and Sojourner Truth were breaking the law when they helped free slaves. Samuel Adams, Patrick Henry, Thomas Paine, and many others were violating the law when they called for an end to British tyranny. Mohandas Gandhi was breaking the law when he defied the British in India, Martin Luther King when he defied the racists in Alabama, Germans when they resisted the Nazis. David Miller's actions were nonviolent. He burned a piece of paper, not another human being, and we supported him absolutely.

Three weeks after Miller's arrest, a young *Catholic Worker* activist and former seminarian, Roger Laporte, sat down on the steps of the United Nations, emptied a jug of gasoline over his body and struck a match. Dan's superiors called Laporte's death a suicide, and warned my brother not to make any public statements about this tragedy.

At a memorial service, Dan asked mourners to ponder whether this young man's death might have been an act of hope, rather than a concession to despair. Perhaps, said Daniel, "Roger's death was offered, so that others might live." Cardinal Spellman's chancery responded to these remarks by ordering Dan to catch the first plane out to South America. They didn't tell him when he could return, and wouldn't allow him to say goodbye to our elderly parents. Just pack up your bags, they said, and head south.

Dan wandered from country to country, experiencing the misery of the poor, observing the collusion between the institutional church and military dictatorships. He met worker priests and nuns who were willing to die for impoverished urban dwellers and *campesinos.* If the church officials thought they would drive Daniel Berrigan to despair, they were mistaken. Through his liturgical innovations— celebrating the Mass in English, and positioning the altar so the priest faced worshippers during Mass; through his writings; and through his outspoken commitment to social justice, my brother had already given great hope to Catholics who wanted a more open and socially engaged church.

Many of these people now rallied to his support. Students from Fordham picketed Cardinal Spellman's residence, the *National Catholic Reporter* and *Commonweal* denounced Dan's exile, and 10,000 priests, nuns, seminarians, and lay people signed a full-page ad in the *New York Times,* protesting his punishment.

After four months in exile, my brother returned to the United States, even more committed to work for peace and social justice.

1965 was a pivotal and tragic year for U.S. involvement in Vietnam. North Vietnamese soldiers attacked the Air Cavalry in the Ia Drang valley, killing more than 250 American soldiers in one battle, the U.S. Third Marine regiment arrived in Vietnam to defend Danang, and the Air Force started using Agent Orange to kill mangrove forests and jungles. That same year, opponents of the war held protests in forty American cities.

I started going with friends to Fort Meyers, Virginia, where the Joint Chiefs of Staff were living. We wanted to present a letter to one of the army generals, hoping this might engage the military in dialogue. We were told to leave the base, and when we refused, the military police arrested us. This was my first act of civil disobedience; my first step across the line separating polite discourse from direct action.

I read about Vietnam in the *Nation,* the *Progressive, Ramparts*, and other anti-war publications, but I most vividly recall viewing the carnage on television. Vietnam was the first, and most definitely the last, television war. Night after night, between commercials, the American public looked directly into the gruesome face of war. Night after night, we heard the screams of burning children, we watched angry Americans burning houses, beating civilians, crawling through fear. We saw adolescent soldiers die, their remains stuffed into rubber bags and stacked in the rain.

Asked why they were in Vietnam, these teenage soldiers mumbled platitudes, or said they couldn't wait to get home. Scared young kids, raised on the heroics of John Wayne and Audie Murphy, just trying to stay alive.

Never again would the war-makers allow journalists to crawl through the muck with American troops, recording their dying moans, capturing their fear, their rage, and their despair on film. Vietnam was napalm-coated children screaming in pain, soldiers blown to pieces by booby traps, bloated rotting bodies dangling from concertina wire.

War had always been ugly, but before Vietnam Hollywood could spin the killing into a pageant or ballet, with beautiful women, heart-warming songs, and a cuddly happy-ever-after ending. After Vietnam, the mud and blood would have to be transformed into a video game or a sci-fi adventure. Edit out the napalm, booby traps, and saturation bombing. Never show search-and-destroy missions. Censor atrocities. Place a clean set of cross-hairs on the screen; quiet little puffs to show where the bombs hit; and smile-face generals bubbling about target-rich environments.

By 1966, Tom Lewis and I, along with other members of the Baltimore Interfaith Council, had come to the conclusion that anything short of direct action was unavailing, untruthful, and unjust. Writing to Congress was futile. Talking to the Pentagon was useless. We attended rallies. We organized seminars, we marched, sang, and chanted; the killing got worse.

In 1967, the year we began planning our raid on the Customs House, there were 485,000 U.S. military personnel in Vietnam in 1967. I had attended a big conference called by the historian and writer Sidney Lens at the University of Chicago. Tom Hayden, Greg Calvert, and other members of Students for a Democratic Society (SDS) were there, and I spent a lot of time listening to them talk about shutting down the Selective Service process.

They were really full of ideas. One bright fellow suggested that they put chains on the buses that were taking 1-A draftees into classification centers. Another said, "You know, those draft boards ought to be raided."

Returning to Baltimore, I thought a lot about draft boards. Eighteen-year-old males had a choice: Register for the draft or go to jail. They weren't asked what they thought about the war, whether they believed in saturation bombing, if they approved of napalm, if they wanted to die in some faraway rice paddy for a people who didn't want them there. They filled out a form, and were given a classification which was kept in a file drawer until the day they were called to active duty.

What if draft boards didn't exist? What if the cards all got lost, or burned, or tossed into the sea? How would the government locate military-age males?

"Yes," I concluded, "raiding those draft boards makes a great deal of sense."

We knew that 18 or 19 draft boards had been brought into the protection of the Customs House. We also knew the people guarding the files were armed. There were six of us, but two dropped out just before we acted.

Before the Customs House action, we talked to Philip Hirschkoff, a civil rights lawyer who kept offices in Alexandria, Virginia. He was shocked when we told him about our plans. Didn't we know that we could get shot, maybe even killed, by security guards? Were we really going to hide out in the Customs House at night, and invade the draft boards under cover of darkness? Even if the guards didn't shoot us, Hirschkoff warned, the judge would consider us vigilantes and throw the book at us. He was very eloquent, and very persuasive, urging us to rethink our plans.

Hirschkoff suggested that we dump paint or blood over the draft files and we agreed on blood because of its Biblical symbolism. We returned to Baltimore, acquired some glass vials from a medical supply outfit, and asked a nurse to help us out. At the first sight of blood, one of our co-conspirators fainted dead away. The rest of us did the best we could, but after a while the nurse gave up, bought a beef liver at a Polish market and squeezed it into our vials, adding the blood of a cow to our own. Later, we were ridiculed for dousing the draft files with chicken or duck blood, even though the FBI's analysis showed that half of the blood was human.

Before the action, sixty or seventy people would meet about twice a month to discuss what to do about the war. We gathered in churches or large halls, where we discussed and sometimes argued about strategy. Leftist groups from the Baltimore area attended, but they didn't understand, or embrace, direct action. We knew that the government was spying on political activists, hoping to sow dissent within the anti-war movement. The FBI was paying students to spy on their professors, recruiting professors to report on campus radicals, and sending provocateurs into peace groups. None of this mattered, because we knew and trusted everyone who came to our meetings.

The night before we raided the Customs House, one of our co-conspirators and a dear friend, David Eberhardt, was married, and I will always feel privileged to have been there. The next morning we gathered in an artist's loft, just opposite the Customs House. We talked, prayed, and tried to center our thoughts; then we started out at exactly 12:00 noon.

Once inside the Customs House, I distracted the secretary by asking to check on people in my parish who were classified 1-A. "Absolutely not," she bristled. They did not, they would not, honor this kind of request.

Three of us broke through this little gate and entered the draft board proper, yanking open draft files and pouring our blood over them. This lasted about a minute, because the secretaries were furious, grabbed us from behind, and locked their arms around our waists. We didn't resist or try to break loose. We sat down and waited to be arrested. Jim Mengel, having made a last-minute decision not to pour blood, handed out copies of the New Testament. The enraged clerks threw them back in his face.

Afterward, we were accused of frightening the secretaries, but I don't remember them showing fear. They were enraged, and when they testified against us they were still angry. We had invaded the state's sanctuary, poured our blood over and burned its sacred files. We had damaged property, a crime far greater than destroying human life.

Before we went to the Customs House, we agreed that we would not accept bail, that we would not resist going to prison, and that we would fast for one week after our arrest. Jim Mengel and David Eberhardt changed their minds and signed out of jail on personal recognizance, while Tom Lewis and I refused to sign any recognizance bond.

We were taken to the Baltimore City Jail, a rabbit hutch packed to the rafters with inmates. Just imagine sitting on a crowded bus that is stuck in a terrible traffic jam. Radios blare. Horns blow. People scream, curse, and cry. The bus is an oven. It doesn't move. The doors won't open. There is no exit. The noise increases. Someone produces a television set, turns it on to blare. Someone else turns a radio on to scream. Odors of sweat and fear and human waste.

I was shocked by the misery and the ugliness of life in jail, but I felt a great satisfaction being there. Jail just made the most sense to me, and it still does, because that is where one identifies with the poor, and where one becomes a spokesperson for their dignity and their rights.

The prisoners in Baltimore City Jail needed us very very badly. They needed someone to talk to, someone who would listen to their anguish, someone they could trust, and who would counsel them. Tom Lewis and I helped them write letters to their judges, and we tried to contact their families. The remarkable thing, to us, was that most of these men were in jail for nonviolent crimes, yet they were being treated like assassins.

So there we were, stuffed into the rabbit hutch, and I had no regrets at all. None whatsoever. We had gone to Baltimore to destroy draft files, in order to save lives. I knew, and I accepted, the consequences of my actions. The state might make the laws, but it did not have a license to kill in Southeast Asia, or anywhere else.

The Baltimore Four were defended by Fred Weisgal, a Jewish civil rights attorney who was highly sympathetic to our actions, and by one other attorney. I'm not sure what we really expected. We didn't know that we could defend ourselves, *pro se,* without an attorney. We had no idea that courtrooms are often like circuses, with the judge acting as ringmaster, whipping the jury through legal hoops, forcing lawyers to dance for their dinner. We would learn all these things, and more.

Meanwhile, our first trial was really quite conventional. It made little difference to judge or jury why we entered the Customs House. Our motives were not important. Napalmed children, poisoned crops, mutilated women, bombed hospitals were totally irrelevant. File cabinets crammed with licenses to kill were unimportant.

We had trespassed, and damaged property. What property? The government's property. Eighteen-year-old American boys belonged to the government. Vietnamese rice paddies, mangrove forests, triple-canopy jungle, villages, hospitals, schools, Buddhist pagodas, all belonged to the Pentagon. Vietnam, north and south, belonged to the United States of America.

Weisgal conducted a protracted *voir dire,* trying to choose jurors who might be fair, but the prosecution immediately struck down anyone who seemed interested in our motives. Judge Northrop was a wealthy landowner from the eastern shore, a trust-fund patriot determined to keep America safe from dissent. The jury listened with a certain bemused boredom, prepared to find us guilty regardless of what we or our lawyers might say.

In Judge Northrop's courtroom, cases of conscience and political resistance didn't fall on deaf ears. Judge and jury could hear very well indeed. They merely sang "God Bless America" loud enough to drown out the crackle of human suffering. As a 19-year-old soldier, I had been trained to do the same thing. I too once believed that God supports war.

In early spring 1968, I was out on bail, awaiting sentencing for the Custom House raid. Dan was working with Rabbi Abraham Heschel and Lutheran theologian Richard Neuhaus to form Clergy and Laity Concerned. He was also a co-founder of the Catholic Peace Fellowship, and had been invited to work with United Religious Work, a small but very dedicated group of theologians and peace activists at Cornell University. We strolled about the campus, laughing and talking and stopping to gaze at Cayuga Lake, a chameleon body of water stretching into the horizon like a fjord, changing colors as the day wore on.

I had come to ask Dan to join me and other conspirators in yet another draft board action. We talked our way through the night, and through a bottle of whiskey. Would the action we proposed offend the church? Of course it would. Might it alienate us from some of our fellow peace activists? Most definitely. Would it end the war? Certainly not. Was it consistent with the spirit of Christ, Martin Luther King, and Mohandas Gandhi? We, the people who were planning this action, believed it was.

The war in Southeast Asia was our country's paranoia and racism metastasized into genocidal madness. Not a mistake. Not a misunderstanding. A campaign to exterminate, not liberate, the Vietnamese. Vietnam was the Puritans hacking their Native American benefactors to pieces. Vietnam was the Christian church sanctioning the slave trade. Vietnam was dropping the atomic bomb on a country already on its knees.

Dan had been arrested in Washington, D.C., at the march on the Pentagon, October 22, 1967, sponsored by the New Mobilization. 500,000 demonstrators appeared in the nation's capital, some in bells and beads, others in suits and ties. Abbie Hoffman told reporters that he and his Yippie friends were going to chant until the Pentagon levitated off the ground. Norman Mailer scribbled notes for his book, *The Armies of the Night*, and got carted off to jail with Robert Lowell and other prominent writers. Journalists snapped pictures of young protesters planting flowers in the barrels of of rifles held, at port arms, by other young Americans.

The Pentagon didn't levitate, though some protesters managed to slip inside the building before federal marshals attacked them. Wearing his clerical suit and refusing to budge when ordered to do so, Daniel was arrested outside the Pentagon and sent to Aquaquon, which is part of the Lordon prison complex in northern Virginia. He spent five days in jail, and was still there on October 27, 1967, when the Baltimore Four invaded the Baltimore Customs House. Dan felt that he should remain at Cornell for a while longer, lending his support to Students for a Democratic Society (SDS), which had a very active, intelligent, and highly motivated chapter on campus. Like other institutions of higher learning, Cornell University kept close ties to the military. ROTC was graduating second lieutenants, pinning brown bars on their shoulders, and seeing them off to fight and die in Southeast Asia. Always anxious to support research that might lead to more efficient killing machines, the Pentagon doled out money for war-related projects. Dan was well aware that Cornell's administration, and much of the University's faculty (though some professors were working with Students for a Democratic Society) held anti-war activists in contempt, but ending the war was the issue, not his own academic image. He met with students, marched, sang, and shouted with them. If that violated the academy's sense of decorum, so be it. Vietnam demanded more than just a new way of thinking; it demanded a new way of being.

Soon after our meeting, Dan flew to Hanoi, along with Boston University professor Howard Zinn, to meet with members of a North Vietnamese peace delegation. They had agreed to bring home three flyers shot down over the North, and they were meeting with the Vietnam Committee for Patriotic Catholics when the first wave of B-52s flew over, showering them with 1,000-pound bombs. The FBI knew Dan and Professor Zinn were there. The CIA knew they there. The White House knew they were there.

Dan hunkered down in a bunker, waiting for the attack to end, wondering if the Pentagon was trying to frighten or even kill him and Professor Zinn. Emerging from the bunker, my brother saw B-52 moonscapes, scorched houses, dead bodies; our government's policy of winning the hearts and minds of the Vietnamese people. He smelled burning flesh, and he stared directly into the terrifying face of war.

Dan and Howard Zinn left Hanoi with three American pilots, but when they landed in Vientiane, Laos, the U.S. Ambassador, William Sullivan, boarded their plane, demanding that the pilots complete the trip home on a military plane. After an hour-long standoff, the ranking officer among the POWs informed Dan and Howard Zinn that he was still a military man and must follow orders. Sullivan was delighted and the POWs walked from the plane, into a crowd of reporters waiting for them on the tarmac.

Dan returned to Ithaca where he started work on *Night Flight to Hanoi,* a book about his experiences in North Vietnam.

On May 17, 1968, my brother and I, along with seven others, walked into the draft board at Catonsville, Maryland. We carried file drawers into the parking lot and poured our own blood over them. We burned the files, prayed, and waited to be arrested. Dan might have stayed at Cornell, holding worship services, counseling students, and teaching a course now and then. He might have built a comfortable niche there, writing poetry, going for tenure, living out his life in genteel, wine-and-cheese obscurity. Instead, he stepped out on an existential limb, knowing that it would break, sending him, and all of us, to prison. My brother was the most valuable, the most insightful, the wisest, and perhaps the strongest member of our group.

Our efforts to communicate with the high-ranking masterminds of mass murder had been futile. We had attended nonviolent demonstrations, written letters to government leaders, and met with government officials, pleading with the government to end its genocidal campaign against the Vietnamese people. Nothing worked. No one listened. "Power comes from the barrel of a gun," said Mao Tse-tung. The architects of the Vietnam War—Lyndon Baines Johnson, Robert McNamara, McGeorge Bundy, Dean Rusk—obviously agreed. We were trying to dialogue with the Mad Hatter; we were attempting to reform Big Brother. Words had lost all meaning. Euphemisms and bureaucratese abounded:

We must destroy the village in order to save it. We must prolong the war, in order to bring about peace. We must support dictators if we wish to promote democracy.

In the context of search-and-destroy missions, saturation bombings, and free-fire zones, what did this convoluted language really mean? When officials insist on using Newspeak, how should people respond? Where is the basis for honest communication? Words didn't fail us. We tried to speak truthfully, without guile. Our attempts at dialogue with the warmakers sank into Machiavellian waters. We were speaking to the powerful, who considered us powerless and, therefore, not worth listening to.

Vietnam, we discovered, was not only a war on people. It was a war on the very meaning of human communication. Manipulating language was just one more means to achieve some Orwellian end. Words were merely rhetorical devices. Expendable as 18-year-old American boys, destructible as the Vietnamese people. The Catonsville Nine knew that we were moving even deeper into some new existential, religious, ethical territory. Escalating our opposition to the war; trying to startle the doves from the hawk's nest of the Catholic church; acting out the Christian mandate to resist evil. We were burning draft records at Catonsville to protest our government's burning children in Vietnam, and we knew that our actions would shock, anger, and alienate not only our critics, but some of our closest supporters, and certainly many Catholics as well.

Thomas Merton and Dorothy Day were outspoken critics of the war in Vietnam, but they could not understand, and did not support, destruction of property. I had read Merton's work, visited him at Gethsemane, and considered him a friend. He was one of the first priests in the country to denounce the nuclear arms race, and he fully understood that the Vietnam War was being waged within the context of the Cold War with the Soviet Union.

Thomas Merton was a very insightful thinker, but he had no experience with direct action. He and Dorothy Day worried that our actions could set a dangerous precedent. After all, if the Catonsville Nine were willing to destroy property, what would keep us from attacking human beings? I fully understood why they might think this way, because unless you can thrash out these breakthroughs, and unless you are willing to pay a great price for these risks (engaging first in deep consideration and prayer) you might find it difficult to understand Catonsville. They had not been through this, and consequently they did not initially understand our action.

While I was teaching in Newburgh, I visited the Sisters of the Cenacle, who had a posh estate on the Hudson River. I met Dorothy Day there one weekend. She was in the company of a wealthy woman, whose husband was chairman of the board of Continental Grain, a major American grain cartel that sent heavy shipments of grain to the Soviet Union. Dorothy was going through a rough time at the *Catholic Worker,* because many of the people who were attempting to join the community, or who were on the margins of the community, were pretty insane.

Dorothy Day and I walked the grounds of the estate, talking about the debacle in Vietnam, and the many ways in which our government drives the poor to despair, and even madness. A brilliant woman, she might easily have accumulated wealth and power. Instead, Dorothy Day chose to live among the homeless. She chose to live among the destitute, listening to their stories, cooking for them, comforting and loving them.

Dorothy Day was never smug or self-righteous, and didn't consider herself a leader of any movement. She and her friend, Peter Maurin, started the *Catholic Worker* newspaper. They sold copies of the paper for a penny, or gave them away to people who couldn't afford even that. They founded hospitality houses, where the poor were welcomed with love and respect.

More than any other institution or individual, the *Catholic Worker* movement influenced Dan and me, especially with its tradition of nonviolent direct action. We admired and respected the commitment of people like Ammon Hennacy, Jimmy Wilson, and David Miller—people who didn't talk one thing, and live quite another. They took a stand, spoke truth to power, and paid the price for their opposition to war.

The Catonsville Nine sat together, waiting for the FBI who soon arrived, irritated by our insouciance and anxious to make us pay for breaking the law. When he saw me, their leader blushed with anger. "Him again," he shouted, pointing one large fist at my head, "Good God, I'm changing my religion."

I thought that perhaps he should discover, or re-discover his religion. In many ways, though he would never acknowledge it, he was a prisoner of the system he so ardently supported.

The President was sending children off to die for dictators in Vietnam, Congress was giving away this man's tax money to thieves and drug pushers in Central America, timber companies were clear-cutting his forests, bomb manufacturers were poisoning his environment. None of this mattered, because the state makes the laws; therefore, the state *is* the law. If the state becomes a polluter, a drug pusher, or war machine, citizens still must obey the law.

But if one accepts this autocratic logic, what happens to the kindom of God? Not the King-dom, but the kin-dom of God. What happens to real justice, to the possibility that human beings will be guaranteed justice and love and real freedom? Those who truly believe in nonviolence, in justice, have no choice but to break unjust laws. The state will retaliate. It will charge you. It will convict you almost by rote. And it will send you to jail. We are all prisoners of an unrepresentative government, and we are prisoners of the means that this government uses to stay in power—thousands of nuclear warheads, CIA assassinations and *coup d'états*, financial support for death squads, training for military personnel who commit atrocities in their own countries.

It is a Biblical theme that change always begins in the desert, which is a metaphor for slums, the jails, the docks when one is in court, those margins of society where people are speaking truth to power.

Tom Lewis and I were brought to the Catonsville trial wearing handcuffs, because we were recidivists now, and might just raid another draft board if we were free on bail. We were kept in the Baltimore County jail, where the warden treated us with respect and genuine kindness. We were all alone in a cellblock, and we were fasting. Warden Foster visited us frequently to see how we were doing, and he even worshiped with us. He was fascinated by the fact that Catholic priests had broken the law, and he had an open mind. He wanted to understand us, and our actions at Catonsville. Warden Foster would call us into his office, give us the latest news account of our action, and regale us with his ideas about running a prison. He believed in rehabilitation, not retribution. He wanted to make sure that prisoners could see their families, and he believed in furloughs, work release, and early parole. He was a very remarkable man.

Six months later, Warden Foster was fired. Some of the prisoners he sent out on work release programs betrayed him by getting back into drugs, but I think the real reason for his dismissal was that he associated with us. Foster was a Catholic, a good, caring person who was deeply concerned about the war in Vietnam. In later years, he has joined us at the Pentagon. He doesn't break the law, but he supports our vigils, and our acts of civil disobedience. We are grateful for his friendship.

The Catonsville action received widespread attention, both here and abroad, and every day more people came to our trial, standing in lines from early morning on, hoping to get in. The Baltimore Interfaith Peace Mission did a wonderful job of organizing local support, and bringing in the wider national community.

A Jesuit priest, pastor of a large church on Calvert Street in Baltimore, opened his hall to us. Every night people gathered there to talk about the trial and to exchange ideas. They sang, prayed, and rejoiced together.

Dorothy Day attended those sessions, and I think that's where she gained a better understanding of our actions at the Customs House and Catonsville. Her own life was a series of flexible acts; she was constantly responding to the poor, and couldn't afford to be rigid or doctrinaire. We said that draft files contained *licenses to kill*. The Nazis kept drawers filled with the names of Jews to be deported to concentration camps. Our own government kept files with the names of young men to be sent to kill and die in Southeast Asia. Draft files represented death, not life; therefore, they were not proper. William Stringfellow also attended, and all of the Catonsville defendants except Tom Lewis and myself spoke there at night.

People weren't just letting off steam at those meetings. They were brainstorming and planning strategy. Soon, there would be draft board actions all over the country, including the Milwaukee 14 action which was planned right there on Calvert Street.

Thomas Merton was at Gethsemane and couldn't travel to those meetings. He was a student of Gandhi, and he always felt that the spirituality of the movement, and the accent on nonviolence, ought to be emphasized. He worried about the strain of violence—which was often little more than revolutionary posturing—in the anti-war movement. And he hoped that people would not substitute political rhetoric for spiritual awareness. Merton didn't understand that an action like Catonsville was not only in the best tradition of nonviolence; it was a gift to spirituality.

I don't know if Merton ever contemplated leaving the monastery, perhaps to engage in direct action. His sudden accidental death in December, 1968, stunned and deeply saddened all of us. He and my brother Daniel were alike in some ways. They had taken vows, and were not going to break them. Dan always said that he wouldn't leave the Jesuits, even when they threatened to expel him. He was determined to hold them to some sense of moral and political accountability.

I'm sure that many of the people who visited Merton at Gethsemane realized that the monastic tradition is not true to the gospel. The monks in Egypt fled to the desert to shake the dust, or the corruption, of the cities off their feet. This was a passive protest, conducted far from the corruption they were denouncing. Jesus was an activist, not a monk. He lived among the poor. He drove the money-changers from the temple, criticized the rich and powerful, ridiculed government officials. He would not have remained in a monastery while his own government was slaughtering the Vietnamese.

During the day, the defendants and their supporters marched through Baltimore, hoping people along the way would join the movement to end the war in Vietnam. The police were out in rather astonishing numbers, but the demonstrators mollified them by asking for higher pay for cops.

Decisions about the trial, that is, who would speak when, and other details, were made by the defendants who were free on bail, and that was fine with Tom Lewis and myself. We loved our fellow conspirators, trusted their judgment, and were delighted they could speak for all of us. William Kunstler was our lead attorney. Bill Cunningham, a Jesuit priest and outstanding lawyer, and Harrop Freeman from Cornell University's law school were also among the defense team.

I was beginning to see just how naive I had been about the judicial system. In theory, courts and judges are there to protect citizens from government tyranny. That's what I had learned in school. That's what everyone learns in school—that there are three branches of the government; these branches are separate; the judicial branch is our guardian against unjust, or illegal power; we are protected by due process, writ of habeas corpus, and the assumption that all defendants are innocent until *proven* guilty.

In reality, the courts protect the government *from* the people. The courts serve the state, not ordinary citizens. The courts exist to maintain order, not to secure justice.

When I was still teaching in the South, I learned a good deal about the priorities of the institutional church. The church enjoys enormous privileges from the state, and over time this evolved into a kind of symbiotic relationship, a set of reciprocal expectations. When the state goes to war, the church either approves, or keeps quiet. When the state persecutes the poor, the church may disapprove, but it doesn't send the faithful to the halls of Congress or onto the floor of the Senate to demand justice. When the rich exploit the poor, the church offers insipid homilies about the rewards of being a good citizen. When the courts act as enforcers for the corrupt, violent, racist state, the church cautions its followers to obey the law.

The church has its set of priorities. The church wants to remain tax-exempt. It wants to make sure its own clergy aren't called to war. The church wants the property of its members honored and ratified by the courts of the land. In all these ways, the church has rendered itself quite useless when it comes to speaking the truth to power. I had concluded all this before leaving New Orleans, and had no illusions that the institutional church would support our act of resistance at Catonsville.

Everything the Catonsville Nine had done, and everything we intended to say in court, challenged this contract between church and state. When he was calling for obligatory military service, Cardinal Spellman declared that "individuals cannot refuse their obedience to the state." The Catonsville Nine turned that statement upside down by arguing that when a government is committing genocide, citizens have not only a right, but an obligation to disobey the state. We also tried to tell the court that the Declaration of Independence is an expression of the gospels, which forbid us from waging war on anyone.

Thomas Jefferson might have been somewhat of an agnostic, but he was quite familiar with the gospels, and he incorporated their values into the Declaration of Independence. Thus, our action at Catonsville was an expression of much that is good about the United States, rather than a violation of the country's most cherished values.

Reaction from the institutional church was swift and uncompromising. We were disowned, repudiated, and denounced. That we were in good standing with the church didn't matter. We were left to hang by our thumbs.

Some rather nasty accounts of our action appeared in *Time* and *Newsweek,* but that bothered us very little. We weren't running for political office, we weren't interested in appearing on some late show, and we weren't negotiating for a six-figure book-film deal. It hardly mattered that *Time* magazine called our action "bizarre." Reading *Time* was a lot like listening to the Voice of America. The same old Cold War refrain. Year after year, the same solipsistic nonsense. A pure and simple market strategy. Boil the world down to a few, easy-to-understand formulas.

Cardinal Sheehan of Baltimore was also quite critical of the action at Catonsville. I greatly respected him, and had visited him before the action to ask for permission to travel to Vietnam. He prayed over his decision, warned me about being soft on communism, and agreed to let me go. But then my own superior refused to give his consent. Cardinal Sheehan was one of the first Catholic Ordinaries in the country to condemn the Vietnam War. He was not a brilliant man, but he was a truly spiritual, always fair, and very decent human being.

Every day they packed the courtroom—nuns, priests, ministers, rabbis, students. They came from all over the country, and all over the world, and they stood in line every morning, rain or shine. We were honored by, and grateful for, their presence. Judge Marion Thompson, unlike some of the judges we would face in years to come, did not try to silence us. We spoke about our religious training, our ethical beliefs, the many roads that had led, inexorably, toward Catonsville and into this courtroom. We told the court that the institutions of this country, and we included the church that some of us had served with great devotion and love, had broken down. We argued that law serves the empire, not the people.

Thomas Melville, a former Maryknoll priest, excommunicated because he had married, told the court how he had gone to Central America in the fifties, determined to spend his life helping the poor. He discovered that the United Fruit Company owned vast tracts of land in Guatemala, some of which was lying fallow, not used at all. After winning the presidential election in 1951, Jacobo Arbenz expropriated some of this land and gave it to peasant farmers, an act that infuriated officials in the Eisenhower administration, particularly those who held interests in the United Fruit Company.

Thomas Melville and his wife, Majorie, talked about the Central Intelligence Agency's overthrow of Jacobo Arbenz in 1954. They described the misery in which the majority of people in Guatemala were living, condemned to see their children die of hunger and disease. Arbenz had given them hope for a better life, but after the coup, the military assumed absolute power. There was no redress for grievances. Union organizing was considered a subversive activity. Opponents of the dictatorship were tortured, murdered, and "disappeared." Anyone who objected to the oligarchy was tortured and murdered, their mutilated bodies left beside the road as a warning to others.

When he was a Maryknoll priest, Melville received many invitations from the United Fruit Company, asking him to be the company's guest. Officials offered to send a plane to fly him, and other priests and nuns, to a resort where they could swim, play golf, and be waited on by servants. They would be treated like royalty, and indoctrinated with the United Fruit Company's, and the United States government's, propaganda. Father Melville refused these offers.

The Melvilles talked about the Guatemalan military's search-and-destroy missions in the countryside. Government soldiers were raping and murdering Indians, burning down their houses, and destroying their villages. They told the court that the U.S. government was supporting the killing in Guatemala.

Some courageous nuns and priests supported the peasants, while the official church sided with the military. The killing in Central America, and the genocide in Vietnam, reflected the United States government's war on poor people throughout the world.

Marjorie Melville told the court (excerpted from Daniel Berrigan's play "The Trial of the Catonsville Nine"):

We were asked to leave Guatemala
in December of 1967
We went to Mexico
trying to help the peasants
and student leaders
who also had been expelled
Their lives were in danger
Being associated with us put them in danger
In fact I found out
that their names
were on the Secret Police lists
and they would have been murdered
as 4000 people had been murdered
in the last 2 years
It is impossible to describe that.

JUDGE
Well, we are listening.

THOMAS MELVILLE
Eighty-five percent of the people of Guatemala
live in misery
You don't live in misery
perhaps that is why

you don't worry about it
They live in misery
because two percent of the population
are determined
to keep them that way
Those two percent
are aligned with business interests
in Guatemala
especially with the United Fruit Company
The United States government
identifies its interests
in Guatemala
with the interests of American big business
and with the Guatemalan two percent
who control the country
So if any peasant movement
does not conduct itself
according to their wishes that is to say
if such a movement
is not completely ineffective
they start screaming
'They are communists!'
and begin executing these people

Judge Thompson asked Father Melville if the United States government had sent troops into Guatemala. Melville answered that U.S. troops were sent to Guatemala in late 1966 and in January 1967. "And you say that the United States executed people there?" Father Melville said "Yes, this was reported even in *Time* magazine." Another defendant, George Mische, had started a collective in northwest Washington. He had been involved with a Catholic lay organization called the Association for International Development, a kind of counterpart to the government organization of a similar name. I knew George quite well from my own travels through the Midwest, and trusted him implicitly. He welcomed all these people who had been run out of various parts of the American empire, and that was where Tom Melville, Marjorie Melville, and John Hogan were living after they got kicked out of Guatemala.

After we put out a call for people to join the action at Catonsville, George Mische did all the organizing with John Hogan, Mary

Moylan, and the Melvilles. David Darst, a Christian brother from
St. Louis, also joined our resistance group.

THOMAS MELVILLE
We wish to say lastly
why we went to Catonsville
Americans know
that their nation was born in blood
we have expanded our frontiers
and pacified the Indians
in blood

MARJORIE MELVILLE
The creature of our history
is our fatherland today
The history we create today
will form the minds and hearts
of our children tomorrow

THOMAS MELVILLE
I hear our President confuse greatness with strength
riches with goodness fear with respect
hopelessness and passivity with peace
The clichés of our leaders
pay tribute to property and indifference to suffering
We long for a hand of friendship and succor
and that hand
clenches into a fist
I wonder how long we can endure

Daniel Berrigan told the court about surviving a bombing raid in
North Vietnam.

DANIEL BERRIGAN
In Hanoi I think we were the first Americans
to undergo
an American bombing attack
When the burned draft files
were brought into court yesterday
as evidence
I could not but recall
that I had seen in Hanoi

evidence of a very different nature
I saw not boxes of burned papers
I saw parts of human bodies preserved in alcohol
the bodies of children the hearts and organs and limbs
of women
teachers workers peasants bombed
in fields and churches and schools and hospitals
I examined our 'improved weaponry'
It was quite clear to me
during three years of air war
America had been experimenting
upon the bodies of the innocent
We had improved our weapons
on their flesh.

Judge Thompson allowed us to talk about our lives, what had brought us to Catonsville, and why we were willing to spend years in prison for a symbolic act of nonviolent civil disobedience. The prosecutor in the Customs House case had been Steven Sachs, a Jewish attorney who would later become Attorney General for the state of Maryland. At Catonsville, the prosecutor was an African-American by the name of Murphy, but he was rather inept. Judge Thompson overruled most of his objections to our testimony.

My brother read a statement summarizing all our feelings and, in a powerful and poetic way, explaining why we destroyed draft records at Catonsville. He said:

Our apologies good friends
    for the fracture of good order the burning of
        paper
    instead of children   the angering of the orderlies
  in the front parlor of the charnel house
    We could not so help us God do otherwise
        for we are sick at heart   our hearts
            give us no rest for thinking of the Land of
                Burning
                        Children.

I spoke to the court about the Catonsville defendants' attempts to convince government officials to end the war in Vietnam.

I made a proposal to Senator Fulbright
suggesting it might be a good thing
to investigate the war
in light of the moral opinion of the nation
We planned to bring a team
of theologians   to testify
before the Foreign Relations Committee
Fulbright was partial to the idea
but he never had political leverage
particularly from the churches
so of course our idea died aborning.
At Christmas of 1967
I also spent two hours
with Secretary Rusk   I went to his office
with another clergyman
We discussed all aspects of the war
He was very gracious
but he did not tell us anything
he had not said before
and that was not enough for us
Yes   I came
to the conclusion
that I was in direct line
with American democratic tradition
in choosing civil disobedience
in a serious fashion
There have been times in our history
when in order to get redress
in order to get a voice   vox populi
arising from the roots
people have so acted
From the Boston Tea Party
through the abolitionist and anarchist movements
through World War I   and World War II
and right on
through the civil rights movement
we have a rich tradition
of civil disobedience

DEFENSE
Will you explain why, with a jail sentence staring you in the face,
you felt impelled to act again at Catonsville?

PHILIP BERRIGAN

Neither at the Customs House   nor at Catonsville
do I wish my actions reduced
to a question   of acquittal or conviction
Rather I   and all of us
desire to communicate
with the bench with the prosecution
with our country
We have already made it clear   our dissent runs counter
to more than the war   which is but one instance
of American power in the world
Latin America is another instance   So is the Near East
This trial is yet another
From those in power we have met
little understanding   much silence
much scorn and punishment
We have been accused of arrogance
But what of the fantastic arrogance   of our leaders
What of their crimes against the people   the poor and powerless
Still no court will try them   no jail will receive them
They live in righteousness   They will die in honor
For them we have one message   for those
in whose manicured hands   the power of the land lies
We say to them
Lead us   Lead us in justice
And there will be no need to break the law
Let the President do   what his predecessors failed to do
Let him obey the rich less   and the people more
Let him think less of the privileged
and more of the poor
Less of America and more of the world
Let lawmakers   judges   and lawyers
think less of the law   more of justice
less of legal ritual   more of human rights
To our bishops and superiors we say
Learn something about the gospel and something about
illegitimate   power
When you do   you will liquidate your investments
take a house in the slums   or even
join us in jail
To lawyers we say

Defend draft resisters   ask no fees
Insist on justice   risk contempt of court
got to jail with your clients
To the prosecution we say
Refuse to indict
opponents of war
prefer to resign   practice in private
To Federal judges we say
Give anti-war people   suspended sentences
to work for justice and peace
or resign your posts
You men of power   I also have a dream
Federal Judges   District Attorneys   Marshals
Against the War in Vietnam
You men of power   you have told us
that your system is reformable
Reform it then
and we will help
with all our conviction and energy
in jail and out

The trial lasted a week and when testimony ended, Judge Thompson told the jury to ignore our testimony. The issue was whether or not we destroyed government property. Nothing else mattered.

On October 9, 1968, the jury, which had deliberated for about two hours, found us guilty as charged on each of three counts: destruction of U.S. government property, destruction of Selective Service records, and interference with the Selective Service Act of 1967. In November, all nine were sentenced to three years in prison and, with the exception of Tom Lewis and myself, released on bail. Tom and I were sentenced to six years in prison for the Baltimore action, and a three-and-one-half-year concurrent term for Catonsville.

Richard Nixon defeated Hubert Humphrey in the 1968 presidential election, claiming that he had a secret plan to end the Vietnam War. Earlier that year, the Tet Offensive had shocked and demoralized even the war's most ardent supporters, leaving little doubt that the National Liberation Front intended to keep fighting. Lyndon

Johnson returned to Texas, a tired, broken man. His war on American poverty had turned into a war on the poor in Vietnam, and at home.

Dan and I went to prison because we believed that Christianity and revolution are synonymous. Jesus Christ was a nonviolent revolutionary; therefore, Christians have a duty to subvert society in order to create a world where justice prevails, particularly for the poor who must be treated with fairness and love.

I am committed to nonviolent revolution, and I supported the struggle of the National Liberation Front in South Vietnam. The Front's uprising was violent, great numbers of people were being killed, and some Americans joined the guerrillas. I thought about joining the National Liberation Front, but I had already been a soldier and I vowed never to pick up a gun again, not even for the most righteous cause.

I supported the struggle to liberate Vietnam, not the killing. It seems to me that the people who are fighting for justice ought to choose their own means to that end. They are the ones who are being tortured, raped, robbed, and executed. How can I ask them to lay down their arms, when that means certain death for their families, their village, everything they love and hold dear. It is one thing to preach from a distance, quite another to live and die in a war zone.

I know this troubles some people, because it sounds like I am condoning violence. And yet, I have sworn *never* to pick up the gun, no matter how much I might support liberation struggles.

For many years, U.S.-supported death squads roamed El Salvador, torturing and murdering tens of thousands of innocent people; U.S.-backed terrorists raped and pillaged their way across Nicaragua; the Guatemalan military burned hundreds of Indian villages, raped and murdered Indian women and children.

In Guatemala and El Salvador, the oligarchies still murder people who resist fascist domination. In Nicaragua, hungry people scavenge dumps looking for food, their dream of a just society shattered by U.S.-backed mercenaries. I applaud courageous people who struggle to overthrow dictatorships and oligarchies. I support resisters, pray that they will prevail. Their witness is powerful. Their willingness to speak truth to power is inspiring. Their cause is just.

APOLOGIA FOR CAT
written in Allentown federal penitentiary, 1968
from *Journals of a Priest Revolutionary*

"Humanity is skin deep in most of these guys—you'd better believe it!" The guard spoke with conviction, and—I must admit—a certain authority. He had broken up deadly fights and legislated petty quarrels, and witnessed the effect of racism and anti-Semitism, and he had tried to deal with the daily routine of theft and homosexuality. Having often seen men at their worst, and seldom at their best, he believed thoroughly that their failures in prison were extensions of their failures in society.

There was something in his remark, however, that was deeper than observation—resentment at the thankless, sterile job of a policeman. (American GIs in Vietnam have essentially similar feelings about themselves.) Even if he did not explain the interplay of forces, he sensed that police are caught in a frightening no-man's-land between rulers and ruled; exhorted and criticized by one side, they are hated and resisted by the other; their defense of the rulers is at the same time oppression of the ruled.

Moreover, the bulging population of federal jails might suggest a much more serious development than do statistics about mounting crime—the readiness of police to identify with oppression, to use force more and more arbitrarily, and to unite informally with vigilante elements of the right. Apparently the police suspect that leftists may be right in arguing that power ultimately means control of the army, that the police are an occupation army, and that, therefore, they are the first line of defense—and first target.

One must, nevertheless, be fair to the guards here. They are, for the most part, uncomplicated and solid men—several being ex-farmers who still work little plots of ground. It is a tribute both to them and to an unusually sensitive warden that they consistently practice understanding and service to the men. A few are superb amateur psychologists who will amaze one with their offhandedly accurate judgments on prison mores. Among them I have often found compassion and a practical balance between harshness and indulgence.

"Humanity is skin deep"—the remark was significant, and I could not forget it. Moreover, an experience with an inmate forced me to ponder it at length and to wonder if it did not deserve to be applied to men at large, and to me particularly.

Marshals had moved Tom Lewis and me from the federal penitentiary at Allenwood to Baltimore County jail in preparation for our complex though legally hopeless trial. Room had to be made for us; consequently, while one guard processed us, another removed an inmate from a neighboring cellblock. The object was, of course, to keep us together; but however beneficial that might be to us, it was burdensome to the man moved, who was uprooted and forced to acclimate to new people and conditions.

Our addition brought the block to capacity—an effect like that of stacking Harlem liberally with refugees. To varying degrees, the territorial imperative went to work; old acquaintances greeted us with restraint, but strangers expressed more hostility than welcome. The reason was simple: our arrival meant less room and less freedom of movement, plus the likelihood of abrasiveness and hostility. As newcomers we were sure to add burdens to backs already bowed!

One man (we did not know him) was called "Cat" or "Cotton," from his loose-jointed way of ambling around, and his taffy-colored kinky hair. He was light enough and Negroid enough to be a rare hybrid. (I thought upon seeing him that he could never "pass" and would often be a curiosity to his own people.) During our first evening here, we saw little of Cat, but heard him talking animatedly with another black youngster at the end of the cellblock. I remember the suspicion that they were "up tight" with one another and that the old racist themes were openly at work.

After lights out, however, our real initiation to Cat began. For something close to an hour he tormented us with a series of weird and prolonged cries, which our astounded and unaccustomed ears could not distinguish as laughter or crying. I lay in the bunk above him desperately trying to fathom this new phenomenon—had Tom or I provoked him in some way? Was this a new kind of emotional safety valve? Were these cries born of despair? Was he simply mad? Whatever the case, he finally grew weary and fell asleep, leaving me to an uneasy doze and more questions than answers.

Next morning I asked one of the whites what "gave" with Cat. His answer was contemptuous and abrupt: 'Hell, he's on his way to Patuxent!' (A state mental institution.) The manner of delivery indicated that the sooner Cat left, the better the speaker would like it.

That evening, verifying my worst fears, a similar performance began. Nerves were taut by now—I had noticed during the day how preoccupied and touchy the men had become, and helplessness had exaggerated my own irritation. Consequently, after another period of this unearthly howling, my patience evaporated and with scarcely controlled anger I ordered Cat to stop his mad noise and to allow others to sleep.

Now, we had with us in jail a cab driver—let's call him Jensen—jailed on the charge of raping his common-law wife. No one could have been less equipped for jail—he had a bad ulcer and enough hypertension to keep it bad; he could neither sleep at night nor stomach the coarse, starchy food.

He was hardly an attractive figure, constantly repeating his story, whining and complaining as if the only problem in the world was his. But when his hands trembled more day by day, and he confided to me over and over that if he were not released on bail he would crack up, several of us asked the guards to get him to the hospital. They, however, thought that he would adapt; as one said to me, "People in here gotta adapt. Jensen'll make it!"

Jensen didn't make it. The night in question, when I told Cat to shut his mouth, he was pacing our tiny cell, chain-smoking begged cigarettes. (There is something eerie about a man pacing in an eight-by-eight-foot cell while three others attempt to sleep. On two earlier occasions I had been shut in with men on cold turkey, a witness to their terrible nausea, muscular constrictions, and insomnia. They would pace up and down, do deep knee bends, retch, and try to sleep; finding this futile they would get up and repeat the performance.)

Despite Jensen's pacing and mumbling, I fell asleep, whereupon Cat, doubtless furious because of my rebuke, turned upon Jensen, reviling his ancestry, morality, and his whole life, while repeatedly threatening to beat him. When I awoke for breakfast, Jensen was cowering at the end of an upper bunk, a big, frightened rabbit. Later he told me of the night's terror, and sobbed at the memory of it. Suddenly, the last remnants of control vanished; trying to restrain him was like trying to hold a pet bear when it first smells the forest. Then the guards came, he quieted down, and they led Jensen away. It was the last we saw of him.

Since Jensen was both helpless and harmless, Cat's persecution of him seemed the worst depravity. My resentment was encouraged by the continuing campaign against me. He slept most of the day and was awake most of the night, when, between spasms of mad laughter, he would whisper stealthily from the lower bunk, "Devil, devil, devil, devil!" and, "Go, go, go!" At those odd moments when he was awake during the day, he would steal a glance at me, look quickly away, and explode into wild sobs. He would take my slightest word or gesture, and mimic it for the general enjoyment. There was a request to have him moved, but the guards refused, suspecting that Cat wanted to avoid charges by pretending derangement. We had told them nothing of Jensen's persecution, and they apparently wanted us to handle Cat. "He's your problem," they said.

He was, indeed. What frightened me most was the fact that I was beginning to share his violence. He was no physical match for me, and if it ever came to a fight, I was sure I could hurt him badly. Therefore, I waited for a chance to challenge him and to bring affairs to a climax. A brief struggle, I surmised, and it would be over; he would be educated and I would be relieved. Anything seemed better than what was happening. On three occasions it nearly came to such an end, despite the fact that I was aware of the consequences—denial of the Gospel and nonviolence, exacerbation of black-white relations in jail, scandalous conduct for a priest, possible serious physical harm to another man.

I was nearly helpless before my anger—all the discipline of the years, all the fine, sensitive convictions I had learned from books and friends, were forgotten. Trapped by a giant primitivism that I could neither understand nor cope with, I was simply helpless to pursue alternatives that would break the vicious stalemate between us. I could not bear to speak to him, to take him casually or jokingly, to have the slightest normal thing to do with him. The only communication between us was his readiness to harass me, and mine to break him if the occasion offered. It was a murderous impasse, making a mockery of my thirteen years of work with black people.

The danger is over now. It probably wore itself out from its own inner fury. I deserve no credit for the change, except that somehow I found the strength to control myself. It is now possible to see more clearly what Cat is about, and what I am about. The former gives me hope, while the latter appalls me—which may be a healthier state of affairs than before.

Philip and Daniel in Ithaca, New York, March 1970.
Photo by Bob Fitch, Black Star.

A downed U.S. flier in North Vietnam, receiving treatment for his injuries. Photo courtesy of Cornell University, Carl A. Kroch Library, Division of Rare and Manuscript Collections.

SIX

Letters from the Gulag: Waging Peace in Prison

great power flows from us,
luminous, a promise. Yes! . . . Then
great energy flows from solitude,
and great power from communion.

DENISE LEVERTOV

L
ewisburg Penitentiary is a dark, brooding, and impenetrable
fortress. A hard rock maximum-security prison where some
of America's toughest criminals do time. Smart, wily guys
who run their scams inside the walls, learn new skills, teach younger
cons a few tricks. When their time is up, they stroll out the gate, right
back into the game. The majority are poor, many are black. Guys
who began the race not only way behind the starting line, but with
broken legs, club feet, half blind. Uneducated, but not stupid. Beaten
and abused at home. Assaulted and raped in reform school. Knocked
to a pulp in the back rooms of police stations. Prison is simply a
reflection of their neighborhoods, their schools, and their families.
A mirror in which they see past, present, and future.

Even the most remedial inmate knows that Lewisburg is the reality behind Miss America's charming smile.

Tom Lewis and I arrived there in June 1968 chained together in
the back seat of a federal marshal's car. The marshals stopped for
lunch, but they refused to remove our shackles so we had to balance

hamburgers and cokes, spilling more than we put in our mouths. These guys weren't brutes. Just civil servants doing their job. Putting in their time until retirement. Quite a few were Catholics, and as such were really pissed at me. After all, priests belonged behind the altar, not at anti-war demonstrations. Priests should be blessing babies, hearing confessions, conducting marriage ceremonies, not burning draft records, and not embarrassing the church by going to jail. I frightened them, violated their sense of values and security. I had stepped out of their fold, become the black sheep of *our* family. I had broken some sacred trust, some inviolable agreement, and to make their point they refused to address me as "Father Berrigan," calling me "Berrigan" instead.

Tom Lewis, co-defendant in the Catonsville and Baltimore trials, had been cooped up with me in the Baltimore County jail for a couple of months. Too dangerous, said the government, to be let out on bail. Now, we stood waiting just outside the joint, the slammer, the house of the dead. The prison's high brick walls were built by WPA labor, and I couldn't help laughing at that irony. Would my own dad, that fiery champion of the working man, have helped build places like Lewisburg? Great forbidding warehouses in which to store the bodies and destroy the spirits of our fellow human beings? I couldn't blame Tom Berrigan if he had laid a brick or two for a prison wall. Hunger drives people to all kinds of extremes.

We were packed in tight. Chained wrist to ankle. Sweating. Anxious to get the hell out of that car. The marshals talked to the guardhouse, and the guardhouse talked to "Control" inside the prison, guiding us slowly and carefully toward the fortress. We got out of the car and shuffled toward one gate. Prisoners were watching us from their cells, sizing us up, spreading the news. By the time we were inside, everyone in Lewisburg knew who we were. I was the first Catholic priest in American history to be tried and imprisoned for a political crime, and a bit of a celebrity in Lewisburg. But I neither expected, nor did I ever ask for, special treatment in that seething pit of human misery.

The warden, J.J. Parker, was a Notre Dame man. An isolated figure. Not particularly hated or feared by the prisoners. Just a functionary who let subordinates run the prison while he was away attending Notre Dame football games. He lived outside the walls in a mansion built by Lewisburg inmates in the mid-'thirties. Prisoners acted as servants for the warden and his family, doing the housework, mowing the grass, tending the flowers and shrubbery. When he entertained, Parker ordered a suckling pig or a slab of veal from one of the farm camps, had it dressed and delivered to his convict chef.

We were taken into a small room, ordered to strip. A guard stuck a flashlight into our mouths, probed orifices, gave us a handful of lice-killing soap, and led us to the shower. Cons helped process us into Lewisburg; they were friendly enough, telling us whom to trust and whom to look out for, talking in a kind of subliminal mutter. My clerical clothes, which I had been wearing since the Baltimore action, were taken away and I was given prison togs. Two sets of blue, the fit didn't matter. Shirts, pants, prison shoes.

I spent several months in Lewisburg, without any real trouble, before being released on bond just before Christmas '68. A Jesuit attorney named Callahan managed to spring me on appeal, and our lawyers took the Catonsville convictions all the way to the Supreme Court, but the good justices refused to hear our case. So it was back to jail for the nine defendants. Three years for Daniel. Six years for me.

Robert McNamara's promises of the "light at the end of the tunnel" turned out to be more government hubris. The killing in Vietnam, and the violence at home, continued unabated. Richard Nixon, very much alive, kept urging the American people to share his fantasies about victory in Vietnam. Meanwhile, the Weathermen were calling for violent revolution, and the Weather Underground commenced their own bombing campaign, attacking banks and other symbols of U.S. imperialism.

We had taken our stand at Baltimore and Catonsville. Stood up. Said no to the madness. We were out on appeal for almost two years. Then what? Should we surrender quietly to federal marshals? Should we play the state's game and allow mass murderers like Richard Nixon to toss us back into the lion's den?

In April 1970 four of the Catonsville Nine decided to go underground, knowing that our refusal to cooperate with the authorities was another calculated break with traditional nonviolent strategy. Our actions would confuse, anger, and alienate some of our fellow peace activists, some of whom refuse to speak to us even now, more than twenty-five years later. Shortly before we were scheduled to give ourselves up, the Catonsville defendants met at the Catholic Worker House in Baltimore to discuss what we ought to do. Should we surrender to a government that was committing genocide in Vietnam, or go underground and continue our resistance to the war? How could we allow ourselves to be shackled and led off to prison, when we had broken neither international law nor God's law? Our actions were just; the law was unjust.

A superficial view of nonviolence would argue that you have to take the consequences of your actions. We've always done that, but sometimes there is a larger point that needs to be made. By going underground, we were rejecting, totally and unequivocally, the "justice system." We did not respect, and we could not obey, laws that condoned and courts that supported genocide.

Our trial had been a farce. We weren't judged by a jury of our peers, and the conclusion was inevitable. The judge never instructed the jury that it could set the evidence aside, and decide our innocence or guilt on the basis of their conscience, a tradition called "jury nullification." The Catonsville trial had nothing to do with justice.

As Christians, and as peace activists, we needed a new vision in which to ground our actions. Something deeper than political analysis. Increasingly, we were taking our inspiration from the gospels, and from war resisters like Dietrich Bonhoeffer, Franz Jagerstaetzer, and other courageous Germans who refused to cooperate with Hitler, even when their resistance meant certain death. We didn't see ourselves as martyrs or heroes, but as ordinary men and women who were called to give our lives to peace and social justice.

David Eberhardt and I took off together. George Mische was hiding somewhere in the Midwest. Mary Moylan would stay underground for nine years. David Darst was killed in a car accident, driving the icy back roads in Minnesota on his way to visit a friend at Sandstone federal penitentiary. John Hogan, Tom Lewis, and the Melvilles reported to the authorities and had their sentences reduced.

Dan gave the FBI a run for its money, popping up like the proverbial fox, dodging well-laid traps, making fools out of J. Edgar Hoover's agents. He was meeting with the Black Panthers and the Weatherpeople, preaching anti-war sermons in churches, and engaging in other acts of resistance.

One night, my brother showed up at a huge anti-war rally in Cornell University's Barton Hall. He was wearing a Darth Vader helmet and riding on the back of a motorcycle. When the lights came on, Dan gave a short rousing speech to the ten thousand stomping, screaming, clapping students. Masquerading as hippies, Hoover's agents waited to pounce, but suddenly Dan was enveloped in a huge Bread and Puppet puppet, made to resemble one of the twelve apostles; he fled from Barton Hall.

Elizabeth McAlister and I had secretly married, and she offered to hide David Eberhardt and myself in a summer house belonging to her religious order. The house was on the Atlantic Ocean, and we stayed there for about two weeks before moving to the home of a very generous and remarkable family by the name of Smith. About a week before we arrived, a very tragic thing happened. A teenage boy living just a few doors from the Smiths rose early one morning, sat on his front lawn, and immolated himself. He was a very wonderful, sensitive, young man, and he left a note saying that he could no longer live with this terrible war. His father was about to leave for work when he discovered his son's charred remains.

David and I were invited to address a big peace rally at St. Gregory's, a Catholic church in Manhattan. One more rousing speech, and we would submit to arrest. We trusted the priest who had arranged this with the FBI, and we trusted the FBI to keep its word. We came in from western New Jersey in the wee hours of the morning, had something to eat, and managed to get a little sleep at the priest's apartment, which was right above the church.

The rally was scheduled for that evening, and during the day I met with a remarkable young leader of the Young Lords, a militant Puerto Rican group in New York City. He said that he knew a way to get us out of the church after we addressed the rally. We walked around for a while, talking about the war in Vietnam, and the war on New York City's streets. He explained that the Young Lords were willing to help us. He was really convinced that we could outmaneuver Hoover's troops one more time.

Dan had been with us shortly before, but he grew suspicious and took off, hiding out for awhile in Elizabeth McAlister's family home in Upper Montclair, New Jersey. When Liz's brother found out, he threatened to call the FBI, forcing Dan to find other safe havens.

By mid-afternoon, more than a hundred FBI agents had surrounded St. Gregory's. They were standing on rooftops, sitting in cars, walking the sidewalks. They burst into the priest's apartment, guns drawn, hoping to catch Dan and me in the same net, angry that one of their prey had escaped. Hoover was taking no chances. His agents chained David and me together, and at least 20 agents escorted us to FBI headquarters in Manhattan.

Warden Parker was not happy to see David and me back in Lewisburg. We had exposed the judicial system's bias and corruption, and taunted the FBI. We had spoken freely about the cruel conditions inside U.S. prisons, had accused the U.S. government of being totalitarian, had called for the release of all political prisoners in U.S. jails. Parker suspected me of having contacts with activist groups outside the prison, and he was determined to break me. Guards opened my mail, constantly shook me down, recruited stool pigeons to spy on me. They searched my cell, and denied me the right to receive legitimate visitors. My letters to Elizabeth McAlister, a Catholic nun with whom I had fallen in love and secretly married, were intercepted. Prison authorities passed copies to the FBI.

Tired of all the petty hazing, David and I refused to line up for the noonday meal. A guard reported us, and a disciplinary committee threatened punishment, but still we refused to work, telling them, ever so politely, to shove their orders. We were sentenced to solitary confinement. There we continued our resistance, fasting the entire time.

I lived in quiet fury, knowing that as I sat in that sweatbox the killing in Vietnam went on and on. Knowing that the judicial system served the masters of war, not the American people. Knowing that 18-year-old kids were being dumped into pits of despair like Lewisburg, beaten, raped, driven to the brink of despair because they wouldn't kill for God and country. I wasn't about to plead with the judge for a return to court, throwing myself on the state's mercy, groveling with contrition. I thought about Gandhi and King and so many people who suffered beatings and jailings and killings; people who stood fast, refusing to resort to violence, putting their bodies and souls behind their words.

Prior to this incident, the guards shook down the chapel, trying to find contraband they suspected I was hiding there. I was allowed to offer the Eucharist, every day and all alone, but they thought my real purpose was to hide subversive anti-war stuff.

Who, I asked myself, was to fly this material over the high walls? Super priest? The guards entered our cells, threw books around, and ripped clothing apart. They found nothing, and they left more angry than they came.

Teamsters boss Jimmy Hoffa was doing hard time in Lewisburg. The word had obviously come down from Washington: Make the little bastard suffer. Hound him. Harass him. Make him wish he had kept his big mouth shut. He was sewing mattress covers inside this cage, and when prison officials were giving a tour of the prison, they always made sure their visitors saw the Teamsters boss: sewing, inside his cage.

Like many white-collar criminals in Lewisburg, Hoffa was a devout Catholic, a regular attendee at mass and the sacraments. He respected priests absolutely, and he hated the government for putting me in prison. Jimmy knew a lot about the Baltimore Four and Catonsville Nine actions, and he considered us fellow political prisoners. He told me that he had people over in Allenwood, people at the farm outside Lewisburg's walls, and people inside Lewisburg itself. If anyone gave me trouble, just let Jimmy know. If I needed anything special, he would see that I got it. If I was given a shit detail, he would ensure better duty.

Hoffa came up from the streets, and he knew exactly what lies behind the glitter and glamor of Washington. He was no idiot. He could have taught labor law at any college or university, and he wasn't in awe of the ivy league boys who despised him as much, if not more, than he hated them. They might have impeccable manners and charming wives, but Hoffa didn't think they differed very much from the bone breakers he knew.

When the Justice Department wants to take you down, said Hoffa, they wire your phone; they start rumors, hoping to get you killed; they threaten your friends and family, and they put a price on your head. And the media makes it look so sweet. All that good versus evil bullshit. Jimmy Hoffa didn't read between the lines. He lived there. O.K., he said, maybe the Teamsters do have a few bone breakers, but the government uses the FBI to do its dirty work. Sure, the mafia does use hit men to make a point, and the CIA tortures, disappears, and assassinates people all over the world. Once you strip away the tinsel, said Hoffa, there's not much difference between the cons doing time in Lewisburg, and the crooks doing crime out of the White House.

Jimmy had an extraordinary network in Lewisburg, and outside in Allenwood. Teamster loyalists. Friends from the United Mine Workers. Little-time mafia figures. Big-time mafiosi. His people in Allenwood were always scheming to see him. They would play sick or claim to have an abscessed tooth, but once inside Lewisburg they managed to slip away for an audience with the boss. I listened to their complaints and confessions, and I maintained a good relationship with Jimmy's people. They were sympathetic to me, even though they knew my views on violence. I never took Hoffa up on his offer of protection.

When our supporters found out that David and I were fasting in the hole, they created quite an uproar, demonstrating and picketing just outside the prison. After awhile, the prison authorities ate crow, offering me a job teaching in the education department if I would end my fast. I agreed, even though the associate warden who made me the offer was a snake. I didn't trust him at all.

I was always writing about the war, and other political matters, and in those days that was absolutely forbidden. If the authorities caught you, they confiscated your work and you never got it back. I knew prisoners who wrote books, only to have them seized and, most likely, destroyed.

David Eberhardt and I went back to work, but the harassment continued, so I wrote to New York Senator Charles Goodell (God bless him, he was a decent guy), telling him about our treatment. A young Cornell intern named Judy Poole rescued my letter from the slush pile. She passed my note on to Goodell, who started maneuvering to get me, David Eberhardt, and George Mische (Catonsville defendant) transferred to a less hostile environment.

Daniel was still underground, the chase more mean than merry. He kept playing hide-and-seek with J. Edgar Hoover, showing his sly Jesuit mug in unexpected places, then slipping away with another peace chicken between his teeth. Hoover was furious, and Dan kept spreading the word that good old Uncle Sam was a terrorist, holding me hostage in Lewisburg, banging away at my body and soul, looking for my breaking point, trying to force me to call a news conference where I would burst into tears, urge my brother to come to his senses, and beg him to give himself up. Through channels the government couldn't uncover, I kept urging my brother to stay underground.

Harvard psychologist Robert Coles arrived at Lewisburg to check out a rumor that David and I were on the verge of cracking up. Dr. Coles arranged to meet with us privately, but one of the associate wardens, a devious and hypocritical character named Hendricks, insisted on sitting in. We weren't about to talk about our treatment in front of that creep, so after about thirty futile minutes, Coles gave up. He stopped in to see J.J. Parker, who ranted and raved, telling Coles that political prisoners are grandstanders, trouble makers, obsessed with getting attention. Hendricks tossed a fountain pen onto the warden's desk. "You see this," shouted Parker, waving the pen in Dr. Coles's face, "this is why we shake down Berrigan's cell. This is why we shake down everyone's cell." The pen was a concealed knife. It had never been in my cell, could never be there, unless the guards decided to plant it under my pillow.

Coles told friends that David and I were in pretty bad shape. Highly emotional. Near psychological collapse. About to go over the edge. This infuriated us. We might have looked a little green around the gills, and we were rather thin and pretty damn tired after two weeks of fasting in the sweatbox. But near the edge? Not at all. We just wanted to talk about some of the misery Parker was putting us through. We just wanted the bullshit to stop flowing in our direction. Coles came highly recommended. He had intervened at Parchmont, Mississippi, on behalf of civil rights workers, and he seemed to know the score. But the more time you spend in prison, the more you realize how similar it is to combat. You can read about it, see films and hear stories, but you can never quite understand until you're there.

Later, I heard that the warden threatened Coles, insisting he accept a metal tray the prisoners made in shop, warning him that the prison gates didn't always work, implying that he might be trapped all night in Lewisburg. Coles called the warden's bluff, telling Parker that he would love to spend the night in the joint. J. J. gave in and let him go home.

Dr. Coles meant well. He just didn't understand our witness, and the price we were willing to pay for it. Coles was a liberal. He still believed that the American system could be modified, reformed, saved from itself. Those of us the news media had dubbed "the Catholic left" no longer shared his optimism. To us, reform was a misnomer, a bad joke played and re-played on good people. The system must be taken down altogether, replaced by something altogether new, something vital and life-giving—a world where love, not war, prevails.

We were talking about revolution. Not with guns. Nor would we imprison the people who had imprisoned us. We didn't want to kill the people who were orchestrating the massacre in Vietnam. Christ said we ought to "Turn the other cheek," not retaliate when someone hurts us. He told us we must learn to love, not try to kill our enemies. We wanted the church to come out of its government-supported, state-sanctioned coma. To get off the rhetorical Pentagon dole.

In November 1966 the American bishops had stated that the Vietnam war met the criteria for a just war, but those men weren't going to die in some leech-filled rice paddy. Cardinal Spellman wasn't going to walk point through triple-canopy jungle, waiting for a sniper to blow out his brains or a booby trap to send him home in a chocolate box. Those horrors were for young working-class men, not the church hierarchy. A revolution of spirit is what we were seeking.

Most war resisters were placed outside of Lewisburg wall on the hog farm, or sent to Allenwood 17 miles away. The few who got left behind in the big house were abused by older cons. Verbally harassed and beaten by inmates who were doing time for rape, murder, and armed robbery. Cons who had dedicated their entire lives to crime chanting "My country 'tis of thee" as they pounded on war resisters' heads. A fascinating phenomenon—that victims of oppression are often willing to kill and die for their oppressors. I was transferred to Danbury federal penitentiary shortly after FBI agents, disguised as bird watchers, captured my brother on Block Island. Dan was soon brought to Connecticut, and we considered it a great blessing that we would serve our sentences in the same prison. Inmates weren't allowed to practice their profession in federal prisons. Doctors couldn't practice medicine, lawyers couldn't do law, and Dan and I couldn't be priests, though we were permitted to teach. We set up a

Great Books club for inmates, and started a discussion group with draft resisters and other prisoners, most of whom were doing time for nonviolent crimes. We branched out into more controversial texts, starting with the Gospel according to Matthew, then on to *Bury My Heart At Wounded Knee, Sisterhood Is Powerful, Soul On Ice*, and other powerful social, political, and religious books.

We had a tight, resolute group of about twelve to fifteen prisoners, and after a time we decided to put our theories into practice, right there, inside those prison walls. We knew the risks: solitary confinement, reduction of good time, sudden transfers to troublemaker prisons. Still, we had to continue our resistance to the war. We were determined not to lose our voices. Our imprisonment, we knew, pointed out the big lie. Power might or might not come from the barrel of a gun, but justice never does.

In the fall of 1970, I confided to Dan that Liz McAlister and I had secretly married two years before. This was after the first indictment came down for the Harrisburg conspiracy, charging Liz, myself, and others (Dan was listed as an unindicted co-conspirator) with plotting to destroy utilities under government buildings, and with conspiring to kidnap President Nixon's National Security Advisor, Henry Kissinger, or some other important government official. Dan was shocked by my disclosure. Not because I, a priest, had married a nun, but because I hadn't trusted him. I obviously didn't hold him in high enough regard to tell him that Liz and I were man and wife.

The second indictment in the Harrisburg case charged me and others with conspiring to destroy the entire Selective Service System on the east coast. Anti-war activists had been busy, invading draft boards in Boston, Baltimore, Wilmington, and Washington, D.C., and it appeared that J. Edgar Hoover thought I was masterminding these actions. Some of these raids were highly effective, destroying hundreds of draft records and making it difficult, if not impossible, to send 18-year-old boys off to war. Conspirators also mailed draft cards back to their owners, with a note attached suggesting that they not re-register for the draft. That was probably the best news a lot of young men received during the war years.

It started to snow in late November, spreading over trees and fields around Danbury, closing us off from the outside world. 1970, and the madness in Southeast Asia, and at home, continued. The CIA replaced Cambodia's Prince Norodom Sihanouk with General Lon Nol. The Pentagon raided Son Tay Prison in North Vietnam, but failed to free American POWs. The Ohio National Guard killed four students at Kent State. J. Edgar Hoover sent a secret memo to Henry Kissinger, and to White House aide John Ehrlichman, warning that the Catholic left was plotting to kidnap Kissinger, who was shuttling to Paris for secret talks with the North Vietnamese.

Dan and I walked around the prison's compound, trying to reflect on what the Harrisburg indictment really meant. Would we spend more years, perhaps even the rest of our lives, in prison? That was a distinct possibility. The charges were so absurd, and the government so deadly serious. Would I ever see Elizabeth McAlister again outside Danbury's walls? Would my elderly parents die without my giving them one last hug? I was beginning to understand how ruthless and cruel our government can be. Imperial states are about ripping people apart, chewing them to pieces; that's what the government was doing in Southeast Asia, and that's what it was doing at home.

I made peace with myself. If I had to spend the rest of my life behind bars, so be it. I was prepared for the worst, and I wasn't going to make any deals with anyone except my God, and my conscience.

We had looked at the utilities under government buildings, in order to investigate how we might shut off the heat to government buildings. We felt that government workers, at least those who remained silent about the killing in Southeast Asia, were conspiring with Richard Nixon to pursue the war. We would shut off the heat and then, as workers left their buildings, hand out leaflets denouncing the war in Vietnam. We weren't going to risk anyone's life, and we never talked about blowing up heating ducts. That was the government's version, which had nothing to do with reality. I did look under a couple of buildings in the capital to see how we might shut off utilities, but the FBI was looking for me and I couldn't pull this action off. No one else wanted to, and that ended our conspiracy.

Henry Kissinger was a war criminal, but we never planned to kidnap him. We had discussed a "citizen's arrest," which seemed very much in the American grain. When the judicial system fails to prevent someone from committing egregious acts of violence, citizens have a right to take action. Kissinger strutted and fretted his bloody hour. No one could stop him. He wasn't accountable to the American or Vietnamese people. He had no respect for international law, or the law of God. We were merely talking about one way to hold him accountable for his crimes against humanity.

Elizabeth McAlister had written to me at Danbury, asking what I thought about the idea of arresting Henry Kissinger. She had attended the meeting at which this strategy was discussed, and wanted my views. I replied that it wouldn't be possible. Kissinger never went anywhere without armed guards. It just wouldn't work.

The government was engaged in thought control, which is why our letters were read in court. I did think about arresting Henry Kissinger, but I did not approve of this plan. Richard Nixon was massacring Vietnam's children, and trying to send me to prison for life. My crime: having unacceptable thoughts.

This, of course, is the basis for totalitarianism. Our lawyers told us that when all else fails, prosecutors will throw the conspiracy net, hoping to snare more than one person. When the net is full, they convene a grand jury, collect some tough indictments, and start cutting deals, offering immunity to people who agree to turn state's evidence, or simply lie on the witness stand.

We've come a long way since the 'sixties and 'seventies in this regard. The legislation that is on the books now, and the penalties, are far more stringent than when we were tried at Harrisburg.

The FBI must have thought, "What the hell, Dan and Phil are brothers, they just have to be in on this thing together." Dan was at Catonsville, and he always approved of what I did, just as I approved of his actions. That's why the government decided to throw him in as a co-conspirator in the Harrisburg fiasco.

Soon lawyers began arriving at Danbury to help us prepare for J. Edgar Hoover's latest vendetta, and my brother was far more articulate, more witty, and more clever than me. Everyone seemed to be paying more attention to him, laughing at his jokes, taking his picture, asking him for a good, pithy quote. Devoured by jealousy, I accused him of grandstanding, and of trying to hold on to center stage. I called him a "dime store liberal," questioned his commitment to ending the war, and warned him that he was about to sell out. Not only the movement, but his own brother. Like a spiritual boll weevil, envy was eating me hollow, draining my vitality, and leaving me a dried-out shell. Dan was in great pain, and when he questioned me I came to my senses. My charges were groundless and unjust. I apologized and asked for his forgiveness, which he readily gave.

Hoover was desperate to send me away for life; to the executioner, if he could. On Friday, November 27, 1970, he met behind closed doors with members of a Senate Appropriations subcommittee, telling them about our two "plots": to plant bombs somewhere in and around Washington, and to kidnap a high-ranking government official. Only two members of the subcommittee—Senator Roman L. Hruska (R–Neb.) and Senator Robert C. Byrd (D–W. Va.), attended this meeting, and neither thought to ask Hoover just who the government official might be. The subcommittee released Hoover's charges to the news media, but federal prisoners weren't allowed to speak to the free press, so Dan and I couldn't respond to these charges.

Two weeks later, on December 9, 1970, William R. Anderson, a Democratic Congressman from Tennessee, stood up to address the House of Representatives. A graduate of the U.S. Naval Academy, a commissioned officer who served in the Pacific on eleven submarine combat patrols, Anderson commanded the *Nautilus,* the world's first atomic submarine. In August 1958 he took that sub on an under-ice Arctic crossing, passing from the Pacific to the Atlantic Ocean, under the North Pole. Congressman Anderson was a member of the American Legion, the American Veterans of World War II, and the Veterans of Foreign Wars.

And there he stood on the floor of the House, demanding that Hoover prove his charges against the Berrigan brothers; denouncing the vendetta against Dan and me; describing how Danbury officials tried to force us to make weapon components for the U.S. government; telling his colleagues how the Justice Department kept shuffling Daniel from prison to prison, without even a court order, holding my brother incommunicado, keeping him in solitary confinement, moving him about in leg shackles and waist chains so tight he couldn't even blow his nose.

Congressman Anderson came to see us in Danbury. He read our books, wrote us letters, asked many questions about our religious and political beliefs. Anderson was willing to look beyond the news media's caricatures of peace activists. He listened to our views, and he got to know us as priests, writers, and thinkers. He came to know us as fellow Americans, and as human beings.

Anderson had voted for every military appropriation and every war measure to come before the House, but during a fact-finding mission to Vietnam he saw the pits into which the Saigon government threw its opponents. At Con Son, he saw women, old men, and even children, massed together in tiger cages. Guards tossed lime on their heads, urinated on them, tortured and murdered them. Anderson learned that American boys were fighting and dying for a dictatorship that condemned its own citizens to die, slowly and painfully, in underground cages.

Hoover stood his ground and the Harrisburg trial went forward. Others accused in the conspiracy were: Eqbal Ahmad; ex-Josephite priest Tony Scoblick, and ex-Notre Dame nun Mary Scoblick; Neil McLaughlin and Joe Wenderroth, both Baltimore priests; and Ted Glick. With the exception of Wenderroth, who planned on doing an action later, all were draft board invaders. All were radically against the Vietnam War.

Wenderroth and I had gone into the tunnels under Washington, D.C., and I had asked him to ask some engineers what they thought about shutting off the utilities to government office buildings. I said, "Joe, you know we don't want to hurt anybody. We just want to shut off the electricity and the heat for awhile, to make a point with the workers." It would have been a good action.

In a loud mocking voice, the prosecutor read my love letters to Elizabeth, and her love letters to me. Boyd Douglass, the informer who smuggled my letters out of Danbury, and promptly gave copies of them to the FBI, spun absurd tales about intrigues and plots, claiming to have been privy to the Berrigans' violent schemes. On and on he talked, day after miserable day. The classic forked-tongue informer was saving his neck by selling friends and family down the river. Lost in his own wonderland of lies and deceit, never quite explaining how we were going to plant bombs in Washington while locked behind bars in Connecticut. Never quite revealing how we might kidnap Henry Kissinger, with our wrists cuffed together, cuffs chained to our waists, a chain holding our ankles.

Ramsey Clark, the former Attorney General who once helped send Daniel and me to prison, was our legal advisor during the Harrisburg debacle. He told us that talking to a kangaroo court wouldn't help at all. He advised us not to legitimize this comedy of errors, urged us not to respond to the judge's taunting, and encouraged us to ignore the ludicrous ranting of government witnesses. We kept silent while the Catholic judge, who would have loved to burn us at the stake, urged the prosecutor forward. We said nothing when his honor tried to browbeat the jury into finding us guilty. Nothing when the pack of lies rose higher and higher, wobbled, and collapsed.

I met Boyd Douglass in Lewisburg, trusted him, and went to considerable pains to clear him with people at Bucknell University. Dick Drinnon, professor of history at Bucknell, was a good friend of mine, and was very active in the anti-war movement at the college. There was also a great librarian at Bucknell, who was caught up in this conspiracy net, and jailed because she refused to talk to a grand jury.

Boyd Douglass was allowed out of prison to attend Bucknell, and he had enrolled in one of Drinnon's classes. Douglass was the only prisoner in Lewisburg who was allowed outside the walls on a daily basis, and he had been trying to ingratiate himself with me, worming his way into my confidence. Drinnon said not to worry. Douglass was solid, someone I could trust.

I also knew a lot of the old cons at Lewisburg, guys who were doing double life, thirty years for robbing banks, a dime for bashing in someone's skull. They had a very tight community in prison, played bridge together, and read a lot of heavy books. I liked those people, and used to talk with them all the time. When I asked what they thought about Boyd Douglass, they said, "Don't worry, Phil. He's no stool. He's all right. You can trust him."

After that, I started to confide in Douglass. I told him that we had discussed the possibility of "arresting" Henry Kissinger. I talked about the tunnels under Washington, D.C., and said that I had checked them out to see if our plan might work. And he said, "Look, Phil, I'm a Vietnam veteran. I'm a demolitions expert, and I know all about primer cord." I didn't know anything about primer cord. "Well," said Douglass, "It's explosive. You can use it for a very limited, concentrated explosion." I told him that we had no intentions of hurting anyone. That wasn't our style, and we would never do it, even if it would mean an end to the Vietnam war.

Douglass had agreed to carry my letters outside the prison, and he did deliver them to Elizabeth—after making copies for the FBI. As an indicted conspirator in the Harrisburg case, Liz wasn't allowed to write or visit me in Lewisburg. No problem, said Douglass. He would carry her letters inside the prison. My conversations with Douglass, and my letters to Liz, provided Hoover with enough "evidence" to launch the Harrisburg trial.

The Harrisburg trial was covered by the national and international press. William Kunstler visited Dan and me in prison, offering to help. Thousands of people rallied and demonstrated their support, including Congresswoman Bella Abzug, Ralph Abernathy, and Daniel Ellsberg, who was facing serious charges for having given the *Pentagon Papers* to the *New York Times*.

On the morning the trial was to begin, I asked Judge R. Dixon Herman for permission to make a statement. When he refused, I attempted to dismiss my attorneys in order to act as my own lawyer. The other defendants and our attorneys approved of my request, which was consistent with the Sixth Amendment guarantee of self-defense, if a defendant requests this before opening testimony in a trial.

I intended to offer a "note of sympathy" to the jury over their sequestration, to say

> As you know, the defense opposed it from the beginning. Forgive me, however, for thinking that I too am locked up; forgive me for concluding that all of us are locked up for a good cause. Possibly that can console and strengthen us in the long weeks ahead.
>
> Furthermore, let me express for the defense our pride and satisfaction in you as the jury. You have freely taken upon yourselves a noteworthy responsibility—that of judging us as our peers. But what does that mean? In the concrete, it means understanding the lives of a Third-World scholar, an expert on the aspirations and movements of the world's poor (two-thirds of humanity); the lives of four ghetto priests, who on one hand, have dedicated their ministries to justice for blacks, and on the other, to the abolition of war as an instrument of foreign policy; the life of a nun, a college professor, who with one or two others, has represented over 100,000 Roman

Catholic sisters in their hopes for peace; the life of Mary Cain Scoblick, who has expended her Christian life in the education of black children, in the struggle for black rights, in the fight for peace.

We possess the utmost confidence that you can judge us fairly and impartially; that you can distinguish between conspiracy and acts of conscience; between plotting and responsible discussion—discussion allowed by the Constitution which we judge a grave moral and political duty; between government warmaking and our peacemaking. We have the fullest confidence, I assure you, that you can distinguish between these two realities—that we have never conspired to bomb or kidnap anyone; while the government *has* conspired to bomb and kidnap. In fact, it has bombed and kidnapped—bombed Indochina until, as one of our pilots said, "It looks like a lunar landscape"; kidnapped millions of Indochinese by the simple expedient of bombing them out, to forcibly relocate the survivors in refugee camps. It has virtually kidnapped millions of young Americans through its Selective Service Act—a certainly immoral and possibly illegal piece of legislation—coercing them to kill and possibly to be killed.

Facts like these are the dominating facts of this indictment, not the government's counts, not an enumeration of overt acts. We stand before this dock because we have non-violently resisted our government's warmaking in Indochina. *That* is the reason; there is no other. We are confident you can perceive this—and conclude it.

I had planned to tell the court that I grew up on a farm during the Depression, a period of dire poverty and hopelessness. I was going to talk about being an enthusiastic soldier in World War II, and then describe four experiences with war that helped educate me, helped to lead me to resistance, to non-violent civil disobedience, to federal prison, to that dock.

The first had to do with my second night in France during World War II. We were outside Brest, and the Germans began to shell us, lightly and intermittently—more of a nuisance than anything else. In any event, a light tank company in the next hedgerow panicked—they were green troops like ourselves—and began to fire at shadows, sounds, and eventually one another. My introduction to war was the spectacle of Americans killing one another. I saw dead and wounded men the next morning, and blood-splattered half-tracks.

Later on in Germany, while the Bulge raged southwest of us, I watched a convoy of American dead go by, perhaps a dozen trucks and one hundred and fifty bodies. It was near New Year's 1945, bitterly cold—the corpses frozen, rigid arms and legs bumping on tailgates as the trucks bounced over the cobblestones. "Where is the glory of war for these men," I thought, "or the honor and reverence normally given the dead?" They had been unceremoniously picked up from the battlefield, blood frozen on their death wounds—perhaps near Bastogne—and transported like carcasses of beef to obscure and lonely graves.

Still later in 1945, I returned to Germany an officer, having volunteered for infantry school outside of Paris. Without dwelling overmuch on my attitudes—I was an efficient young killer, an expert with rifle, carbine, sidearms, bayonet—eager to imitate the exploits of my three older brothers. While being screened for Officer's Training, I was warned that the combat expectancy of a rifle platoon leader was something under several minutes, before he was hit or killed. That made scant impression on me—I believed in the war, believed I had to do more to win it.

After commissioning in France, I went to Munster for assignment to a unit. The war had just ended—a personal disappointment to me. But Munster proved critical to my education—its devastation overwhelmed my senses. Saturation bombing had reduced a large and gracious city to dust and rubble. What sickened me the most, however, was not the unremitting, tedious destruction. It was the smell of the dead, the cloying, nauseous odor of those killed in the terrible hysteria of bombing. There they rotted in the warm summer sun—with no one to dig them out, no one to bury them—women and children and old men, a familiar pattern. And I thought vaguely and worriedly—must we win at this price? History tells us that the Romans salted Carthage after overwhelming it, so that the city could not rise again on that spot. I remembered that fact from high school Latin, and felt we must have had the same ruthlessness in bombing Munster as they did.

Had Judge Herman allowed, I would have described my conversations with the men responsible for U.S. policy in Indochina. For example, I had lengthy discussions with Secretary of State Dean Rusk, and corresponded with Secretary McNamara; also, Walt Whitman Rostow, President Johnson's foreign policy advisor. I conferred with Senator Fulbright, with Alain Enthoven, Assistant Secretary of Defense, with numerous Congressmen, State and Defense Department officials. I debated experts from the great universities. I pursued all constitutional channels; I believed in the system; I believed our leaders were honest, decent, and humble men. I believed that peace would take time, but that it would come.

But I changed, as people must change, under stress of conscience and event. I discussed with people as agonized as myself the resistance of Socrates, of Christ, of Henry David Thoreau, of Gandhi and King and Muste. They all emphasized obedience to the higher law of God; they made clear distinctions between the rights of responsible conscience and the rights of the State. They called for, and did, non-violent resistance to government; not as conspiracy or subversion, but to assert the democratic ideal of government of, for, and by the people; an ideal seldom reduced to concreteness by men in power.

I asked myself what Gandhi and others would have done, if faced with Cold War dangers, with the waste and dishonor of the Indochinese war? I had planned to say:

> I ask myself that question as I ask you. U Thant, former Secretary General of the United Nations, often remarked that if the American people knew the true facts of the Vietnam war, they would stop it. Stop it not necessarily as I tried to stop it in Baltimore and Catonsville; or as the other defendants tried to stop it, but according to the best dictates of their consciences and politics.
>
> But I committed civil disobedience and waited for arrest twice in Baltimore and at Catonsville, not because I hoped that destroying draft files would arrest the American war machine, but because it was the only convincing way of saying that what we did to the Indochinese, we did to ourselves—as we ruined their environment, we polluted our own; as we killed their young, we killed our own at Kent State, Jackson State, and at Attica; as we drove the Indochinese from their homes, so also we drove our young men into exile, or underground.
>
> I waited for arrest twice because I was ashamed of young men taking the heat for me. They had nothing to do with the Bomb, or Cold War, or Indochina, but they had to fight, to flee, or go to jail. As for me, who had helped build the terror (my silence was necessary for it), I lived in comfort and security.

I waited for arrest twice because a man must live what he believes and take the consequences. In Christ Our Lord, word and deed were one—one life. He never said anything that He didn't do; He never believed anything that He didn't live.

I waited for arrest twice because it would be necessary to explain why we had defaced draft records with blood—for the blood wasted in Vietnam; and destroyed them with napalm, for the burning of children. What I attempted to say—the other defendants as well—was simply this: I reject this war; I will neither support it nor remain silent in face of it.

For which pains I received an extravagant and vindictive sentence of six years; Lt. Calley, in contrast, is under house arrest for the premeditated murder of 22 civilians at My Lai—children, women, and old men—while the other 24 charged with the massacre there never came to trial or were acquitted. Meanwhile, other veterans of a hundred other My Lais go free and proudly show their medals; and policy makers, who sent them to kill and destroy, run for re-election.

We have in effect, added new horrors to Guernica, Auschwitz, and Hiroshima. Never before has a war been attempted against children like the war in Indochina. Because of bombing, napalming, shelling, search and destroy operations, interdiction artillery, food denial programs, and other similar acts of charity, over 50% of the Indochinese children don't reach five years old. One American officer puts it this way: "We are at war with the 10-year-old children;. It may not be humanitarian, but that's what it's like." An eyewitness account of an American correspondent illustrates his point. "In a central Vietnam village, I saw a group of children run toward an open fire which laborers had made of uprooted grass. One boy threw a handful of something into the fire, the rest waited. As I was approaching them out of curiosity, one boy used a stick to get the things out of the fire and the rest swarmed over him, snatching them up. The things were baby rats. In near frenzy, the children began to pursue one another again, some tossed the hot rats between their two hands, others gulped them down whole." (*Ecocide in Vietnam*, Barry Weisberg).

Samuel Butler once said that Christians are equally horrified to see their religion practiced, or to see it doubted. All over this land some Christians have been horrified by our lives. Which is their choice, except that most offer nothing real to stop the killing, to outlaw war before it ends civilization. Let them judge us, let any court or government judge us when they have a better idea. For this

government has no intention of ending the killing, ending the
Indochina war or the Arms Race. It builds ABM, MIRV, Poseidon,
and God knows what other doomsday weapons. It withdraws our
troops, employs more mercenaries, computerizes the battlefield,
steps up the bombing, and changes the color of the corpses.

Hoover had ordered his lieutenants to keep him informed about
the trial and even to rouse him from sleep when the verdict came
down. Dan and I were the first Catholic priests in American history
to get in serious trouble with the government. Hoover was a Catholic,
which might help explain his personal vendetta toward Dan and me.
We had violated his territory. The FBI was sworn to protect the Selective Service System, and Hoover believed we were trying to destroy
it. We had gone underground, moving about rather freely, making
fools of Hoover and his agents, proving they were not invincible.
He hated us.

The jury wouldn't buy the government's lunatic vision of the
"Catholic Left." Boyd Douglass had been sequestered with FBI
agents for more than a year. They had prepped him for the Harrisburg trial, trying to turn a con artist into a credible witness. He had
spent his life swindling banks, so surely he could pull the wool over
a jury's eyes.

Liz and I were found guilty of one crime—smuggling our own
love letters to one another. J. Edgar Hoover died a short time after
the five-month Harrisburg trial had ended. Even after the trial, my
letters, and letters to me, were intercepted, xeroxed, and placed in
my FBI file.

I didn't think we would be acquitted. Boyd Douglass was a bad
witness for the prosecution, but he was the only real evidence the
government had to convict us. The jury was out for more than a
week. One juror was a member of the Church of the Brethren, and
her son was a conscientious objector, so we were just astonished that
the prosecution accepted her on the jury. We thought she would be
sympathetic, only to find out later that she was most emphatic about
convicting us.

Hoover was a consummate politician. He kept files on powerful
people, and used the dirt he gathered to blackmail, and control, them.
He was able to intimidate the President of the United States, so I

never doubted that he might send me to prison for life. On the other hand, I knew enough about the criminal justice system to realize that things change overnight. I'd seen people released from jail when there was absolutely no indication this would happen. And people remained in prison, when no one really knew why.

The Harrisburg conspiracy has to be seen in the context of Hoover's attempt to crush the resistance movement in the United States. By this time, his agents and agents provocateurs were everywhere. They had helped kill Black Panthers Mark Clark and Fred Hampton, infiltrated Vietnam Veterans Against the War, indicted some of their members on trumped-up charges, and threw conspiracy charges against Dr. Spock, William Sloane Coffin, Michael Ferber, Mitch Goodman, and others. They were willing to use guile, deceit, bribery, threats, assault, blackmail, just about anything to sow paranoia, fear, and dissension within the movement.

Their strategy was quite solid and well thought out. Not because they were able to indict and convict activists. They lost every case, either in the courtroom or on appeal, but they succeeded in forcing the peace movement to invest great amounts of time and money to free defendants. The government spent tens of millions of dollars on conspiracy trials, and I always thought they invested their money wisely, since their goal was to continue the genocide in Southeast Asia.

Mitch Snyder, who would become a prominent and absolutely devoted advocate for the homeless, joined our book group. And another great resister, John Bach, was also a participant. I was in Danbury about two and a half years, and during that time our discussion group turned into a very tight resistance community. We started having frequent political meetings, we organized fasts against the war, we sponsored prisoners to climb the water tower, from which we hung anti-war banners, and when our friends were punished with transfers to other, more secure, prisons, they kept up their resistance.

Some of our actions in Danbury actually received international attention, and I'm sure made some contribution to ending the war. I was at trial in Harrisburg when, in the spring of 1972, the community I was working with struck the compound. They shut down work at the prison, refusing to do the laundry or clean the cell blocks.

They just wouldn't work, and they kept that up for nine days, protesting against making anything at Danbury that might aid the Pentagon. Convicts, working for 17 to 46 cents an hour, were making parts for Trident submarines, and other war-related things, and we wanted that to stop. Moreover, some of the prisoners were highly skilled workers, and they were being paid slave wages to make things for war contractors, who were getting very rich off prison labor. We wanted the profits from prison industries to be reinvested in the prison, for better dental and medical care, better library facilities, and better food. That was the original conception of prison industries. George Meany, head of the AFL-CIO, was on the board of directors of prison industries, but as the demand for war-related products increased, so did profits, which wound up back in the U.S. treasury, not in the prison.

John Bach kept up his peace work when he got out of prison, co-founding Jonah House, the community in which Liz, myself, our three children, and many other resisters have lived for more than twenty years. Bach also founded a peace community, the Whale's Tale, in New England, and he has been one of the most dedicated, outspoken, and consistent peace activists in that part of the country.

While I was serving time in Danbury federal penitentiary, Richard Nixon sent troops into Cambodia, widening the war he claimed to have a "secret plan" for ending, way back in 1968. National Guard troops opened fire on student protesters at Kent State, killing four and wounding 13. At Jackson State, the highway patrol fired on students, killing two. Photographs of the massacre at My Lai flashed around the world, Vietnam Veterans Against the War marched into Washington, D.C., ripped off their medals and threw them onto the steps of the nation's Capitol, the American Catholic Bishops started to question whether Vietnam did meet St. Augustine's criteria for a Just War. Thousands of young Americans were in exile in Canada, Sweden, and Australia. Desertions, AWOLs, drug abuse, and fraggings were ripping the U.S. military apart. Sick at heart, more divided than our nation had been since the Civil War, the voters re-elected Richard Milhous Nixon, who kept promising that the Viet Cong and North Vietnamese would be defeated by the gallant South Vietnamese army. American troops were coming home. The burning and bombing, the laying waste in Vietnam went on and on and on.

THE CHURCH IN CHAINS, September 1971

We began our hunger strike in Danbury federal penitentiary on August 6, 1971, the anniversary of the bombing of Hiroshima. In July 1971 Dan and I had appeared before the Federal Parole Board, after having served one third of our sentences; Dan, one year, myself two. With unmistakable distaste and hostility, the examiner tried to question us minutely about Catonsville, ignoring our protest, our conscience, the war, ignoring too, our many months in prison. Parole decisions in our case arrived within one week. Most federal prisoners wait six to ten weeks. Decision: a CTE (continue to expiration) for Dan, a rare 18 months setoff for me (next parole consideration in 18 months). No reasons offered, and none available.

Our hunger strike turned into a prison-wide work-strike to protest the parole board's arbitrariness and secrecy. We wanted Congress to investigate the Parole Board. We also wanted the tiger cages in Vietnam dismantled.

Five days into the protest, eleven prisoners, myself among them, were transported to the federal prison hospital in Springfield, Missouri. We were kept in isolated cells, guarded twenty-four hours a day, and we continued our liquids-only fast for about a month. During that time, the local Bishop, William Baum, paid me a visit. He asked that I write a letter in which I reflected on questions of priesthood and world justice. Bishop Baum was scheduled to attend the Catholic Bishops Synod in Rome, at which issues like the ones I wrote about would be discussed. This is what I wrote from prison.

Dear Bishop Baum,

Here are the few ideas I promised you. They are qualified, of course, by my status and by the two years I have already served. But I possessed them before imprisonment, my books are full of them, and, it goes without saying, I believe them profoundly enough to stake my life on them. I have not found many men who can say that about their ideas.

So if you find the following negative, caustic, angry—remember that they come from one who has questioned domestic racism and modern war for ten years; who has lived in the slums and seen the anguish of the poor; who has resisted militarism and war-making repeatedly; who has experienced not only prison but solitary confinement and long fasts; who has endured the charade of three political trials and who faces a fourth; and who probably will be in and out of prison for the remainder of his life. In sum, my experience has been out of the ordinary, and it comes purely from attempts to answer the question, "What does Christ ask of me?"

Despite the fact that we come from different frames of reference, and that the Berrigan view of the Gospel (Dan's and mine) is radically different from the hierarchy's, we will not admit that our own responsibilities differ from yours. In fact, we might even suggest that the Bishops have a deeper obligation to costly witness than we do because of the magisterium, their pastorship and charisma. I tend to state the matter bluntly. On the issue of modern war, the hierarchy's default is very nearly total; it is so bad, in effect, that nuclear exchange would find Bishops unprepared to discuss anything but the morality of defending a shelter with a shotgun.

Apart from these observations, which I offer only in introduction, please convey our love and fraternity (Dan's and mine) to the Pope. It strikes me that we speak for those unable to do so, those sisters and brothers around the world—priests, religious, laity—in Latin America, Africa, Europe, Indochina, the Marxist world. We constitute the church in chains—advocates of resistance to naked power, disproportionate wealth, racism, war-making. We want to express our fidelity to the Church and to the Chair of Peter, even as we sorrow over Christian myopia, hardness of heart, and even cowardice.

With these preliminaries, let me offer a few general observations as well. It impresses me that thinking in the Church today—now that we are over the Vatican II euphoria—is stereotyped, cautious, quasi-despairing. Bishops, theologians, and clergy are obviously operating under the house-keeping assumption: from top to bottom, from Rome to parish, more synods, councils, democracy, and guitars will see us through present world crises. We operate as though, under a divine and magical star, we will muddle through with minimal losses while grace and providence work for us—providing, however, we pretend hard enough that nuclear overkill does not exist, that genocide in Indochina has not been carried out, that the North Atlantic community does not control one-half of the world's wealth, that wealth and power are not identified with the white world, and poverty and desperation are not identified with the so-called colored world.

Those Catholics—clergy and laity—who have expressed disillusionment with such realities by leaving the Church altogether are leisurely marking time, maintaining low profile, avoiding controversy, shoring up obsolescent structures, talking a species of ecclesiastical doublespeak, and rejecting any involvement in the social horrors of the day. Apparently they take lightly the admonition of a witness like Paul: "Bear the burdens of one another, and you will have fulfilled the law of Christ."

Implicit in attitudes like these, shockingly pervasive as they are, is a dreadful and ill-defined fear—fear that we're not going to make it; fear that the Church will go down with the Powers of this world; fear of questioning, initiative, creativity, courage; fear of sacrifice, loneliness, criticism; fear, finally, of self, of neighbor, of Gospel, of Christ. I remember President Johnson saying, with an off-the-cuff honesty quite foreign to him: "Peace is going to demand more than we counted on!" In the same manner, Catholics are discovering that Christ will demand more than we counted on. And generally, the thought fills us with dread.

The Church in America—in fact, in the West as a whole—has accepted as religion a kind of cultural syncretism, culminating in near-perfect allegiance to the State. Not a few of its more prominent Bishops have even waited upon the Presidency like court jesters. And now the culture is being violently challenged, and the State doesn't so much govern as rule by force. To whom do we turn?

A case in point is the Catholic response to the Indochinese war. It is a classic case of burning incense to Caesar. After twenty-two years' involvement in Indochina (President Truman committed American support to the French in 1949); American dead (Pentagon figures are probably half the total); after war expenditures of 300 billion; after documented ecocide and genocide; after all this, thirty-two American Bishops have finally condemned the immorality of the war. In a tragedy of this magnitude, worldwide in its ramifications, the American Church, supposedly the most vital expression of universal Catholicism, mustered thirty-two tepid, episcopal voices, most of them recent. This, despite crushing evidence of the war's illegality—United Nations Charter, Geneva Accords, the SEATO agreement, the U.S. Constitution. Why so long for episcopal word, why so late and feeble? So late, in fact, that few listen and few care.

We have obviously surpassed the German Church in negligence both moral and criminal. (Resistance to Hitler, for example, meant totalitarian reprisal, which would not quite be the case here.) Despite the clarity of Paul VI's stand, despite constitutional protections, no

Bishop has challenged the illegality of the war in serious fashion; no Bishop has broken patently immoral laws (the Apostles were martyred for refusing to obey the law); no Bishop (except Parilla of Puerto Rico) has advocated non-violent resistance to the war (Mayor Lindsay of New York City, a nebulous liberal at best, advocated such a course two years ago). And only two or three Bishops have visited Catholic resisters in jail, at least two of them virtually apologizing for their action: "This visit is a spiritual work of mercy, which I would perform for any of my flock." More to the point would be an explanation of why they themselves were not in jail.

Furthermore, no Bishop has questioned the marriage of Big Business and Big Military in Big Government, and how the marriage results in government by and for the wealthy and powerful. No Bishop has condemned the American rape of the developing world, nor the arms race in horror weapons, nor American arms salesmanship, nor the division of the world by superpowers.

On the contrary, the American episcopacy has docilely and silently stood by while their countrymen and spiritual sons established the American empire and ruled it with ruthless might. They stood by as spectator, or advocate, while their country plunged into perpetual hot and cold warring, spent 1 ½ trillion dollars on war and weapons since 1946, and filled up Arlington Cemetery with the dead of Korea, the Dominican Republic, and Indochina. And yet the Church they lead, like the Savior, is come "to give life, and to give it more abundantly." What a gross irony!

Do I exaggerate? Perhaps. Some Catholics, who have suffered for dedication to Gospel and Church, would go much further, however. One layman I know—a superb student of Gospel politics and Gandhian non-violence, currently in jail—would say this with a snort: "Shepherds? There is not one in the American Church! They are upper-management people for the most part. And they are the State's sheep!" Of him, I would suggest that he remains loyal in a sense that most Catholics and most Bishops cannot understand.

Perhaps in the above you might perceive my difficulty in speculating about the priesthood, and how it might serve man as physician and prophet. For who will finally legislate as to training, experience, freedom? And who will provide what is most crucial of all—example? The men and women who can address the subject realistically are concerned mainly with witnessing against institutionalized terror and death—and they are in severe jeopardy of jail.

Moreover, there is this factor to consider. If Dan and I can serve as examples of repression from the Church—for nearly ten years now we have engaged in a constant, painful, running skirmish with Church authority, encountering ridicule, outrage, exile, reassignment, mistrust—the scales have, nevertheless, slowly balanced out. Today the Episcopacy tolerates us as under the jurisdiction of the State. But Episcopal hypocrisy has cut very deeply. Catholics who are today developing for themselves and their brothers "the freedom with which Christ has made us free" are extremely skeptical of Papal or Episcopal pronouncements. They even tend to ignore them as shallow and devious. They want the pronouncement of action, feeling that it is very late for words.

In effect, thinking Catholics make little distinction between treatment by Church and State. They know that both desire malleability and conformity, that both fear conscience, that both are self-righteous and dogmatic, that both are ruthless in handling deviants. To be fair, the Church is quicker to forgive and to forget. On the other hand, the State may be quicker to learn. But the point is that Catholics increasingly tend to ignore the official Church since it says so little real about the questions of life and death, and lives less than it says. How could it be otherwise? they ask. The official Church is not about the Gospel, or the plight of what Pope John called "the majority of men." Therefore, how can it speak to either issue?

The understanding from this quarter is simply this: both Church and State are vast, sprawling bureaucracies which share an insufferably arrogant assumption that they are the fundamental answers to the human condition. The understanding, further, is that, despite claims to the contrary, Church and State have brought Western civilization to its nadir, and have destroyed other civilizations in the process.

Critics have learned, or are learning in swelling numbers from history as well as from the Gospels, that nothing much makes sense except death to self and conversion to Christ and brother. All the virtues exemplified by the Lord—poverty, freedom in responsibility, the politics of community, willingness to risk jail and death for the exploited person—all these attack head-on the conceptions and realities of bureaucracies whether in Church or State. The goals of bureaucracies are simply not the goals of Christ.

To apply all this seriously to contemporary problems of priesthood—especially as an American—is enormously difficult, simply because we are so cut off from the mind and life of Christ. About all one can do is fumble with a few critical questions, and then labor with the complications of response.

The Catholic priest in America—and in the West generally—is more of a cultural phenomenon than he is a Gospel man. He is nationalistic, white supremacist, and uncritical toward affluence and its source. His training reflects nuances of these cultural fixations, but, beyond that, it schools him merely in neutrality toward life. By that I mean, he tends to take a purely institutional view of threats to life, whether they be its abuse or destruction. Indeed, if he is sensitive, he will go through immense pretensions to escape such brutalities. Or if he is hardened, he will advocate them, or remain casual in face of them.

Therefore the problem becomes—how to instill convictions strong enough to resist dehumanization in himself, in others, in structures. How to instruct him in non-violence as a way of life, as mark of the "new man," as instrument of human revolution and social regeneration? How to teach him the realities of power in all its nuances, from the will to dominate others to the will to exploit whole nations and peoples? How to toughen him so that he will understand and accept persecution, contempt, ostracism, jail, or death on account of conscience and (above all) on account of the suffering brother? How to acquaint him with such a sensitivity to human rights and dignity that he will test violence in every turn of his life—in himself, in the culture, in the State? How to convince him that Christ's man must integrate word and act, in full recognition that this might lead him to death, even as it did his Lord?

I don't know, because one can neither teach the above nor administer it. But the Church can beg the grace of God, the Church can provide the setting; even though it be modern catacombs, the Church can begin, realizing that her life must always constitute beginnings, and never endings. And if such fidelity means a vocation of opposition to Powers and Principalities as they operate in government and in the circle of prestige for which the government exists, so be it. If it means the outlawry of the Church, persecution...the Lord spoke of that too: "The time will come when those who kill you will think they are doing a service to God." But in the process, the Church would serve humanity, would even help to give humanity a future on this planet which it could not otherwise have.

As for the impending deliberations on world justice and peace, I have anguished questions about them. Do the American Bishops accept the implications of their country's control over one-half the world's productive capacity and finance? Do they realize that, despite our affluence, we have institutionalized poverty for perhaps one-quarter of our own people, plus millions in the developing world? Will they admit that these appalling realities are not accident, but cold calculation; that they follow the logic of profit and policy? Can they comprehend that war, particularly modern war, decides what nation or "security bloc" will control the profits, and that on the success or failure of the Indochinese war hinges the American Open Door to the developing world? (Policy-makers fear that if the Indochinese force us out, certainty will spread among the world's poor that wars of liberation can succeed.) Do they understand that a few hundred American corporations, with hundreds of billions in assets and international holdings, are empires in their own right, exerting political and economic dominion wherever they are? To deliberate justice and peace while overlooking such realities would be both ignorant and dishonest. Just as it would be dishonest to deny that while most men starve, most Bishops live in comfort and affluence, welcome the dividends of offending corporations, and remain discreetly silent before the excesses of capitalism.

In closing, I hope and pray this letter is a source of help to you, and not a cause for pain and shock. Obviously you love the Church as I do. But before the tragedy and ruin of the times we must love the Church more—enough to criticize honestly and charitably, enough to pick up heavier burdens, enough to lose everything in order that others may discover life. In essence, what would the wretched of the earth have us do to offer them hope, to lift from them the horror of war and starvation, to extend a sense of dignity and destiny in God and human community?

Our prayers go with you. And our wishes for the light, the strength, the peace of Christ.

BUYING AND SELLING AND OTHER POINTS OF COMMERCIAL INTEREST

Two stories, please, which point up the national preoccupation with huckstering, with cash registers, even with slave blocks.

The first is told by two young Frenchmen, Jean Pierre Debris and Andre Menras, in their book *WE ACCUSE: BACK FROM SAIGON'S PRISONS*. Debris and Menras, as an alternative to their military service, taught in South Vietnam in the late '60s. Appalled at the suffering they witnessed, and the stupendous waste of America's blundering following France's, they prepared to demonstrate against the war at the end of their teaching obligation.

In early 1970, they climbed one of Saigon's tallest statues, flew an NLF flag and scattered tracts written in Vietnamese to the people. They lasted one half-hour before being pulled down by the police, beaten, and jailed. At one court appearance before sentencing, they had this experience. Let them tell it: "There were American, French, Vietnamese journalists there, representing among others Agence France Presse, Reuters, UPI, CBS, with whom we were able to exchange a few words. One of them said to us, 'It was suicidal, your gesture! It's completely pointless.' And then, 'YOU were paid!'

We answered him, 'It would never occur to you that one might do something other than for money.' His answer, 'In any case, in the world we're living in, if you don't sell yourself, someone buys you.'"

A second story. Missionaries to India tell of a practice sometimes observed in coastal cities before independence from Britain in 1948. The poor, and members of the poor castes, generally Untouchables, fell prey to it. It was, in effect, an abominable form of slavery, invariably done to women.

When a girl child is born, she is enclosed in a tiny jar and raised there. The jar grows with the child, which is to say, it is outgrown, broken and replaced with a more commodious one.

The imprisonment causes a fetal-like crippling of the limbs and trunk, which assume the exact dimensions of the jar's interior. Parents sometimes introduce nuances to the brutality—like pinioning the hands below the chin, palms up; or blinding the unfortunate creature. Anything to evoke pity, and alms.

What emerges at maturity is a fearfully hideous caricature of a human being—deformed, retarded, frequently blind—a spiritual and physical basket case, capable only of inspiring nightmares, guilt, charity. The parents then set her out on a likely street corner to beg, or sell her to an agent for the same purpose. One could call the practice a sadistic form of commercialism.

Which practice strikes the reader as worse? The journalist sells himself, or is bought (by his own words). But the Indian is sold; she has no say in the matter. For the first, the degradation is voluntary; for the other, involuntary. The journalist is sinner, and morally culpable. The Indian is innocent.

But the journalist's words remain, "In the world we're living in, if you don't sell yourself, someone buys you." An extraordinarily apt and perceptive observation, suggesting (1) that commercialism is so rampant in the West (or U.S.) that virtually no one acts for compassionate or altruistic reasons; (2) that implicit in the marketing of goods and services is marketing in lives; (3) that one sells oneself voluntarily or one is bought involuntarily; (4) that selling is preferable to being bought.

What the journalist is blindly and painfully attempting to discuss with Debris and Menras is freedom. Which is to say, the respective states of their souls. In another setting, where the use of abstraction eliminates threat to one's mode of living, he might admit that truth frees one. But his life—bought, sold, imprisoned?—prevents him from seeing the freedom of the two Frenchmen, freedom won because they did what they ought to have done. (Or the best version that occurred to them). The journalist was a commodity and that prevented him from seeing anything else than buying and selling. And so, he could only utter a frightened snarl: "You were paid!"

The journalist had no freedom to be a brother, i.e. to take the cause of those warred upon by the war merchants. He had no freedom because for ten thousand times he had sold himself in little or large ways, until now, he had nothing left to give. And therefore, no freedom.

The reader may still sense some obscurity on the point, i.e., that most of our countrypeople sell themselves, or lacking that, are bought. I recall a saying current in federal prisons: "90% of any given compound population can be bought, sold, or rented." Meaning what? Precisely what it means outside the walls, privilege—a better shot at parole, added "good" days, a better cell or job, the meanest wormwood crumbs off some functionary's sorrow-laden desk. What else? Enrich the privilege, up the ante, add another silver piece right up to, and beyond, thirty, and most prisoners will hand over their soul, will go State's evidence, will join the "rat" squad, will even play a Judas role to the hilt—informer, provocateur, entrapper.

Now, if this applies to people notorious for non-conformity and individuality, however suspect, what of the ordinary citizens exempt from the enormous spiritual and physical pressures of walls and bars, cells and locks? The privileges lose some of their stark simplicity, becoming emoluments like a higher class, a coveted woman (or man), another step up the spiral of ambition, power, or a "place in history." Or merely, for the vast majority—security of income and old age.

I once asked a teacher in a federal prison—who verbally opposed the Indochina war—if he could take that position publicly. He admitted that he couldn't. "Can you campaign for one of the political parties before general election?" "No." "Can you write a letter to an editor about any public issue?" "NO." "Isn't that a terrible price to pay for a job?:" He didn't dare answer that one, for fear I would laugh at him for his (NO!), or report him for (YES!).

Silence, acquiescence, passivity, complicity—influence (bought) by a job. Conscience nullified by acculturation to a standard of consumption. Or better still, replaced by a standard of consumption. As it amounted, the teacher's biggest contribution to his prisoners was a personified helplessness. In him, the system "worked," having first made a commodity of him.

Is our friend's case unique? Hardly. The most significant word in the American lexicon today is "mass"—mass education, mass media, mass religion, mass values, mass ethos, all adding up to mass culture.

Essentially, our friend's position differs only in degree from that of his President "surrounded by a gang of zealots and thugs who shook down companies for millions of dollars, bought elections, sold services and decisions of the Government, conducted illegal wars, harassed so-called "enemies," committed burglaries and forgeries, provoked violence, engaged in spying on fellow Americans, ordered mass arrests in violation of the Constitution, and assisted organized crime in evading legal punishment." (Washington Watch: After Watergate; Reform). Ethical retardation exemplified in both cases, allowing on the one hand, a job to buy silence and public neutrality. And on the other, ambition to justify high larceny and mass murder.

How much silence and public immobility must be bought until the government can, with impunity, spend $1.3 trillion on warmaking since 1946? Or $300 billion on what has come to be called the Perpetual War in Indochina. What is the price of apathy toward two to four hundred thousand South Vietnamese political prisoners? How many lives must the wealthy buy before they buy government, now existing virtually for them. No one can say, while nonetheless, one can comprehend that essentially the main commerce traffic is not in goods and services at all. It is in the spirits and lives of people. They bring a rapturous jangle from the cash registers.

Recall the excuses offered in the Gospel to explain absence from the wedding feast—a wife, a farm, oxen. Today, the excuses from a clear call for resistance to the murderous war policies of Washington are similar— a job, the good life, a wife and kids, fear of separation, loneliness, prison. One wonders at the lesions of soul which allow such craven merchandising, which sells freedom so cheaply, which abandons so many innocent to the clutches of American or Soviet Junkers, or of power-mongering ad men like Nixon.

All of this is in some contrast for Christians, who must recall Christ before Pilate. "Reentering the Praetorium, Pilate said to Jesus, 'Where do you come from?' But Jesus made no answer, Pilate then said to him, 'Are you refusing to speak to me? Surely you know that I have the power to release you and I have power to crucify you?' 'You would have no power over me,' replied Jesus, 'if it had not been given you from above; that is why the one who handed me over to you has the greater guilt.' (John 19:10–11) Which is a profoundly tactful way of saying, "You have no power over me at all!"—since your power doesn't come from God; your power isn't moral.

The power of any Herod or Hitler or Nixon over us is precisely what is in our heads—no more, no less. If we claim that Nixon's power is illegitimate because of foreign genocide and domestic corruption, we are saying in the same breath that his power—or that of his lackeys in the police state apparatus—is immoral, non-objective, nonexistent. He possesses only so much over us as we give him.

Finally, we will give Nixon—or his like—whatever power our idolatries require to nourish and sustain them. In a Biblical sense, idols are what we love when we fail to love God with all our being, and our sister or brother as ourselves. Since we are insecure in our failure, plagued by doubt and guilt, most promptly substitute ersatz for real. We long for the leader, for the official magician who will make our lies true by greater lies, who will let us keep our toys and security blankets, who will make us grateful for contempt, betrayal, and mass ripoffs.

That is what government is about—the protection of our idols. That is why we sell ourselves—to possess idols. And that is why the destruction of idols—and freeing ourselves from their brassy charms—is also to resist Nixon's pomps and circumstances, his deceits, bombs, and minions. Suddenly Nixon (or anyone) can't buy us any more. And we ain't sellin'!

Philip Berrigan and Elizabeth McAlister, 1973. Photo by Ron Schumacher, courtesy of Cornell University, Carl A. Kroch Library, Division of Rare and Manuscript Collections.

SEVEN

Meeting and Marrying Elizabeth McAlister

Once we knew the world well.
It was so small it could fit in a handshake,
so easy you could describe it with a smile,
it was ordinary as old truths in a prayer.
WISLAWA SZYMBORSKA

T he earth didn't move, time didn't stand still, and there was no eclipse of the sun when I first saw Elizabeth McAlister. Nothing like that. It wasn't love at first sight.

We talked about Al Uhrie, a mutual friend who was walking home from a meeting in Manhattan when a group of teenagers accosted him. They demanded money, he tried to tell them that his pockets were empty, and they stabbed him to death mid-sentence. That was in 1966, one year after the Marines landed at Danang; one year before three friends and I invaded the Baltimore Customs House.

I offered the funeral mass, and had just spoken a few Psalms at the graveside. Al Uhrie's father-in-law, a prominent Boston lawyer, was sobbing. Naturally, I assumed that he was commiserating with his daughter, but suddenly he grabbed the lapels of my coat, shook me once or twice, and shouted, "Would you please speak to her about this goddamn nonsense she's into!"

I broke loose, saying something innocuous about the nobility of the *Catholic Worker,* and his daughter's desire to live simply in

community. Al's wife could have had a comfortable, even luxuri-
ous life. She chose to live in a Catholic Worker house, feeding, clothing, and housing the poor. Moreover, she refused to prosecute the
young men who murdered her husband, a courageous stand which
seemed to upset her father.

We laid our friend to rest in Ossining, and returned to Tarrytown
to share our grief and tell stories about Al's work and life. That is
where I first met Sister Elizabeth McAlister, a nun in the Religious
Order of the Sacred Heart.

Elizabeth was in her twenties, I was forty-three. She had been a
nun for ten years, perhaps longer. In some ways our backgrounds
were quite similar. She was distinctly Irish-American Catholic, her
parents having immigrated from County Antreim in northern Ireland.
She had six brothers and sisters, and her father was a contractor. Our
backgrounds differed in that I grew up in poverty, while she lived
in Upper Montclair, an affluent New Jersey community. My own
father was hard working, but unstable, while Liz's father was a stable,
energetic man, who earned a good living for his family.

Liz joined her order in 1959, and was sent to study art at Hunter
College, where she earned a master's degree before returning to teach
at Marymount in 1963. She was a dedicated teacher, with little interest in politics. Nevertheless, the world outside the convent was
changing too rapidly, and too dramatically to be ignored. Assigned
to keep the convent's current events bulletin up to date, Liz began
reading newspapers, magazines, and religious publications.

Everywhere she looked, Elizabeth found controversy. Dr. King
was rattling white America, breaking laws which, he said, perpetuated slavery and protected bigots. Vatican II was shaking the dust
from scripture, challenging clergy and lay people to reexamine their
commitment to social justice, and creating space for Catholics to
transcend indifference and apathy.

Elizabeth was lecturing on symbolism in art, when one of her students suggested that David Miller's burning his draft card might be
an example of symbolism. She agreed, and was soon embroiled in
controversy, forced to defend what had initially been an academic
rather than a political statement.

Elizabeth took a hard look at her own beliefs, asking herself
whether she would be willing to kill and die in Vietnam, or in any

other war. She concluded that under no circumstances would she take a human life; she declared herself a pacifist; in biblical terms, a maker of peace.

That same year, my brother Daniel visited Marymount College. He denounced the war in Vietnam, stated his unequivocal support for resisters like David Miller, and urged students and teachers to join the anti-war movement. Inspired by Dan's talk, Liz vowed to do more to oppose the war. Sister Brendan McQuillan, president of Marymount College, showed her support for Liz's decision; they went together to a vigil against the war. Sister Jogues Egan, dean of Marymount and later provincial in Liz's order, invited many anti-war speakers to campus. Nuns and students came together to talk, debate, and organize into a community of resisters.

The nuns in the Religious Order of the Sacred Heart took part in legal demonstrations, wrote letters to Congress, and marched against the war in Vietnam. Their superior and provincial was highly intelligent and fair-minded, a genuine progressive who encouraged the nuns to support me and other defendants in the Customs House trial. The nuns also supported the Catonsville Nine, attending court sessions, rallies, and strategy sessions.

I spent eight months in prison, before our Jesuit lawyer, Bill Callahan, convinced Judge Thompson to allow us out on bail. Thompson ordered me not to leave Baltimore or the state of Maryland without permission, but I continued to move about as I pleased, paying no attention to the court's restrictions. My religious order did not restrict, or try to restrict, where I went or with whom I associated. They understood that I would eventually go to prison. And this meant that, relative to the Society's work, I was in limbo. I moved to our headquarters and they left me strictly alone.

I was in New York on an anti-war errand, and though I'm not sure how our paths crossed, Elizabeth McAlister and I met again. After that first meeting, we hadn't called one another, or corresponded by letter, though we did meet at rallies and demonstrations. This time, we talked about our feelings. I had grown to love her, she had grown to love me. I wasn't frightened at all, because two people confided mutual respect and admiration; shared, through words, the deep love they felt for one another. It was really the most natural thing in the world.

I had been struggling with my relationship to the priesthood for quite some time. Not wanting to break my vows, yet realizing that mandatory celibacy was a form of coercion, even violence. The issue was not whether I remained chaste, because I never had trouble doing that. Yet the more I studied nonviolence, the more convinced I became that mandatory celibacy is a violation of the human conscience.

In the early years of the Vietnam War, I thought that peace activists should practice celibacy. Later, when I began to question the very idea of enforced celibacy, I turned to Gandhi, who wrote that our consciences are always changing, always evolving; we can only hope to become more dedicated to the truth, more mature, more able to think critically and judge ourselves and others fairly.

I'm not advocating situation ethics, just trying to express what my conscience dictated at that time. I fell in love with Elizabeth McAlister *after* I had concluded that mandatory celibacy is coercive, an act of violence by the church toward Catholic priests and nuns. Only after extensive reading and much careful thought did I change my views on celibacy, and even then I didn't want to leave the church; I just couldn't stop the church from leaving me.

Elizabeth didn't want to leave her community either, and I respected her decision. I was facing six years in prison, the Supreme Court had denied the Catonsville defendants appeal, and I had been ordered to report to federal marshals in April, 1970. Liz would then be alone, without financial and moral support from her religious order. We agreed that a public announcement would not be a good thing, and she remained with her order until we announced our marriage three years later.

It has been difficult to explain my early relationship with Elizabeth McAlister. Did we try to resist our love for one another? We saw no reason to do that. Did we quarrel, or ride through storm clouds, on our way to true love? Not at all. Our hearts and minds met. On some deep level, we communicated about moral questions, religious issues, existential choices.

First and foremost, our love was an expression of our mutual respect. We met as Catholics and dedicated war resisters; we met as man and woman living through difficult times. We were not trapped. No one was writing our script. We weren't delusional, and hadn't lost perspective on ourselves, or the world around us. We fell in love and we married, leaving judgments to others, never believing for a moment that we were doing wrong.

I'm convinced that Liz and I had a certain authority for acting the way we did. The New Testament militates against oaths and vows; therefore, the celibacy that Liz and I had accepted was a dictum of Catholic officialdom, not an expression of the word of God. The Sermon on the Mount speaks against oaths and vows, stating that conscience should evolve under the two commandments: Love of God, and love of neighbor, including enemies.

This helped me understand why I placed no great emphasis on the vow of celibacy, even though, before meeting and falling in love with Liz, I had never broken this vow.

When we were married, I felt no guilt about changing the course of my life. I was still a Josephite priest; still dedicated to working for justice and peace. Liz felt much the same way. She was in good standing with her order. She was a fine teacher, a loving friend, a compassionate and caring person. The church might withdraw its love from us; we weren't going to withdraw our love from the church.

In early 1970, Liz and I met at St. George's, an Episcopal Church in the Bronx. John Grady, who would later be arrested and tried for raiding a draft board in Camden, New Jersey, was using this church as a center for organizing against the war. A great man, with five small children and a big Irish heart, John invited us to his office at the church. We loved and trusted him absolutely.

Liz arrived from her provincial headquarters on West 76th Street in Manhattan. We sat together, praying, talking, pledging our love and respect, promising life-long fidelity. We sat alone in a small, quiet, cluttered office. So far away from, and so very close to, the war in Vietnam.

We married one another.

Organs didn't thunder, angels didn't sing. We weren't showered with rice and presents. There were no witnesses. Nevertheless, we were married, because the essence of marriage depends on the free acceptance of the parties involved. Our marriage was secret, known only to ourselves and to God. We meant it to be permanent, until death would part us. We have remained faithful to the commitment we made that afternoon more than a quarter century ago.

The FBI was monitoring us rather closely at this time. Strange-looking men in trench coats and Converse sneakers loitered about anti-war gatherings. We suspected that the phone at Liz's provinciate was monitored; and I knew that my phone in Baltimore was tapped. We even suspected that our mail was being censored.

Still, we managed to meet once a month, or once every two months. We were working hard, organizing resistance to the war, and felt no great need to visit one another.

Our country was committing genocide in Vietnam. One day, perhaps, when the slaughter ended, and I was released from prison, we might be free to ramble by the sea or spend a quiet evening together by a fire. With the FBI shadowing our moves, and no end to the war in sight, we could only dream of such things.

I felt no guilt or confusion over our clandestine meetings, though I do bitterly regret keeping our marriage a secret, particularly from my brother Dan, my sister-in-law Carol, and my brother Jerry. Our secrecy is the only default I felt uneasy or unsure about. We were well aware that once our marriage became public knowledge, the church would excommunicate us, though we had done nothing to harm our fellow priests and nuns; nothing to harm the church.

We expressed our love for one another, promised fidelity, and agreed to extend this love to the world, to our church, our friends and family, especially to Americans and Vietnamese who were dying every day of the war. We considered our love to be a gift to our church, not a violation of its trust.

Before we announced our marriage publicly in June 1973, I visited my superior in the hospital, where he was undergoing minor surgery. He was deeply shaken when I told him that Liz and I had been married for four years. I confided that we intended to announce our marriage in favor of honesty and public responsibility. He wanted to know why we would make a public issue of our union; I replied that not doing so would be tantamount to our merely having an affair. Under no circumstances would I agree to that. He advised continuing secrecy. I insisted on public disclosure.

In June 1973, we renewed our vows at Liz's home in Upper Montclair, New Jersey. Our lawyers were present, as were Dan and a large gathering of friends. After the ceremony we returned to Dan's apartment in New York, and held a press conference with reporters from the *Baltimore Sun, New York Times,* and other papers.

Church officials wasted no time; they excommunicated us a day later. The secular press underscored the consequences of our terrible deed: We were no longer able to receive the sacraments; I was no longer able to preach, to administer the sacraments, or to function officially. In a real sense, we were banished from the community of belief.

I had served in World War II, attended college, and studied in the seminary. I had been a Josephite priest in good standing for nearly 20 years, working in the Deep South with caring priests and nuns, serving under a largely racist hierarchy. I had been reprimanded for my views on civil rights, silenced for pointing out the connections between genocide in Southeast Asia and racism at home. My stands, my views, and my commitment to social, political, and economic justice seemed to me absolutely compatible with the teachings and life of Jesus. The church felt otherwise, and we often were at loggerheads.

Liz and I wasted no time licking our wounds. The Vietnam War continued, and there was still much work to be done. Richard Nixon's prolonged campaign of terror bombing had failed to intimidate the North Vietnamese. His plan to "Vietnamize" the war, a scheme by which the South Vietnamese would, miraculously, defeat the National Liberation Front, was a complete failure.

Year after year, hundreds of B-52 bombers had pounded North Vietnam, destroying towns and schools, demolishing Bach Mai hospital, which covered five acres and had a faculty of 250 doctors and 800 medical students.

All over the world, people demonstrated against the destruction of Vietnam. The governments of Sweden, Denmark, Finland, Belgium, Italy, Canada, Australia, and New Zealand criticized first Johnson's, and later Nixon's, terror tactics. Speaking to a close aide, Richard Nixon said he wanted the Russians and Chinese to believe him a madman, because this would force their leaders to talk the North Vietnamese into capitulating before the war spread to other countries.

Just before the Harrisburg trial opened, Liz and I met at Danbury federal prison with our lawyers, my brother Dan who was an unindicted co-conspirator, and Paul Mayer, an old friend. Our lawyers and several priests witnessed the renewal of our vows. Some of our friends and family, and some members of our respective orders, were hurt by our disclosure, because we had not been as forthright as, perhaps, we should have been.

We never intended to cause pain. We met, we talked, and in time we grew to love one another. We conspired to injure no one; were resolved moreover to devote our lives to ending the genocide in Vietnam.

In retrospect, our little secret pales before the crimes our government was committing in Southeast Asia. Few people realized, and few know even now, that the U.S. Air Force had been bombing Laos since 1964, forcing hundreds of thousands of people to live in caves and underground tunnels, unable to emerge at night because napalm and anti-personnel bombs were raining over the countryside, destroying every town, school, farm, and home in vast areas of that small country. Few Americans knew about CIA plots to kill Prince Norodom Sihanouk, fewer still knew about the tiger cages at Con Son, or the CIA's Phoenix Program, which tortured and killed tens of thousands of Vietnamese suspected of being National Liberation Front cadre.

Liz and I endured the cauldron of the Harrisburg trial and emerged stronger than before. The United States would never win the Vietnam war, because it's impossible to "destroy a country in order to save it." And after Vietnam, there would be more wars, more killing; the government would continue building nuclear weapons, the CIA would assassinate more leaders, and overthrow more governments.

Liz and I agreed that opposition to war and violence would be one expression of our love. Our love for one another would inspire us to form a community of conscience. We would not retreat into solitude, build fences around our hearts, or put our souls in an interest-bearing account. We would own no property and pay no taxes, making what money we needed honestly and without harming others.

God in His providence has given us three wonderful gifts—Jerry, Frida, and Katie. We have often stretched ourselves to provide for these three, and to remain, at the same time, active in the movement. We have lived in community, sharing our lives with other resisters.

In retrospect, I realize that I could be rather hard on people who were new to the faith and resistance movement. I was impatient, even intolerant at times. I granted no doubts or uncertainties, wanted everyone to be absolutely dedicated to the Kingdom of God.

I did feel confused and uncertain, at times, about community life. The best account of community in scripture is from the Acts of the Apostles. Every now and then, the early Christians would go through a crisis, struggling over the meaning of nonviolence, over persecution from the state, and their own superficial, essentially violent, interpersonal relations.

Our community too was destined to go through a series of crises; we lost members, and people left in difficult circumstances.

Today Liz and I are veterans of four or five deep crises in community; if anything has shaken and confused me, it is the departure of dear friends, with whom we had worked and gone to jail.

I attribute my lack of confusion, doubt, or perplexity about anti-war work to two sources. One is the word of God, the scripture, which I believe is spoken directly to us, a standard of quality against which to measure our lives. The second is community. Commentators assert that in the life of Jesus the cross took two forms. Nonviolent confrontation with the state, ending in His crucifixion. Living in and bearing with community.

Experience shows that community life is tough, exacting, and sometimes utterly frustrating, but always immensely rewarding. One must deny the constant urgency of the ego. One must agree to hold all things in common, to share a common purse, to have a communal bank account, to work with one's hands to support the community.

Throughout the years, Elizabeth has always been at the center of community. A comrade and confidante, riding fully and competently with others the roller coaster of life.

Whatever I may have done to further peace or social justice, whatever I may have tried to do that was nonviolent and loving, God was always present. I have also been lavished with the love of my family, particularly from my brother Dan, from Jerry and his wife Carol, and from Rosalie and Jim. Each has been magnificent in their steadfast love over the years; and they have been active in their own right, all of them. Daniel is one of the most notable nonviolent anti-war figures in the country. My brother Jerry has been arrested many times at the Pentagon and Griffiss Air Force base. Jim, too, has come to Washington on several occasions when I and others were arrested, and he has stood at my side, a brother, a peace activist, and a friend.

God has given me the grace to continue resistance, with the loving care of Her word, with a loving community, Elizabeth McAlister, and my family.

STATEMENT FROM LIZ AND PHIL, APRIL 1973

Elizabeth McAlister and Philip Berrigan have known one another since 1966 and have worked together in the peace movement almost since that time. We became aware of our love for each other in the spring of 1969 and by mutual choice married one another in trust and gratitude.

For nearly eighteen months, we kept our marriage private, without the knowledge of families or intimate friends. We formalized our union in January 1972 at Danbury Prison; it was witnessed by the Harrisburg defendants, Sister Jogues, and Father Daniel Berrigan.

Our love has deepened through the last four years—we've paid dearly for it, as have our friends. We have considered our relationship a service to the victims of American aggression, to other Americans, to our families and friends, and to one another. We have lived these four years married in every sense but life-style (having no common home) and public knowledge.

From the outset, we agreed on certain lines of commitment: a guarantee of freedom in the service of resistance, with its requirements of discipline, risk, separation, jail. We have refused to allow personal considerations to interfere with our dedication to Gospel and to people. So we met infrequently and never considered abandoning our work or evading its consequences. At the same time we sought an opportunity to share our marriage with the Church and with the public.

By 1969, resistance to the war had become a way of life for Philip (three political trials and a six year prison sentence). Elizabeth had pledged her life to her religious community as a college educator and resister. Our lives converged in community and non-violent resistance, particularly to our country's warmaking in Indochina. Community and non-violent resistance defined the religious life for us.

The Church has made celibacy the spirit of religious commitment, if not its heart. We had hoped that a time would come when religious communities would invite both celibate and married people to a situation of mutual support and service to the Gospel and to suffering people. But the present Church vision, policy, and leadership make that impossible. Nonetheless, we cannot but question and resist the priority of celibacy over mature conscience and the spirit of the Gospels. We have tried to live responsibility since our contract—in separation, in jail, in legal jeopardy, in official attempts to disgrace us. Separation from our religious communities has not been our choice for we believe that in our case, as with others, celibacy is not the issue. Responsible freedom is.

We see our marriage as a radical assertion of our faith. With God's grace and the help of our friends, we hope to continue to live the Gospels— in poverty, in community, and in nonviolent resistance, convinced of the contribution of religious resistance to humankind.

We realize that many friends will be disappointed and hurt by what we now reveal. We owe them an explanation as to why we have kept this truth from people for so long.

At first, we wanted our relationship to clarify itself without pressure. In the midst of that process, Philip went to prison (April 1970). At that point, public disclosure was impossible, since it would have put the total burden of explanation upon Elizabeth. Later in the year, we did speak to friends and family and their pain at our secrecy revealed that that had been an error in judgment on our part. As the Harrisburg trial approached, we contemplated disclosing our union but we felt that a free admission on our part would confuse both the substance of the trial and our relationship itself. Following the trial and up to the point of Philip's release in December, the separation of prison further prevented any public acknowledgement. Since that time, we have sought opportunities to publicize it and to share it with friends.

As we evolved our plans over the past five months, some friends encouraged us to announce this day (May 28) as the beginning of our marriage. Such a course would be easier on us and on the public. But we decided against this, feeling that it would not serve either the truth or others whose love is apt to be tested, as ours was, by separation, trial, and prison. Finally, we felt that such a decision would fail to serve the public, who all too infrequently hear the truth—without ambiguity and varnish—from any public person.

Today we celebrated our marriage with our families and with those defendants and lawyers who shared the events of the past three years; civil disobedience, the separation of 32 months of prison, and the Harrisburg trial. (On June 23, we will hold a general celebration for friends.)

The future still holds the possibility of a year's imprisonment for Elizabeth, followed by three years probation. Philip remains on parole until

September 1975. In the last few months, we have worked with a small group of friends growing towards non-violent resistance. We are presently seeking a center out of which that work can continue.

We hope that our ministry will serve the Gospels and the victims of war. We also hope, with all our hearts, that at some future date, the Church will accept our marriage as well as our efforts for non-violence and peace. And we continue to be profoundly grateful for the great gifts of that Church and of our respective religious communities.

Liz McAlister and children, 1976. Photo courtesy of Cornell University, Carl A. Kroch Library, Division of Rare and Manuscript Collections.

EIGHT

Down By the Riverside: Community and Nonviolence

Only the innocent die.
Take up, take up
the bloody map of the century.
The long trek homeward begins
into the land of unknowing.
DANIEL BERRIGAN

After the Harrisburg trial, I waited in limbo. Would Judge Herman, condescending and hostile toward the defendants, add years to my prison term? Was J. Edgar Hoover, bitter over his defeat, pressuring the court to keep me behind bars? Days passed, then weeks and months. I waited; Judge Herman refused to act.

Daniel, paroled from Danbury in February, was fasting on the steps of the federal building in Harrisburg. My brothers Jerry and Jim joined him, trying to pressure Judge Herman to pass sentence. Friends were picketing the courthouse, supporters rallied in New York and Baltimore, Judge Herman was flooded with phone calls and letters. At last, he handed down his ruling: three years, to run concurrently with my sentence for the Catonsville and Customs House actions.

When I walked out of Danbury on a cold, snowy day, shortly before Christmas, 1972, a large crowd met me at the prison gate. They were chilled to the bone, and I was deeply moved by their greeting. My brothers were waiting, along with Abraham Heschel, Holocaust survivor and Jewish biblical scholar. It had been Rabbi Heschel's idea to organize, with Daniel and Lutheran minister Richard Neuhaus, Clergy and Laity Concerned.

Heschel stood by the gate, shaking with cold. He was ill, and risking his life to be there. We embraced, spoke briefly; he raced back to New York City to teach a class that afternoon. Three days later, our good friend, supporter, and mentor, was dead. I think about Rabbi Heschel often, and blame myself for his early death.

A big celebration was planned that afternoon. People rented a hall near Danbury penitentiary, and we held a party, singing, eating, drinking, dancing for hours. Later, we drove into New York City, where Liz and I spent the evening at Dan's apartment with her superior, Mother Jogues, and other good friends. In the morning, we flew to Syracuse to spend Christmas with our mother and family. Our father, Tom Berrigan, had died in 1969, before I returned to prison.

I left Danbury with no bitterness or sorrow. I had protested the killing in Vietnam and gone to prison for 40 months. I met other resisters, we formed a close-knit group, and some of us are still friends.

Prison is designed to silence dissent. We savage people in order to make them better citizens. We torture men and women to make them kinder and more productive. We execute human beings, in order to teach our children respect for human life.

My spirit was far from broken. Prison strengthened my commitment to peace and social justice. It made me more determined to live in a loving community, and more committed to resisting militarism, even if that would mean spending more years behind bars.

Ramsey Clark confided that Richard Nixon released me as a concession to the North Vietnamese. Nixon knew that the Vietnamese people supported Dan, myself, and other imprisoned resisters. Unlike most people in this country, the Vietnamese worried about us while we were in jail, and I even received several exquisite Christmas cards from Ho Chi Minh's successor, Pham Van Dong. After my release from Danbury, he invited me to visit Vietnam, but the U.S. government refused to grant me permission to travel.

My lawyers appealed, arguing my case in Washington, D.C. We lost at the district court level, won at the federal appeals level, and when the case reverted back, again, to the district court, we lost again. Asking the courts for justice is futile; we dropped our case, and I didn't visit Vietnam.

Today, the United States has more than a million men and women in federal prisons, another half million in state, county, and local jails. More people, per capita, than any country in the world except Russia. The Supreme Court expedites the murder of death row inmates. Politicians urge us to persecute the poor, defund our own schools, despoil our environment, and reward the rich. We build more jail cells, construct more killing chambers and speed up executions. Driven by fear, we shred the Constitution. I see little difference between the world inside prison gates, and the world outside. The illusion is that people on the outside are free, because those on the inside are not; outside, people are honest; inside, they are crooked; that outside, people have a future; inside, they have nothing.

A million million prison walls can't protect us, because the real dangers—militarism, greed, economic inequality, fascism, police brutality—lie outside, not inside, prison walls. The war in Vietnam is over; the war we wage on ourselves is escalating.

After 40 months in prison, I returned to the anti-war circuit, speaking at rallies up and down the East Coast. I was risking a quick trip back to the dustbin, but my parole officer was a decent fellow and he refused to punish me for traveling outside a prescribed area. FBI agents attended my talks, scribbling surreptitious notes which they mailed to the parole office in Baltimore.

They were wasting their time, and the taxpayers' money. I wasn't saying anything new. My talks were very clear. Prison reinforced my view that we must resist, by all nonviolent means, the state's homicidal policies. I kept repeating this; federal agents kept writing it down.

Years later, when some of my anti-war friends sued for their dossier under the Freedom of Information Act, I discovered that the FBI had collected several cabinets of Berrigan brothers' memorabilia.

On March 10, 1972, the North Vietnamese and Viet Cong mounted a massive three-wave offensive in the northern provinces of South Vietnam. Just weeks before, Secretary of Defense Melvin

Laird informed Congress that such an attack was "not a serious possibility." Army chief of staff Westmoreland was also optimistic, arguing that a Communist offensive would last only a few days. Fierce battles raged for weeks, killing tens of thousands of Vietnamese soldiers and civilians.

On April 15, Nixon ordered more bombing raids on Hanoi. On May 8, the U.S. Navy commenced mining North Vietnamese ports. Anti-war demonstrations continued here and abroad. Four months after the Watergate break-in and subsequent arrests, President Nixon won a landslide victory over George McGovern. The killing in southeast Asia continued.

In spring 1973, I spoke at a huge anti-war rally in Washington, D.C., and along with several other well-known peace activists marched past the White House. We were hoping to exert nonviolent pressure on the President to end the war. Nixon had withdrawn several hundred thousand American troops; but the master magician pulled one more trick from his hat.The South Vietnamese army, said Nixon, was about to do what 500,000 U.S. troops, thousands of B-52 strikes, free fire zones, and massive defoliation had failed to accomplish. Vietnamese would keep killing Vietnamese; Nixon called this "Peace with honor."

In Danbury, John Bach, myself, and other members of our resistance group had often discussed nonviolence. Outside the walls, the peace movement was going through a painful struggle. Martin Luther King was dead, American cities were war zones, activists were frustrated and angry. President Nixon ridiculed dissent, expanded the killing fields, and encouraged his supporters to attack peaceful demonstrators. Disillusioned and bitter, the Weathermen and others were calling for violent revolution. Nonviolence, they said, had failed. Fire must be fought with fire, violence with violence.

Nonviolence was not defunct. We just needed to envision new ways to work. Not as individual peace activists, but as extended families, working and living together, sharing our love, our talents, everything we might have, supporting one another for the long haul; that is, for the rest of our mortal lives.

During my years behind bars, I had seen young men succumb to despair. Arriving with high ideals, they broke under the strain of prison life. Some compromised to shorten their sentences, vowing never to break the law again. Others withdrew into sullen shells, devoured by anger and loneliness. They had taken a principled stand, but without the support of a loving community they couldn't withstand the brutality of prison.

Before he left Danbury in late 1972, John Bach had agreed to join Elizabeth McAlister, myself, and others in forming a faith-based community in Baltimore, Maryland. For twelve months, Liz met on a weekly basis with some of the wonderful people who supported us at Harrisburg. Through these meetings, and our discussions inside prison, we formed Jonah House.

Judith Lafemina, a Mercy nun from Connecticut, Jim La Croce, a diocesan priest from Harrisburg, and Tess Kohlenberg, John Bach's partner and comrade, a dropout from Wesleyan University in Hartford, all joined us in Baltimore.

Resisters cannot persist and survive without community. Sooner or later, they will be frustrated and crushed. That's why we invested so much time, effort, and money into starting Jonah House. We wanted a place where people could share meals and ideas, study scripture together, and support one another through the long haul.

When friends went to prison, we would care for their children. When they left jail, we would welcome them home. If someone was upset or depressed, we would listen to their problems, give them a hug, let them know that we loved them. We tried to be a loving family, committed to the spirit and the reality of nonviolent resistance.

This, I think, was one of the failures of the anti-war movement. Activists didn't spend enough time building community. When we did form support groups and communities within prison, the results were extraordinary. We felt a collective hope, our spirits lifted. We broke through the barrier between the world outside, and our own circumscribed existence. We were able to continue our anti-war work inside prisons like Allenwood, Danbury, Lewisburg, and Petersberg.

During 1973-74, I and others in the community raced about the country, returning home on Friday nights, leaving again late Sunday afternoon or early Monday morning. Up and down the East Coast we went, giving talks, attending meetings, mapping strategy with groups of activists.

Month after month we swilled junk food, slept in strange beds and swept into Jonah House, suitcase in hand, only to dash off hours later. We were certain that this was the best contribution we could make to the peace movement, and to our community at Jonah House.

In 1974, our community development efforts collapsed, forcing us to analyze why this happened. We were inexperienced and not fully prepared for the life we had envisioned. Moreover, we underestimated the influence of a culture that is anti-communitarian and foreign to gospel values. We assumed that we could transcend social conditioning. If we lived our ideals, everything else would fall into place. Our attachment to property would diminish; we would relinquish our egos, cancel out a lifetime of conditioning in others.

So went the dream. But reality intruded. Communities in Connecticut, New York City, Long Island, New Jersey, Washington, and Baltimore collapsed within a few months.

At this time, we were conducting dumpster prowls several times a week, collecting day-old bread, dented cans, soggy vegetables and fruits; distributing most of it to the poor, keeping little for our own needs. During the Great Depression, restaurants had doused their garbage with kerosene, and citrus growers burned mounds of oranges to keep them from starving migrants. Now, to prevent our scavenging, Washington's food chains began putting crushers on their dumpsters.

We protested this waste to no avail and, with other advocates for the poor, resorted to guerrilla tactics against the chains. We wanted to embarrass them, and to undermine their profits by shoplifting food. We also lifted tools, which we intended to use for repairing and painting houses.

After a couple of months, I was arrested in a food store, then Judith Lafemina and Elizabeth McAlister were arrested for trying to steal tools from a Sears & Roebuck outlet. News of Liz's arrest flashed around the world, but my escapade was ignored. The store security slapped handcuffs on me, threatened me repeatedly with arrest and an appearance before a local judge. After several humiliating hours, I was released, told to go home, and warned never to return to that store.

Meanwhile, friends at the Catholic Worker house in Baltimore were questioning the guerrilla campaign. Pilfering from grocery stores, though one way to express frustration with the chains, was not helping feed the hungry. Stealing things we didn't need wasn't helping the poor. We agreed with their observations, ended our shoplifting spree, and never stole again.

Central to the Christian view of life is relationship to the cross of Christ. And that means two things. The first is nonviolent confrontation with the state, in order to hold it accountable, especially, for its abuse of the poor. And secondly, bearing with community life, with diversity of background, experience, and conscience, but also with different approaches in political matters.

We have great difficulty with community, because we're products of a predatory culture. In addition, we know precious little about nonviolence and its application to interpersonal relationships. For example, I happen to be quite good at what I do. Like Elizabeth, I have a great capacity for work, initiative, and leadership. These are talents, but they have a dark side: I'm inclined to compare my own commitment to that of others, to my advantage. I could not understand why some people weren't more productive and more disciplined; I chastised them for not making better use of their time. I insisted that some members of the community make a greater commitment to resistance work.

My confusion, egotism, competitiveness, and impatience led to eruptions and quarrels within our community. Feelings were hurt, there were painful silences, bitter recriminations. We were experimenting with human interaction, and we discovered that we were loving, jealous, caring, bossy, cooperative, and competitive. After 23 years of living within community, I'm a good deal mellower. I've discovered something about forgiveness, mercy, and tolerance. Not as much, perhaps as I should have learned, but more than I knew before. I can accept the deficiencies of other people, just as I can live with my own deficiencies, which, believe me, are legion.

We have experienced several heartbreaking, harrowing community breakups. And I've been responsible for the divorce of numerous people from this community. I tried to impose my standards on everyone who joined us, and when people failed to meet my expectations, I resented them. I was a spiritual drill instructor, driving myself and everyone around me to greater commitment and sacrifice.

There were tears and angry words, wounds that wouldn't heal. People left the community and didn't return. Friendships dissolved. On several occasions, Liz and I proposed to move out with our children and to start elsewhere, if other members would remain at Jonah House for two years. We made our proposals in good faith, as a means to reconcile differences, but no one accepted these terms.

These experiences, though deeply painful, have taught us a great deal. And in spite of our difficulties, we have been instrumental in starting communities in New York City, Baltimore, Toronto, Hartford, and Washington, D.C. After a year or so, all disbanded.

In community we are responsible for one another, which means that we are responsible for the human family. We are all responsible when others are abused, crushed, bombed, or starved. In community, we are responsible for our life together, for nourishing one another, for setting good examples, and for inspiring others.

But how do we make all this accountability work? Should one scrutinize another person? How can we reconcile philosophical disagreements and personality conflicts in a nonviolent manner? How might we fairly measure one's contribution to the community?

Extremely complex questions; in real-life settings, fraught with peril.

For some years, the Jonah House community experimented with "evaluative responsibility," using three categories as a measure: Nonviolence, Community, and Resistance. Once a month, a community member would submit his or her self-evaluation to the group. This helped us acknowledge our strengths and weaknesses. It enabled us to discover how we might contribute more to resistance and community life.

These were highly productive sessions. We assessed the pros and cons of life at Jonah House. We learned to express, rather than harbor, our resentments. We created an on-going dialogue among equals, and developed pragmatic ways to avoid intrigue and territorial disputes. We examined our commitment to the gospels.

Today, if a community member is troubled, he or she calls a community meeting. We sit down immediately, and try to get to the source of the difficulty. This doesn't happen often, but it really helps prevent the kind of volcanic eruptions we experienced in the past.

Elizabeth McAlister and I have always felt that our children were sent by God. We had very little to do with planning their advent. Instead of artificial birth control methods, we practiced the rhythm method; obviously it wasn't foolproof. Our children are precious gifts, all three born in Jonah House.

The community welcomed Jerry and Frida, pledging to help raise and educate them. Until I was jailed for the King of Prussia action, we taught them at home. After that, Liz decided that they should attend public school; we wanted them to see all the colors in the human rainbow, to make friends with children from different religious backgrounds, and to *experience,* rather than just read or talk about, diversity.

Baltimore is a potpourri of wealth and squalor, hope and despair. Anyone, madman or child, can buy an automatic weapon on the streets. Empty buildings decay, the homeless sleep on the street. Workers lose their jobs, corporate profits soar. The city, like so many others, stands on a fault line of social and economic contradictions.

Even if we wished, we couldn't protect our children from their own country.

At Jonah House, we live in voluntary poverty, taking only what we need, giving back what we can. Our children help gather food from dumpsters and wholesale distributors, and they eat well. They wear warm, comfortable hand-me-downs. The community embraces children by expecting them to take a responsible role in communal life.

Not long after Frida's birth, Liz and I were arrested for an action at the Pentagon. Liz was sentenced to six months, reduced to 90 days. I was given 60 days in jail. We served time in the same jail, though we were not allowed to talk or meet. Frida was 18 months old, Jerry about six months. We did our time, confident the community would take good care of them.

Our critics accuse us of neglecting our children. But neglect, it seems to us, occurs when parents observe injustice and refuse to act; when they choose to turn their backs on suffering. Children are perceptive and deeply caring, more sensible and often stronger than adults. They watch their parents closely, and are confused by "do as I say, not as I do" contradictions.

The strength of community is its love for children even in the absence of parents. When children in the Jonah House community cry, someone holds them. When they need a change of diapers, someone does that. They are fed, clothed, and rocked to sleep. In many respects, they are living in an old-fashioned extended family, surrounded by people who take part in their well-being.

We consider our actions the moral equivalent of war.

We don't leave home in pursuit of fame or fortune. We don't go on expeditions to protect an empire that spends $7 billion on child nutrition for an entire year, and $5 billion *each week* on the military. Our children, like millions of others, are being neglected by an empire whose military budget is nearly as large as the combined military budgets of all other nations.

The government meantime is waging war on working men and women. People are being forced to work longer hours for declining wages. Devoted employees at Sears, IBM, AT & T, et al., are "downsized," that catch-all euphemism for greed. Workers are forced to accept cuts in wages and benefits, or lose their jobs. Unable to cope with the stress, many families disintegrate.

The gospel tells us not to consider people related to us by blood as more important than others. In fact, we should consider our relatives as less important than those in desperate need.

Instead, the nuclear family constructs walls, figurative and literal, around children. Families turn into mini-states, at war with outsiders, coveting and consuming the world's resources. Closed in on themselves, families become, in the words of the late British psychiatrist R.D. Laing, "protection rackets."

On April 30, 1975, the National Liberation Front marched into Saigon. America's longest, second-most expensive war was over. The casualties were staggering: More than 58,000 Americans, and 2–4 million Vietnamese were killed. 300,000 Americans wounded, 5 million Vietnamese refugees. Over 2,000 Americans, and 200 thousand North Vietnamese, were missing in action.

The Air Force dropped the equivalent of several atomic bombs on Vietnam—four or five times the amount of TNT we used in both fronts during World War II. During one eleven-day period, 740 B52s and 1,000 other aircraft sorties dropped 36,000 tons of bombs on the Hanoi-Haiphong area. The U.S. doused Vietnam with 18 million gallons of defoliants, destroying 5 million acres, an area about the size of Massachusetts. We razed all five of North Vietnam's industrial centers, thousands of schools, and hundreds of hospitals. At one point, Richard Nixon threatened the North Vietnamese with atomic weapons.

A 1979 Harris poll indicated that 73 percent of the American public, and 89 percent of Vietnam-era veterans, felt that politicians refused to let the military win the war in Vietnam.

Vietnam was a humiliating defeat but hardly a transforming experience for the United States. Lyndon Baines Johnson gave up after one term as president. Richard Nixon left the White House in disgrace. The military was in shambles, politicians became pariahs, a generation of Americans lost faith in the political system.

An impoverished Third World country defeated the world's richest and most powerful empire.

While the peace movement focused on the war in Vietnam, the Pentagon was busy developing "first-strike" atomic weapons. The United States might be humiliated in Indochina, but worldwide, communism would be defeated. Indeed, just a few years after the war ended, government officials were talking about "preemptive first strikes" against, and "protracted" nuclear warfare with, the Soviet Union. This, though scores of Russian and American cities would be destroyed, 100 million Americans, perhaps even more Russians, would die, radioactive fallout would poison the earth.

"Acceptable losses," said government officials.

China was building an extensive underground civil defense system, the Swiss were digging huge bunkers into the Alps, and Russia—the rumor turned out to be false—was constructing bombproof labyrinths under its major cities.

When the war started, millions of terrified people would be evacuated to coal mines and limestone caverns where no technology existed for purifying air and water, or for human waste disposal. Eighteen-year-old males were encouraged to register for possible service in the military. Home owners were advised to leave forwarding addresses, in case the Social Security agency or Internal Revenue Service wanted to reach them.

To prepare for an atomic emergency, the Federal Emergency Management Agency (FEMA) sent teams to small cities like Ithaca, New York. They measured floor space in shoe stores, coffee shops, and fast food outlets. Between 100 and 200 thousand evacuees from the New York metropolitan region would live in these shops. Regional coordinators would secure food, medicine, blankets, pillows, clothes, and psychiatric care for the evacuees. The war over, everyone could go home.

At Jonah House, we listened to Washington's bellicose rhetoric with a growing sense of dismay. The U.S. government killed millions of Vietnamese "in order to save them." Was it prepared to kill hundreds of millions of Soviet citizens in order to protect them from communism?

To express our opposition to this madness, we dug graves on the White House lawn. Graves, we said, for children. Graves for mothers. Graves for fathers. Graves for schools, churches, hospitals. Graves for Americans, graves for Russians, graves for the human family. Graves for the oceans, the forests, the sky. Graves for our friends in the animal kingdom.

The media gave our action extensive coverage; however, much of what we said was censored.

Later, we moved our operation to the Pentagon where we dug graves on the Parade Ground below the river entrance, between the Potomac River and the main building. We dug many graves during 1975, '76, and '77. After that, we poured blood as a symbolic gesture. We wanted Pentagon employees to understand that their paychecks are soaked in blood. We wanted them to know that they are working at the bloodiest place on earth.

I can't remember how many times, leading up to the King of Prussia action, I poured blood at the Pentagon; seven or eight arrests a year at the White House and Pentagon, and quite a few jail sentences ranging up to six months.

Ronald Reagan called his doomsday scenarios "peace through strength." In the name of peace, the United States prepared for mass murder. Building atomic weapons, he said, would demonstrate the government's commitment to a stable world.

Congress refused to challenge this madness. Scientists set to work designing new instruments of mass murder. Pentagon contractors built bigger, more destructive ships, planes, and missiles. The human race hovered on the brink of a firestorm that would burn like hundreds of Hiroshimas, sucking life from mother earth.

Hundreds of thousands of people marched through the streets of Paris, Madrid, and other European cities, demanding an end to the superpowers' mutual suicide pact. Millions of Americans lobbied their elected representatives, pleading with them to come to their senses. On June 12, 1982, more than a million people marched through New York City, demanding that the Soviet Union and United States freeze their arsenals and start listening to the world's people.

The government responded to its critics, as it always does, by launching a campaign to discredit them. The *Reader's Digest* warned that the Freeze Movement was dominated by leftists. Government officials dismissed opponents of the arms race as aging hippies and 'sixties radicals. There had been no dialogue during the Vietnam War; there would be none now.

The designing, deploying, and testing of atomic weapons continued unabated. President Reagan and friends insisted that nuclear war would be a minor inconvenience, similar to a family car breakdown. When the smoke cleared, bulldozers would push 100 million corpses into mass graves, entrepreneurs would begin rebuilding the American economy, banks would open, cities would spring back to life, Congress would declare peace on earth.

To reassure the public, FEMA released a film explaining that everyone should keep at least one shovel in the trunk of the car. When the sirens wailed, drivers could pull off the highway, dig a shelter, place their vehicle over the hole, and wait out the atomic traffic jam.

We of the Jonah House community prayed for peace, and were jailed repeatedly for acts of *divine disobedience.* Our witness reflected the gospel's vision of human life. The state's laws protected atomic missiles, but the state is not God. The state would continue to build and deploy first-strike weapons. And people who resisted the government's madness would be arrested, tried, imprisoned.

We weren't deluding ourselves. Congress wasn't going to stop funding nuclear weapons. War profiteers weren't going to stop exploiting the American people. President Reagan wouldn't stop joking about omnicide. We had no faith in a government that boasted of its own demise.

We saw no purpose in debating the criteria for a "Just War." Whether the state kills one, or one million human beings, it is murder. To the Jonah House community, "Thou Shalt Not Kill" is an imperative, not an academic exercise or political theory.

In *Pacem in Terris,* Pope John XXIII stated that nuclear weapons should be banned. Not diminished, with fewer warheads on each missile, or fewer weapons in the superpowers' respective arsenals. Nuclear weapons must be removed from earth, sky, and sea; destroyed, and forever banned.

One of our early leaflets explained our position: "Yet is the issue simply one of survival? Not at all. The issue is dying inside—it is allowing the bomb to supplant the spirit of Christ. When that is done, the nuclear crematorium, the world, will be a ghostly climax . . . we die inside when we don't resist."

"Rational" people continued to insist that mass murder is a sports event, with clear winners and losers. In underground bunkers, aboard ships, in submarines and on planes, military personnel waited for the signal to attack. The nation's psyche grew numb. The threat of megadeath was turning us into a nation of spiritual cadavers. Jonah House renewed our witness at the war department. The police handcuffed our wrists; they couldn't manacle our spirits. The arms race was killing the poor, terrifying the children, poisoning the environment. Christians and pacifists, we embraced life as peacemakers, offering hope, resisting the empire's efforts to destroy God's world.

BEING DIFFERENT: BEING CHRISTIAN
Claggett Center, December 31, 1991

It is extraordinary—people agreeing to prayer, reflection, communication of the Gospel as a means to close the old year and open the new. It is 180 degrees removed from the pagan celebration marking New Year's—false joy and excessive consumption masking a host of anxieties and uncertainties. When will the economy recover? Will there be another war in 1992 as in 1990 and 1991? Will we have jobs by the year's end? Where is our country going wrong? Perplexing questions indeed! Where does one go for the truth? Who possesses enough authority that one can believe and trust and follow?

Mark, the author of the second Gospel, seems to have understood the need for authority that all of us possess. In the very first chapter, he states unequivocally that his Gospel is the Gospel of Jesus, which is the Gospel of God. God, then, is author, and God is the final authority. We can believe in this authority; we can trust it, follow it, and live it. God never lies to us; never breaks a promise. The culture claims authority, as Our Way of Life; politicians claim it; so do educators, religious leaders, lawyers and parents. But their authority is under judgment by the Word of God, by its truth, love,and justice.

Let's take an example. No Gospel teaching better exemplifies being different, being Christian, than the Parable of the Good Samaritan in Luke's Gospel. You know the setting. A Scribe, or scholar of the law, "tests" Jesus—tries to get him to say something unorthodox—by asking how to inherit eternal life. Jesus in turn, tests the Scribe, asking him how he reads his own law. At this, the Scribe quotes the two great commandments of love of God and love of neighbor. For that, Jesus commends him saying: "You have answered correctly. Do this and you will live." (10:28)

The text continues: "But because he wished to justify himself, he said to Jesus, 'And who is my neighbor?' Jesus replied. 'A man fell victim to robbers as he went down from Jerusalem to Jericho. They stripped and beat him and went off leaving him half dead. A priest happened to be going down that road, but when he saw him, he passed by on the opposite side. Likewise a Levite came to the place, and when he saw him, he passed by on the opposite side. But a Samaritan traveler who came upon him was moved with compassion at the sight. He approached the victim, poured oil and wine over his wounds and bandaged them. Then he lifted him up on his own animal, took him to an inn and cared for him. The next day he took out two silver coins and gave them to the innkeeper with the instruction: "Take care of him. If you spend more than what I have given you, I shall repay you on my way back." Which of these three, in your opinion, was neighbor to the robber's victim?' He answered: 'The one who treated him with mercy.' Jesus said to him: 'Go and do likewise!' "

Let me review some history behind this teaching. The Jews and Samaritans were bitter enemies—the Samaritans considered as schismatics— accepting only the first five books of the Bible and rejecting both the prophets and the centrality of the Jewish Temple in Jerusalem. About one hundred years before Christ, the Jewish high priest had destroyed the Samaritan Temple on Mt. Gerizim.

The Samaritan, then, in Jesus' story, saved the life of an enemy after two Jews, a priest and a Levite, passed by on the opposite side. (The text suggests that both crossed the road to go by the victim, half dead as he was.) He saved the life of one who, in all probability, would destroy him if the chance arose.

The conclusion drawn is inescapable and astounding even to us, nearly 2,000 years later. Jesus identifies the neighbor as enemy. When we love our neighbor as ourselves, the enemy is included. Otherwise, we do not truly love ourselves—the love we withhold from the enemy we withhold from ourselves and from God.

Terry Anderson, the American journalist freed December 5 after seven years as a hostage, candidly related that he bore his jailers no ill will. "As a Christian," he said, "I am required to forgive. And I am determined to forgive!"

In my own case, I remember May 1945, when I came close to shooting two German prisoners of war who happened to be Waffen SS, Hitler's elite bodyguard troops. They stared at us arrogantly and hatefully and cursed us Americans in German as we slowly passed them at a railroad siding, a few days after the German surrender in May 1945. They were unarmed, I was armed, an officer of the victorious American Army—and I could hardly stomach their hatred and hostility. I very nearly shot them, knowing at the time that if I had, a mere tap on the wrist would result as punishment. They were SS scum, unworthy to live. And I was a victor, with the right to shoot them or let them live.

I have come from that level of brutalization as a young infantry officer to today, and the certainty that my relationship to an enemy is precisely my relationship to God. It makes no difference if the enemy has truly harmed me or attempted to kill me—or if the government has picked my enemy—a Communist, Arab, Cuban, North Korean, Libyan. No difference whatsoever. My enemy might be artificial or real—he or she still bears the image of God and what I do to them I do to God.

And so Matthew's Sermon on the Mount has it: "You have heard that it was said: 'You shall love your neighbor and hate your enemy!' But I say to you, love your enemies and pray for those who persecute you, that you may be children of your heavenly Parent, for she makes her sun rise on the bad and the good, and causes rain to fall on the just and the unjust. For if you love those who love you, what recompense will you have? Do not the tax collectors do the same? And if you greet your sisters and brothers only, what is unusual about that? Do not the pagans do the same? So be perfect, just as your heavenly Parent is perfect." (Matt 5:43ff)

Note the authority with which Jesus speaks; he uses the imperative mood to issue a command. He does the same in John's Gospel—"This is my commandment: love one another as I love you. No one has greater love than this—to lay down one's life for one's friends. You are my friends if you do what I command you." (John 15:12)

It is curious that we obey commands from nearly every source—parents, educators, military—except from God. Yet as Paul says—Christ offered his life for us when we were yet enemies of God (Rom. 5:8)—in the hope that such profound love might evoke a response of loving one another.

So much for being different—being Christian according to the Word of God. But there is another aspect to this unconditional love that we need to explore, one that is at the core of being different, being Christian. That is to say, most of us can truthfully say: "I don't hate this one or that one who has abused or injured me. I wish them nothing ill; I will not retaliate in kind." And indeed, we will not retaliate in kind, even given the opportunity. To that degree, we love our enemies.

But what if our enemy is endangered unjustly—what if they are vilified, or beaten, robbed, or terrorized? What if ethnics or nationals declared enemy by our government are bombed, poisoned, slaughtered? Like the Iraqis, like the Panamanians before them? Iraqi casualties—mostly children, elderly, and infirm these days—may number half a million before the infrastructure is restored. What does love of enemies involve there?

We must protect them nonviolently from abuse or destruction—that much is clear. We must interpose ourselves between the unjust aggressor and the victim, according to the Gospel, or nonviolent philosophy, or international law. Short of doing this, justice is lacking, love is an illusion, and human reconciliation is impossible.

While in federal prison, I witnessed a French-Canadian drug dealer being twice assaulted by a band of his clients who had not gotten their regular fix of heroin from him. They not only craved the drug and were in desperate shape without it—but they feared he had stopped dealing and had gone to the prison authorities. After the second assault, they left him with a fractured skull and near death. I watched both assaults, utterly unprepared to do anything.

During the Iraqi war, my course was more clear—constant resistance at the White House, Pentagon, and Department of Energy, culminated in a Plowshares witness aboard the USS *Gettysburg,* a new missile cruiser at the Bath Iron Works in Bath, Maine. Five resisters boarded the *Gettysburg* to disarm the cruise missile launch systems there—because disarmament was a Gospel imperative, and because we had to protect the innocent of Iraq from our military machine.

THE CURSE OF WAR

We have talked about the teaching and example of Christ, who went to the shameful and agonizing death of a criminal rather than pick up a sword. "Put your sword back into its place," he told Peter. "All who live by the sword will die by it." (Matthew 26:52)

So it is that the Gospel provides a standard of interpretation—a vision of life by which to interpret and to confront the works of death. We must, in fact, speak the Word of God to that which threatens humankind most—modern war dominated by the bomb.

Putting it differently—a friend of mine, who was a noteworthy theologian, asserted that he read but two works—the Bible and the *New York Times*. The Word of God analyzed for him the day's events, charging him also with responsibility for them.

Let's take a brief look, then, at the bomb and the reality of modern war, so that we may join them in our lives, becoming a disarmed follower of Jesus Christ.

Sidney Lens once wrote that splitting the atom for war was the greatest single tragedy to befall humankind in its entire history. He then went into particulars—greater in its destructiveness than all the natural catastrophes—floods, tornadoes, earthquakes, volcanic eruptions—disasters causing deaths in the hundreds of millions. Greater than the purges, decimations, genocides of the tyrants of the ages—Attila the Hun, Genghis Khan, Tamerlane, Hitler, Stalin. Greater than all of these, even when combined with natural disasters.

Lens wrote as he did because he knew—scientists today are verifying what he knew—that even if the bomb were never used again in warfare, we have poisoned the planet in developing and deploying it, perhaps terminally. I repeat, we have perhaps gone into a slow suicide of our species in developing and deploying the bomb.

Doctors I know from Physicians for Social Responsibility are now saying what they didn't dare say two years ago—that cancer has reached epidemic proportions globally, and that most of it comes from military-related toxins. That is to say, the disease of spirit which, in the case of most Americans, allowed without a murmur the development, deployment, and use of the bomb has now expanded into grievous physical disease as well. Dr. Rosalie Bertell, an internationally known geneticist, says that the first evidence of species-cide is a growing number of brain-damaged and weakened children who will need extraordinary attention and care, just to help them survive. (In Vietnam—CBU's require five to care for one.)

In an oddly perverse fashion, the bomb has driven us back to the Bible, and has re-taught us the Sermon on the Mount. At the center of the Christian life is the commandment: "Thou shalt not kill!" and its affirmation: "Love your enemies!" These two are restatements of justice and love, and of the nonviolence of Christ.

American Christians—even like yourselves—need to take a firm public stand against killing—killing in war, killing from Death Row, killing the elderly and unborn. Such a stand could save the planet and its people from war and poison, and could bring humankind to rebirth into the kin-dom of God, the nonviolence and peace of Christ in '92.

A protest in Washington.

Philip Berrigan at protest, April 19, 1976, holding daughter Frida.
Photo © by Bob Strawn, NC Photos. Copy supplied courtesy of Cornell
University, Carl A. Kroch Library, Division of Rare and Manuscript
Collections.

NINE

To Be or Not To Be: Beating Swords Into Plowshares

My non-cooperation harms no one, it is non-cooperation with evil, with an evil system, and not with the evil doer. My religion teaches me to love even an evil doer.

MAHATMA GANDHI

SEPTEMBER 9, 1980. Empty parking lots, shards of light, the patter of our footsteps climbing stairs. The plant spreading squidlike and ominously quiet. We race past a security guard, follow John Schuchardt to a door, a sign:

"This is a nondestructible testing room."

Inside, we find nose cones for Mark 12A warheads, the world's most advanced reentry vehicle for ICBMs. These warheads carry an atomic package of 336-350 kilotons; the Hiroshima bomb carried twelve and a half kilotons.

We go to work, beating swords into plowshares, ruining two Mark 12A nose cones before screaming security guards rush into the room. We lay our hammers on a table. No one resists. Our arms are yanked behind our backs, and we are shoved from the room. But not before I manage to pull a vial of blood from my back pocket and splash it over classified blueprints.

Our statement:

> General Electric is the fifth-leading producer of weaponry in the United States. It is draining $3 million a day from the public treasury. We have come to G.E. to beat swords into plowshares, and to expose the criminality of nuclear weaponry and corporate piracy. We want to expose the lethal lie spun by G.E. through its motto, "We bring good things to life."
>
> At G.E., darkness shuts out the light, death reigns over life. G.E. is helping the Pentagon prepare for atomic holocaust.

The Plowshares Eight—Daniel Berrigan, Philip Berrigan, Dean Hammer, Elmer Maas, Carl Kabat, Anne Montgomery, Molly Rush, John Schuchardt —have no illusions about the warfare state. Congressmen and women won't visit us in jail, the Pentagon isn't going to invite us over for a chat, the President will never call to ascertain our motives for invading G.E.'s plant at King of Prussia.

Nothing of that matters; we aren't attempting to reform or overthrow the government. We don't care who sits in the White House, or who walks the hallowed halls of Congress. The King of Prussia action, and Plowshare actions that will follow, are not attempts to offer an alternative policy to nuclear madness.

We pour our blood at G.E. in order to proclaim the sin of mass destruction. In the words of my brother Daniel, we are confronting the "spiritually insane." Confronting not with mere words, but through symbols. Our blood confronts the irrational, makes megadeath concrete, summons the warmakers to their senses.

The authorities react to us with apprehension, even hatred. We fill them with fear and dread, as though we carry a plague. We are locked up. An hour passes, then two. No one speaks to us. We are given no food or water.

Then we are herded into a van, driven back to the General Electric plant, and ordered to disembark. When we refuse, guards roll a wheelchair up to the door and slam one of our group onto the seat. One by one they force us to enter the plant. I ignore their threats. They decide not to drag me from the van.

The others are paraded—some walk, others are carried—before a gauntlet of angry G.E. employees. Bloodstained papers marked *Top*

Secret are scattered about the room. The culprits are identified, indicted, and convicted on the spot. The judge is rage, the jury hatred. Silence, bitter and betrayed, passes sentence.

When one of our attorneys, Charles Glackin, protests this treatment, the authorities throw him out of the plant.

We are returned to jail, stripped of our pants and shoes (the police want to hold them for evidence) and we are ushered again into the jail to await our fate. We know the wires to Washington are humming. We have invaded one of the government's atomic temples, offended the high priests of megadeath, poured blood over the National Security State's idols. Lord Nuke will exact revenge.

No food or water. Around 6:00 p.m., we are ushered, still in our stocking feet, before a judge who charges us with thirteen felony counts. Bail is set at $250,000 for six defendants. Dan and I are held without bond. The charges are ludicrous, the bail absurdly high. Our act of disarmament harmed no one. We scattered our blood on an evil system, not on the men and women who work at G.E. We beat on nose cones, not human beings.

We were kept in the Montgomery County jail, a rather decrepit place offering fairly good food. In time, we were able to settle together. John Schuchardt, Elmer Maas, and I in one cell, Carl Kabat directly across the hall. So we could communicate, and we kept very busy.

John and a jail house lawyer were soon writing legal briefs for prisoners who wanted to plea bargain. Most had been picked up on minor offenses like violating parole, then charged with numerous offenses. Frightened, lacking money, family support, or legal advice, they were overwhelmed by the court's machinations. They copped a plea and were sent to Graterford penitentiary.

Directly across the street from the jail sat the Montgomery County courthouse, a bastion of assembly-line justice. Yawning bailiffs led prisoners into court, bored judges passed sentence, cowed prisoners were handcuffed and taken away. The corrupt machinery of conviction spun its wheels, grinding the poor into submission.

John Schuchardt and the jail house lawyer worked hard to challenge this procedure. They urged prisoners not to plead guilty when, in fact, many of them were innocent. This alarmed the conviction mill across the street, which operated on the assumption that inmates should accept their fate, cop a plea, go willingly to prison. Innocence or guilt was irrelevant. Justice must prevail.

Daniel Berrigan, Anne Montgomery, Dean Hammer, and Molly Rush agreed to accept bail in order to organize support and defense committees for the Plowshare Eight. Outstanding defense committees were organized in places like Pittsburgh, Norristown, Philadelphia, New York City, and Baltimore. We shortly enjoyed a volume of support that went far beyond expectations.

Meanwhile, John Schuchardt's work on behalf of jail inmates was upsetting the conviction mill. Prisoners were pleading innocent, refusing to cop pleas, demanding their Constitutional rights. The courthouse sent messengers across the street to make us an offer. We could leave jail on our own recognizance, no bail required. A promise to show up for trial would suffice.

A rather remarkable offer. Five months before, the government refused to set bail; now, it was offering to release me, and other King of Prussia defendants, with absolutely no bail.

We turned this offer down, stating our intention to remain behind bars until our trial. Desperate to see us leave, the court ordered our jailers to kick us out; to literally eject us. That was the first of two occasions when I've been tossed not in, but out of jail.

We came to trial in April of 1981 before Samuel Salus III, a judge so inept and incompetent that his own associates had considered disbarring him. He was absolutely one of the worst judges I have ever encountered.

Our attorneys were Ramsey Clark, Charles Glackin, and Michael Shields. All dear friends who served us well.

We were familiar with, and had no illusions about, the judicial system. We weren't expecting to find justice in Judge Salus's courtroom. The judge perched on his throne, his black robe swollen with importance. And why not? He understood the game being played out in that room. He was sworn to protect the empire, regardless of what his masters might be doing, or planning to do, to all of creation. He was sworn to crush the weak on behalf of the powerful. He was there not to arbitrate justice, but to perpetuate violence.

Salus ranted and threatened, charged us with contempt of court, hurled invective and insult at us. We tried to talk about the necessity defense, which was not allowed in this trial, and would not be allowed in subsequent trials of Plowshare activists.

That the criminal conduct of which the defendants stand accused was taken to prevent a greater harm to themselves or others, which was imminent.

That there was no effective legal alternative method or course of action available to them that could be taken to avert this so-called harm.

That there was a direct causal relationship between the criminal conduct taken and the avoidance of the alleged harm.

In other words, if a house full of children is burning it is necessary to break down the door to rescue them. This, in essence, is the necessity defense.

In the Plowshare Eight trial, and future Plowshare trials, the government refused to allow the necessity defense, arguing that we could not prove that nuclear war was imminent. We explained that nuclear war could happen at any time. It was imminent because the government was designing, building, and deploying nuclear weapons. It was imminent because our air, water, and food supply were being poisoned with radioactive isotopes; because atomic testing had already killed millions of people worldwide.

We talked about the International Tribunal's judgment at Nuremberg, which states:

Individuals have international duties which transcend the national obligations of obedience imposed by the individual state. He who violates the laws of war cannot obtain immunity while acting in pursuance of the authority of the state if the state in authorizing action moves outside its competence under international law.

The Nuremberg and Tokyo trials are important because they established new guidelines for individual responsibility. Moreover, their conclusions are quite clear: Anyone with knowledge of crimes of state has a responsibility to prevent these crimes. People do not, indeed must not, follow orders that will lead to indiscriminate killing.

We talked about international treaties which prohibit nations from preparing for wars of mass destruction. We told the court that, according to the United States Constitution, these treaties supersede federal or local law. We were not talking about theory, and we were not expressing our opinion. We were talking about law that federal judges resist, continually overlook, nullify, and sweep into the trash bin.

We talked about God's law, which supersedes state and international statues. And we declared that all weapons, nuclear and conventional, reflect the spirit of murder, rather than of hope.

"Nuclear warfare," Judge Salus replied, "is not on trial here, you are."

At one point, we walked out on the farce, leaving Salus to fume. We returned to General Electric's plant number nine at King of Prussia and attempted to continue our civil disobedience there. Bishop Parilla from Puerto Rico, an outstanding resister, accompanied us, but guards kept us outside. The next day, we boycotted the court again, returning to plant number nine where sheriff's deputies arrested us.

In Great Britain and Northern Ireland, IRA defendants would often show their contempt for corrupt court proceedings by turning their backs on judges. After many futile, frustrating, humiliating days, we turned our backs on Judge Salus. He ranted and threatened; we ignored him.

The state has death as its *modus vivendi,* while a Plowshare action insists on the primacy and sacredness of life. A Plowshare action states that we are all sisters and brothers, one race, one people, one family. The scripture says, "One royal priesthood." That's what God made us, what we are attempting to realize through our lives. A disarmament action states the truth, makes it incarnate, makes it real.

Life will always conquer death, as typified by our Lord's resurrection. Sooner or later, life will prevail and disarmament will come about.

Several of the jury were highly sympathetic to us. One man, an auto mechanic, was apparently on the verge of acquitting us, but voted "guilty" instead. Later, he was attacked and beaten for expressing his sympathy with us. We turned our backs on the jury when it brought in a verdict of guilty.

Like other judges who presided over Plowshare cases, Salus made it difficult, if not impossible, for the jury to rule on the merits of our arguments. He told them, as his colleagues would tell other Plowshare juries, that citizens have no standing to invoke international law in relation to foreign policy. Whether the government was planning to kill hundreds of millions of people, a clear violation of international law, was not the issue. The Nuremberg principles were not the issue. Testimony by experts in the field of international law, scientists who had worked on atomic weapons, theologians, and historians, must be disregarded. The Gospels and the Word of God must be ignored.

The defendants had broken the law, damaged property; that alone mattered, was the only issue the jury should consider when deciding guilt or innocence. By narrowing their instructions to the jury, judges stand the Nuremberg principles on their head, arguing that citizens are *obligated* to obey the state, even when its leaders are planning mass murder.

There have been cases, though not Plowshare actions, where a judge was willing to acknowledge that international law is binding on the United States. For example, when twenty-two people were arrested for blocking the entrance to the Great Lakes Naval Training Center in Wake Forest, Illinois, the presiding judge instructed the jury that:

> The use or threat of use of nuclear weapons is a war crime or an attempted war crime because such use would violate international law by causing unnecessary suffering, failure to distinguish between combatants and noncombatants, and poisoning targets by radiation.

In another case, the *United States v. Laforge and Katt,* the presiding judge, Miles Lord, sentenced defendants to six months in jail, suspended if they agreed to probation. In instructing the jury, Judge Lord asked:

> Can it be that those of us who build weapons to kill are engaged in a more sanctified endeavor than those who would counsel moderation and mediation as an alternative method of settling disputes? . . . I would here, in this instance, attempt in some way to force the government . . . to remove the halo—which it seems to hold over any device which can kill—and, instead, to place thereon a shroud, a shroud of death, destruction, mutilation, disease, and debilitation.

These are exceptions. Judges in Plowshare trials have steadfastly disallowed "jury nullification," warning jurors they must not use their consciences to decide guilt or innocence, they must not use their individual judgment, and they must decide innocence or guilt solely on very narrow, circumscribed (i.e., the judge's) interpretations of the law.

We were convicted of burglary, conspiracy, and criminal mischief, and Judge Salus sentenced Daniel and me to serve 3–10 years in prison. Other defendants received shorter sentences. We weren't surprised. Montgomery prosecutors pursued our case with great vigor, the judge was biased and incompetent, and the jury felt it had to follow Judge Salus's instructions.

We might even have been rather grateful for the outcome. This was the first act of disarmament since the Cold War began, a direct challenge to Lord Nuke's authority. We hardly expected that our message—in the name of God and the human family, the arms race must end—would be well received. The National Security State had shown its contempt for the ecology in countless ways. The Atomic Energy Commission had been concealing for years the effects of radiation on human beings. Downwind from Nevada test sites, people were dying slowly and painfully from radiation exposure. Plutonium was escaping from Rocky Flats, Colorado. Drums of radioactive material were leaking into the Columbia River. Fifty thousand radioactive waste sites were scattered across America, and no one knew how many were leaking into the water supply of millions.

We could hardly expect compassion from a government that would deceive and poison its own people.

Elizabeth McAlister, in support of these early Plowshare actions, decided it was time for her to act. With her characteristic purpose and clarity, she set about helping gather a community, and eventually seven remarkable people came together to explore nonviolence, community, and another Plowshare action.

Before every action, Plowshare activists grapple with their doubts. Fear speaks to us, attempting to beguile us with the many rewards of silence. Just acquiesce, says fear, and things will be fine. Don't rock the boat. Don't upset the apple cart. Play it safe. Accept a life of quiet desperation.

In the Gospels, Jesus exhorts His disciples to transcend their fears. He encourages them to leave status, security, friends, and family behind. To embrace the world, with all its pain, dangers, and contradictions. To live in community, serve the poor, challenge injustice.

We can't deny our fears, any more than we can ignore the poverty in our neighborhood. But fear need not dominate our lives.

Indeed, weapons of mass destruction express a deep human terror, a desperate, failed effort to conquer human fear.

Our critics say that attacking atomic weapons with ballpeen hammers is an act of violence. Destroying property, they insist, is a form of violence. At best, it is a curious argument, one I've heard many times before. Warheads whose sole purpose is to vaporize cities are hardly to be thought legitimate property. Bombs that indiscriminately murder millions of men, women, and children are not "property."

The most unrepentant Nazi would call Auschwitz "proper." The most recalcitrant anti-Semite would suggest that the gas chambers at Buchenwald were "proper." Why, then, do we make supersonic bombers and fast-track submarines into idols, insisting that they are "proper?"

Liz knew that she and her friends might well be entering a "deadly force" area, where guards were under orders to shoot intruders. In fact, Liz was "shot" when the group role-played a walk into Griffiss Air Force Base.

Liz spent time praying, deep-breathing, being still. She dreaded being taken from her children. She loved tucking the kids into bed, reading them to sleep and, hearing their rhythmic sighs, joining friends in the kitchen for a bedtime snack. She might well spend years in a penitentiary far from her children, unable to snuggle with them at night, to hear their happy chirping in the morning.

She also understood that, like the raids on draft boards during the Vietnam War, Plowshare actions provoke controversy, stir anger and condemnation. We pour our blood to symbolize the death of innocent human beings. But our actions are meant to be more than symbolic. We pound on bombers and submarines with hammers; intending to damage and, if able, literally to disarm them.

At Jonah House, our faith in God helps us control our fear. We are saying no to our government's atrocious war-making. We are trying to be just; the effort flows from God's enjoining justice upon us, and our knowing that God is just. Faith in God, and in the ultimate goodness of other human beings, helps us control our fears.

Our resistance doesn't stem from self-interest or personal gain. We are not hoping to win theological accolades or spiritual promotions. And yet we are certain that we could not be doing anything more important. We go forward though in fear and trembling.

Shortly before the Griffiss action, one network aired "The Day After," a film in which nuclear missiles are launched. Farmers, housewives, children, look toward the sky, knowing they have only a few hours to live. In one very poignant scene, a woman frantically cleans house. She straightens the curtains and carefully makes the beds, determined to deny the impending disaster.

Liz and I watched "The Day After" with our children. And like millions of others who saw this film, the children were upset. We listened to their concerns, and told them that we didn't want the bombs to go off. As parents, we had a responsibility to see that that didn't happen. We told them that their mother might spend time in prison for acting to end this madness.

They understood and, I think, felt less fearful, knowing that Liz was going to resist the arms race. Frida and Jerry were willing to take this risk, even if it meant being away from their mother for a long time. Katie was two years old and, though a very bright child, couldn't fully understand. Her older brother and sister agreed to help her through the difficult separation from their mother.

THANKSGIVING DAY 1983. Elizabeth and six others climb through a barbed wire fence and walk into the Strategic Air Command base in Rome, New York. They enter a hanger where B-52s are waiting to be retrofitted with cruise missiles, small first-strike weapons designed to fly by sensors on automatic pilot. Each missile has the force of 15 Hiroshima bombs, and each B-52 carries 20 missiles.

The seven protesters—Liz, Dean Hammer, Clare Grady, Jackie Allen, Kathleen Rumpf, Vern Rossman, and Karl Smith—pour their own blood on the hangar floor and over planes, paste photos of children on the sides of bombers, and hammer on bomb bay doors. No one is at hand to arrest them and they walk onto the tarmac, unfurl a banner, pray and sing for nearly an hour.

A security guard approaches. It may be Thanksgiving, he says, but they must leave the base. They reply that he should look at Hangar 101, where they have just done a disarmament action. Soon they are kneeling in the mud, hands cuffed behind their backs, M-16s pointing at their heads. A bus arrives, and they are ushered inside, ordered not to talk, and given no food or water for the next eight hours. When Kathleen Rumpf breaks the silence, she is pulled from the bus and deposited, hands still cuffed behind her bank, in a pool of water.

At the Syracuse Public Safety building the resisters are stripped naked, ordered to squat and cough. Fingers and flashlights probe their body cavities. They are led to a shower, told to scrub clean, and given a rule book to memorize before they reach the cellblock. On the evening news, a reporter announces that "The maximum sentence for the Griffiss action could be 25 years."

One week before Christmas, Frida answers the phone; it is her mother. She is out of jail and will be home the next day. "You mean it's all over?" Frida asks "Oh sweetie," Liz says, "I wish it were, but I'm afraid this is really only the beginning."

We have a fine time between Christmas and the trial in May. Liz is home again, and though we know she will be leaving soon, each day is a celebration. Not with streamers and balloons, but through reflection and preparation for the trial. Liz will undoubtedly be sentenced to prison. She has acted out of love for her children, and for the children of the world. The National Security State considers her a dangerous person.

The Griffiss Plowshares defendants appeared before Judge Howard Munson, federal court judge, Northern District of New York. On behalf of the seven defendants, Liz presented an argument, "On Freedom of Religion and Contemporary Idolatry." She argued that nuclear weapons constitute a religion, and that this violates certain freedoms guaranteed by the Constitution. This, in part, is what she said to Judge Munson and the jury:

> We are dealing with serious constitutional issues—namely, the issue of a national religion having been established in our country in violation of the First Amendment. The religion of national sovereignty or nuclearism is alive and flourishing, and its existence, its

pre-eminence, its rituals, gods, priests, and high priests make serious encroachments on all of us. In fact—and this is the second part of our argument—violating our freedom of religion. This state religion not only compels acts that are prohibited by the laws of God but the state religion itself prohibits the free exercise of religion. The state religion compels a quality of loyalty focused on our acceptance of the existence of nuclear weapons as a necessity. Weapons we are expected to pay for, adulate, thank God for, become sacred objects of worship. And such worship is prohibited by the laws of God. . . .

Nuclearism is the ultimate fundamentalism of our time. Above all, this is the idolatry against which we stand and because of which we stand in this court. And the modern state is the child of the nuclearist religion. In the years since 1945, the modern state has moved steadily in more and more authoritarian directions. The process was subtle. Leaders who insisted that the major stake in international conflict was the fate of democracy were the very ones who steadily eroded democratic content in the name of 'National Security.' Legally, we have witnessed a constitutional antipathy to standing armies give way to an expanding, permanent military establishment with the Pentagon as the cathedral of the nuclearist religion. We have seen the Executive Branch claim privileges to keep national security information secret without any correction from the judiciary. Judge Munson, this nuclear, national-security state is a new, as yet largely unanalyzed phenomenon in the long history of political forms and of civil religions.

Being constantly ready to commit the nation and the planet to a war of annihilation in a matter of minutes created a variety of structural necessities that contradict the spirit and substance of democratic government: secrecy, lack of accountability, permanent emergency, concentration of authority, peacetime militarism, plus an extensive apparatus of state intelligence and police.

Quoting Richard Falk and Robert Lifton, *Indefensible Weapons: The Political and Psychological Case Against Nuclearism*, Liz informed the court that:

No king ever concentrated in his being such absolute authority over human destiny.

'The claim by fallible human beings to inflict total devastation for the sake of the national interests of any particular state is an acute variety of idolatry.

Liz talked about the government's decision to build the first hydrogen bomb. She explained that a "general advisory commission, headed by Oppenheimer in October 1949 came to a unanimous conclusion opposing its development. With that recommendation in hand, and on the basis of seven minutes of Cabinet-level discussion, President Truman announced the decision to go ahead with the H-bomb in January 1950."

No one asked the American people if they wanted to build another doomsday bomb. Congress didn't hold hearings to determine the need for the hydrogen bomb. President Truman and a few of his close associates escalated the arms race; the H-bomb was a *fait accompli*. Democracy was permanently undermined, and violence enshrined. The military gained a powerful voice in the bureaucracy. Moving on to new heights of aggression, the War Department was renamed the Defense Department.

"And, Judge Munson," Liz continued, "this has all been done 'legally,' and it amounts to a congressionally established religion. 'Congress will make *no law with respect to* the establishment of religion. . . .' Yet Congress has passed laws approving and funding the Manhattan Project, the continued arms race including the first strike arsenal of cruise, MX, Trident; the new scenario for winning a nuclear war. It requires that our taxes finance these projects. The bomb and nuclearism have been protected too by laws concerning national security, restrictions on free speech by government employees, loyalty and secrecy oaths required for security clearances. And now the laws of sabotage, laws that protect government property from destruction, and the conspiracy laws are used to punish and prosecute those who, from a perspective of conscience and Christian witness, would speak the truth, would resist the evil of nuclearism and the idolatry of nuclear violence. To so use these laws is to prohibit the free exercise of religion and violates the constitutional guarantee of this freedom."

Liz told Judge Munson that he had the power to contradict this trend. He could act as a check against the imperial power of the presidency, a check against the unconstitutional use of laws to prohibit and punish those who speak the truth, who resist the idolization of the bomb and carry out direct nonviolent acts of disarmament on the ultimate manifestation of the demonic idols—the weapons themselves.

"We submit," said Liz, "that you need to apply to the state the criteria of this court, even as we as Christians, need to apply to the state the criteria of Christianity. And there is a clear basis in Christian political thought from which our criteria can and must proceed."

The jury found all seven Griffiss Plowshare defendants guilty. Liz was sentenced to three years in prison. Things certainly could have been worse. Dan and I received 3-10 years for our part in the King of Prussia action. Judges in the Midwest would impose draconian sentences on Plowshare activists—up to eighteen years for pouring blood and pounding on a concrete missile silo. Comparatively speaking, a maximum of three years wasn't terrible, though it would mean long months of separation from community and family, particularly from her children.

This was a rough time for our children. They missed their mother very deeply, and yet they were struggling to understand the statement she was making: That through her action at Griffiss and her willingness to go to prison, Elizabeth was expressing her love not only for them, but for all of the world's children, who were threatened by this hideous arms race.

When Liz returned home from prison, we watched "A World Apart" with our children. This film is about a family's resistance against apartheid in South Africa. The mother of several young children is locked up for 90 days, released, and locked up for another 90 days. After the film, Jerry said, "Well, she was only in jail for 90 days. Mom was gone for 25 months."

We explained that, even though her mother didn't stay long in prison, this young girl had suffered. She was ostracized, even hated by her community. Jerry tried to understand, but his sense of loss—two years without his mother—prevented him from commiserating with the children in this film.

Elizabeth was confined at Alderson, a federal penitentiary for women about a six-hour drive from where we lived. Once a month I gathered food, kids, and friends, praying that our car wouldn't break down in the West Virginia mountains. Ellen Grady was living at Jonah House with her husband Pete DeMott, and they often came along, singing, telling the children stories, helping the miles fly by.

We spent weekends at a guest house for relatives of prisoners, and were able to see Liz on Friday night, on Saturday until three o'clock in the afternoon, and again on Sunday morning. Then we started home.

Precious time, with many hugs, kisses, and tears. Liz piggybacked the children about the prison grounds, rocking them in her arms, telling them giggle stories. During every visit, she spent time with each of the children alone while I played games with the other two. When the weather was good, we spread a blanket on the grass and ate a picnic lunch.

A number of Plowshare activists, Clare Grady, Jackie Allen and Kathleen Rumpf from the Griffiss action; Anne Montgomery and Christin Schmidt from the Pershing Plowshares; and Helen Woodson from the Silo Pruning action, were doing time in Alderson. They were living and working as a community, keeping the spirit of their resistance alive. We spent time with these noble women every visit, walking with them through the prison's grounds, playing games in a little yard off the visitors' room, giving and receiving lots of hugs.

They talked about life in Alderson. The majority of inmates were doing time for nonviolent drug-related crimes. There were no Pentagon contractors, CIA agents, or State Department operatives in Alderson. Many of the inmates were from urban war zones, most were poor; throw-away people who, after years behind bars, would return to throw-away neighborhoods.

Our children suffered terribly when these weekend visits ended. They wrapped themselves around Elizabeth, reluctant to let her go. One last kiss and they would leave their mother, knowing that another month must pass before they could see or touch her again. They wept, as children do, with a heart-breaking passion.

On the way home, things would calm down a bit. We didn't pretend. Their mother was in prison, and she would not be coming home soon. But she was alive, she was well, she loved her children, they loved her. And what a gift to see her, to hear her voice, to feel her warm spirit, even if only once a month. We were extraordinarily blessed to have Elizabeth as mother, wife, and friend.

We felt her presence with us in the car, she would be with us at bedtime, and in the morning around the breakfast table. The state might keep Elizabeth behind bars; it would never imprison her spirit.

Frida and Jerry were at a difficult age. To urge them to share their thoughts, we almost had to know what they were thinking. If we wanted to understand their feelings, we had to *know* what they felt. They lived in community, but weren't about to accept a substitute mother, although Frida did develop a close big-sister relationship with Ellen Grady. Jerry wouldn't do that.

Katie was only two and a half years old when Liz went to prison. She was cute, cuddly, and able to express her needs which were almost always met. For example, one night Ellen was cooking in the kitchen when three-year-old Katie rushed in. "I *need* you to read me a story right now," she cried. Not, "Could you, would you, or I want you" . . . but "I *need* you to read to me right now."

Everyone in the community gave Katie time, attention, and devotion. She was ill for quite some time while her mother was in prison, and Liz and I wondered if she might be going through a stage of mourning. But then she bounced back, cheerful, open, friendly and loving.

One morning, I was trying to get Katie ready to go to Head Start. She was running through the house, laughing, shouting, refusing to get dressed. I picked her up, sat her on the bed. "Katie," I said, "You're making it difficult not just for me, but for everyone in the community. You ought to think about them, not just yourself . . ."

She listened quietly for a while, then said:

"I know it must be very hard on you, daddy, having mommy in jail."

Liz and I have often laughed over this episode, marveling at a child's ability to turn the tables on adults.

Katie learned to read when she was three and a half. No one taught her. One afternoon, Ellen Grady found her turning the pages of a book. "Do you want to hear me read?" Katie asked. "Of course," said Ellen, astonished when Katie actually read the text.

Liz wrote to the children every day from prison, telling them stories, often accompanied with drawings, always about things she thought might interest them. Katie learned the alphabet through Liz's drawings: "A" for Noah's ark. "B" for bear. "C" for cat. The animals danced and sang for Katie, and the stories cheered our older children when they were feeling downcast.

These letters were bridges over loneliness and unhappiness, a place where Liz and the children could meet to share love and joy.

During our 26-year marriage, Liz and I have often been separated. Altogether, we've spent ten years apart while one of us was in prison. I've spent over seven years in jail, Liz about four. During all that time I never needed to question her moral, psychological, spiritual, emotional support. Nor need she question mine.

Our children grew up in a resistance community. Their parents and friends poured blood at the Pentagon, attempted to disarm airplanes and submarines, attacked missile sites with hammers. When we were tried and sentenced to prison, our children were in the courtroom. They listened to the prosecution, heard our testimony, and learned how the judicial system works.

We hid nothing from them; nor did we demand that they follow our path. Jonah House is a community, not a cult. Children are encouraged to think critically, to discuss and debate and come to their own conclusions. Resistance shows the violence and criminality of the American empire. Through resistance, our children learned to deconstruct the myths and counter the lies of their culture. They were empowered to distinguish between truth telling and obfuscation.

Were we to live our lives again, we would do very little differently. The Plowshare Eight convictions were appealed all the way to the Supreme Court, which refused to review the case, returning it to a lower court which set a resentencing date. Most of us were opposed to this litigation. The courts protected the rich and powerful. They perpetuated violence and injustice. They shielded weapons whose only purpose is to protect wealth and privilege. We were not in favor of keeping the case in the courts.

Our lawyers argued that this was one way of keeping the issue in the public domain. We consented to that, and allowed the case to drag on year after year. We were deeply moved by the dedication and friendship of our lawyers who were working *pro bono,* and would never receive monetary reward.

After nearly ten years of appeals, resentencing was set for April 10, 1990. Our friends at Brandywine organized a "Celebration of Hope" inside Philadelphia's University Lutheran Church, and it was a joy to see so many supporters and close friends there. I sat beside my brother Dan, my daughter Frida between us, wondering whether we might spend the rest of our lives in prison.

The celebration was part revival meeting, part wake. People were sorrowful. The sentence had been fragrantly unjust, our friends would miss us; no one likes seeing friends go to prison.

Gandhi, of course, would see all this in an entirely different way. He would say that it's a cause for rejoicing when people are going to prison for justice and peace. Genuine resistance means that we must be willing to accept the consequences for our actions, and that often means going to prison. We must enter prison, says Gandhi, the way a bridegroom enters a bridal chamber.

A final prayer, and we formed into a procession to General Electric's Aerospace division at 32nd and Chestnut. A young girl handed out white candles, which flickered in the wind. Dan, John Schuchardt, Molly Rush, and I stood at the entrance to G.E., holding a banner that read:

GENERAL ELECTRIC—THE CRIME IS HERE.

Security guards dashed in and out of the building, snapping polaroid photographs of us and our supporters. We sang and prayed for peace. In spite of the wind, most of the candles stayed lit.

The Pennsylvania Supreme Court may be the worst in the country. Nevertheless, it ruled that Judge Salus must be barred from our resentencing. His tantrums, blatant contempt for the Plowshare Eight, and most of all, his legal incompetence, apparently embarrassed a number of his colleagues

Each of the Plowshare Eight defendants gave a short statement before being resentenced for disarming two Mark 12A warheads. Ironically, on that same day and nearly at the same time, some of General Electric's executives were scheduled to go on trial for using graft and bribery to secure war contracts. The corporation itself had already been fined millions of dollars for cheating the government.

I focused my remarks on G.E.'s criminality, pointing out that this corporation claimed to be defending the United States, while it systematically cheated the country's taxpayers.

G.E. managed, through the power of money and influence, to postpone its own trial; thus avoiding the rather embarrassing predicament of being tried on the same day as the Plowshare Eight.

Robert Jay Lifton, professor of psychiatry at Yale University, appeared as an expert witness at our resentencing. He talked about examining survivors of the atomic bomb; people whose suffering, said Lifton, had numbed their psyches. They survived as the living dead.

Sister Anne Montgomery, who was doing time for taking part in the Thames River Plowshare action, was brought into court in handcuffs. She told the court that Ramsey Clark, Robert Jay Lifton, Howard Zinn, and other expert witnesses had helped her to better understand her opposition to the arms race. But her inspiration, she said, was neither international laws, nor history, but the Word of God, the call of the the prophets and Jesus to beat swords into plowshares.

When Judge Buckingham asked her if she planned to continue her actions after resentencing, Anne answered:

"Well, I *have* been upholding the law. But I hope there will be disarmament, so I won't have to."

I had mixed feelings when Judge Buckingham let us off with time served. General Electric had stated that it was highly unlikely we would return to their plant in King of Prussia. And, nine years after we invaded plant number nine, Buckingham stated there was no point in sentencing us to jail. But I am convinced that someone ordered the judge not to send us to prison.

Had we gone to prison, people would have noticed and perhaps been curious about the Plowshare movement. This way, we were taken out of the public's hearts and minds. We would be forgotten, and so too would G.E.'s war making, before the week ended.

Since our first plowshare action in September 1980, there have been fifty-two Plowshares actions in the United States, Europe, and Australia. Some have been disarmament efforts, most have been Plowshare actions, the distinction being that the Plowshares trace our inspiration to the second chapter of Isaiah, or the prophecy of Micah in the fourth chapter.

The Plowshare movement began, and it must continue, because the government has no intention of disarming its nuclear arsenal. Atomic weapons protect the rich and powerful. That's why they were designed, built, tested, and deployed. That's why the establishment is willing to threaten other countries, and our own people, with atomic annihilation.

The Biblical view of the law, the courts, and the state is profoundly radical. The Bible looks upon the state as a kind of rebellious artifice; it is spurious, a human creation in rebellion against God.

In the Old Testament, when the first state is proposed in the person of Saul, the first King of Israel, God tells the prophet Samuel that this project spells rejection of God. The state and its legislation are in rebellion against, or rejection of, God. Its courts are a human fabrication, cannot promote justice and peace; they are founded in violence, and legalize violence.

The state holds together through police power, against the citizenry.

The state, conceived in violence, and backed by violence, will never achieve true peace.

Plowshare activists maintain that there are two great historical commentaries on the law. First, Christ was condemned in accordance with law. The Judean leadership told Pilate that, according to their law, Jesus must die for declaring himself the son of God. Our Lord was completely innocent. He spent his life teaching the good, healing the sick, and feeding the hungry. He preached nonviolence, urging his followers to love their enemies.

Second, in our day the law legalizes nuclear weapons. The slaughter in Hiroshima and Nagasaki was legal. The spread of nuclear weapons has been legal. Atomic warfare that threatens to spawn a nuclear winter, destroying life on earth, is legal. The poisoning of millions of human beings, and the contamination of our air, food, and water supplies, is legal.

THE WORK OF HOLY WEEK AND BEYOND
THE NEW YEAR ONE MAY 1995
reject denial
put up the sword
identify with the victim
embrace the Cross
stand at its foot with the women

> *A little later, a bystander came over and said to Peter:*
> *"Surely you too are one of them; even your speech gives you*
> *away." At that he began to curse and to swear, "I do not know the*
> *man!" And immediately a cock crowed. (Mt. 26:73,74).*

In *American Ground Zero: The Secret Nuclear War,* Carole Gallagher wrote of "manic denial" in Nevada Test Site workers who were dying of cancer contracted from exposure to radioactive material. She interviewed several who frantically denied any connection between their work and illness, even as they lay dying.

By the same token, one could call Peter's three-fold denial of Christ "manic." Hours earlier, at the Last Supper, Peter had boasted of his allegiance to Christ. "Peter said to him, *"Even though I should have to die with you, I will not deny you."* (Matthew 26:35) It appears that Peter's fear was so profound, after the arrest of Christ that it erased memory and friendship, leaving him "manic" and paralyzed.

Peter is not alone in his denial—American Christians practice it habitually. We warm ourselves at the imperial fire as Christ is haled before a kangaroo court, keeping ourselves anonymous, maintaining a distance, unaware that the fire is a metaphor for nuclear lunacy, glorification of wealth, bloodshed for profit, and violence as a way of life. The fire burns us terribly, but we are unaware. The fire makes impossible any allegiance to Christ, any standing with him—makes everything impossible except denial.

The test *"Surely you are one of them"* might come from family or friends or strangers or from the people of power.

And the test might be couched in events like the atomizing of Hiroshima and Nagasaki, or genocide in Vietnam, or US leadership of the Doomsday Race, or the Desert Storm "turkey shoot," or extracting profit from our addiction to violence and war. *"Surely you are one of them"* terrifies us as it did Peter. Worse still, it finds us numb. *"I do not know the man"* takes the form of silence before power, paying for war with taxes, income from warmaking, or sacrificing our children to Mars.

Peter wanted a fellowship with Christ without consequence—official reprisal, ostracism, torture, execution. We want citizenship in the empire and its attendant goodies—a "deterrent" nuclear blanket and the "right" to consume seven times our share of the world's output, without consequences—war, ecological devastation, death in the Third and Fourth Worlds.

We Christians forget (if we ever learned) that attempts to redress real or imagined injustice by violent means are merely another exercise in denial—denial of God and her nonviolence toward us, denial of love of neighbor, denial of laws essential to our being. *"I do not know the man"* takes many forms, suffers many translations. But all end the same—a denial of our humanity, our daughtership or sonship in God.

The mid-April 1995 tragedy in Oklahoma City is another instance of denial—this time by fratricide. Whoever bombed the federal building there apparently sought revenge against the federal government, but ended up killing over 100 innocent people, many of them children. In this cowardly act, *"I do not know the man"* takes the form of punishing further those already victimized. One might call it a perfect formula for slavery, Americans turning against one another—Americans doing the oppressor's work.

A rough parallel now exists between two communities—the African-American and White Middle Class. The traditional oppression of African-Americans by dominant Whites drove blacks to turn against one another. Now, the same trend asserts itself among whites. The oppression of a non-representative government armed with thermonuclear weapons, a government which is patron of the 1% superrich controlling 40% of American wealth, a government which has infested the planet with war and weaponry as no other has—this increasingly fascist, terroristic apparatus is driving whites into the denial of fratricide. The American empire oppresses people everywhere, but especially its own. And they, with no clear perception of this complex, pervasive monolith called government, turn on one another—judges, road workers, forest service rangers, the innocent in Oklahoma City.

The drama of Christ's last days directed us during Holy Week to reject denial, to put up the sword, to identify with Christ the victim, to embrace the Cross, and to stand at its foot with the women. That led us to the sites of oppression—The World Bank on Holy Thursday, the Pentagon on Good Friday, and the White House on Holy Saturday.

At the World Bank, five of us—Carol Gilbert, Ardeth Platte, Art Laffin, Mike Walli and Phil Berrigan—poured blood on the exterior logo, then proceeded into the lobby, where we placed the picture of a famished child on the floor and anointed it with blood. We intended to expose the World Bank's nefarious structural adjustment schemes for the Third World, and its usurious gain of $5.00 for every $1.00 invested in poor countries. The police arrested us, charged us with a felony, and held us over 24 hours.

On Good Friday, we re-portrayed Jesus' Way of the Cross, from Pilate's court to Calvary. Liz McAlister and Jim Keane used blood—Liz along the Way and on the River Entrance steps; Jim on the War Department logo at the River Entrance. A harsh reminder was offered—the Pentagon whose task was more expedient ways of bloodshed and killing, must eventually bow to the nonviolent will of God.

At the White House on Holy Saturday we addressed Clinton's decision to continue the sanctions which have already caused the death of a half million Iraqi children. (Fatalities from Desert Storm and an aftermath of economic sanctions now exceed 800,000.) Kathy Shields, Rose Harper, Paul Magno, and Bill Frankel-Striet did street theater dramatizing the sanctions in a restricted zone on the White House sidewalk. When ordered to leave by the Park Police they refused and were arrested.

With periods of reflection, planning, acting, and evaluating, the assembled community sought to learn from Peter's denial, and to confront our own. Perhaps in time, those who claim the name Christian will learn how to say "NO!" to death and "YES!" to life. Instead of the other way around.

Philip Berrigan with Jeremy Scahill at Jonah House.

TEN

The Revolution Isn't Over:
Working for the Long Haul

*One does not make wars less likely by formulating rules of warfare.
War cannot be humanized. It can only be abolished.*
ALBERT EINSTEIN

In August 1980, I flew to Ireland with my brothers Daniel and Jerry. Dan had been to Ireland several times, and had contacts with people in the North. Jerry, a college professor, was working with H-Block Committee to raise money for the families of Republican prisoners. George McLaughlin, an Irishman living in Brooklyn, organized the trip. He had close contacts with the Republican movement, and he raised the money to pay our way.

We planned to visit IRA prisoners who were protesting against the British government's refusal to treat them as prisoners of war. These men and women, some of whom had been years in jail, were refusing to bathe or wear prison clothes. They smeared the walls of their cages with excrement, and wore only a blanket over their nakedness. Their excrement was symbolic, depicting British oppression as shit of the spirit.

If the British left Northern Ireland and reunification resulted, it would mean a neutral Ireland, denying bases and ports in case of war. Neither Britain nor the U.S. wanted that.

We were met at Shannon Airport by movement people from Dublin, most of them labor organizers and nationalists who supported the IRA's struggle to drive the British out of Ireland. In the South, we stayed at an Inn on the outskirts of Dublin, but in the North we were taken in by Republican families on Falls Road in Belfast. I spent several days with a family whose father had just been released from prison.

I spent only one week in Ireland, but learned a great deal about the civil war that broke out between supporters of the Free State and Nationalists, after the northern six counties were ceded to Great Britain in the Anglo-Irish treaty of 1921. I learned about the Orangemen who live in Ireland, but swear allegiance to England. And I learned why, after centuries of Anglo-Irish conflict, the British government was clinging to a piece of Ireland, and how our own government was conspiring with Britain.

I loved Ireland, where the people are truly gracious, friendly, and generous. I loved the roses that you find almost everywhere, the emerald fields, and the magnificent stone walls that, leaning at odd angles, seem to defy gravity. I particularly loved the feel of Dublin, and all the people we talked with on the streets. My sense was not of coming home. I'm an American, three generations removed from my Irish roots. Still, it was great to be there, if only for a short while.

Our tour of the North was supported by staff members of the IRA, young men and women who had been in jail for their opposition to British rule. All were deeply committed to the movement, and had suffered greatly for their beliefs. Wherever we traveled, our hosts introduced us as nonviolent revolutionaries. Ireland does not have a great tradition of nonviolence, and I suspect some people thought we were rather naive, unschooled. Our experience in the North helped us understand that victims of violent oppression find it difficult to appreciate nonviolence.

Authorities in Northern Ireland denied our requests to visit Long Kesh and the women's prison at Armagh. We returned home and the IRA prisoners continued their hunger strike. Bobby Sands, elected to Parliament during the hunger strike, starved to death. Nine other IRA prisoners, among them a draper's assistant, mechanic, upholsterer, and milkman, died before the strike ended.

The world watched in horror as one by one these men went blind, lost their hearing, and slipped into coma. Their families mounted bedside vigils, their supporters demonstrated, and Margaret Thatcher, the British prime minster, refused to acknowledge the status of Bobby Sands and his friends as prisoners of war. Even as the hunger strikers lay dying, in agonizing pain, she insisted on calling them criminals.

Power always blames its victims. Mrs. Thatcher was sworn to protect Britain's interests in Northern Ireland. False arrests, beatings, torture, assassination, these were not enough; she must transform Bobby Sands and the hunger strikers into monsters. Demagogues, megalomaniacs, dictators speak the same Orwellian language: *The state is powerful; therefore the state is good.*

Opponents of the state must be jailed, starved, tortured, and killed.

The Cold War is over, but the United States is not disarming. We are still spending 262 billion dollars per year on the military. This money must be financed, which means that the real costs are more like *one half trillion dollars* a year. The American people arc paying for a military which takes them as nuclear hostages. The enormous outlay offers no security.

The United States government initiated the arms race, led it for fifty years; and we continue to pay a terrible price for this folly.

Some Christians argue that a nuclear war would cleanse the planet of evil and bring about the Kingdom of God. This is the supreme insult to God. Is she responsible for cutting down our rain forests, poisoning our rivers, lakes, and oceans? Does she start wars, build concentration camps, and engage in ethnic cleansing? Did she design, test, and deploy nuclear weapons?

For Christians to argue from the Book of Revelation, or some other text, that it is God's will to purge the planet and end the world on the plain of Armageddon (whatever meaning that might have) is sheer delusion. Seldom is there an honest inquiry as to what the text says. It is easier to impose on the Scripture one's moral paralysis, hopelessness, and cultural lunacy.

In somewhat the same vein, Christians who reason this way seem driven by a death wish. They are dangerous, mixed up, and deluded. They operate under a veneer of Christianity, while they advocate, support, and pay taxes for the ultimate violence. To suggest that God's will is the destruction of the earth in order to cleanse it of evil, is pure insanity.

Critics of the Plowshare movement point out that we've been arrested countless times, and yet the United States refuses to disarm its arsenal of nuclear weapons. We've prayed and pleaded, poured our blood and pounded upon atomic weapons; and yet our government continues to kill people, here and abroad, in the name of peace and justice. Conclusion: our actions are useless. According to such critics, the outcome of conscientious activity must always be measurable and quantified: *A cup of success, a spoonful of failure. Two hours of success, one week of failure.* There must be a scoreboard to determine who is winning or losing.

Yet it is impossible, we maintain, to measure results stemming from integrity. We act because working in a nonviolent way for justice and peace is right, proper, essential. Moreover, our actions do make a difference in people's lives.

How many lives, how much of a difference? We can hardly measure that. But it is clear from the many friendships we've formed over the years that some are influenced, perhaps even inspired, by our nonviolent witness.

Moreover, by our refusal to be complicit with the war machine, we have avoided becoming a cog in the military-industrial gear box. The killing has not been, will never be, in our name. We leave it up to others to measure our success or failure.

But why am I so certain that the revolution isn't over? After all, I'm told, the 'sixties are dead, the left is in disarray, the peace movement is an anachronism. Revolutionaries are dinosaurs, extinct without our even knowing it.

My justification for nonviolent revolution stems from what I and other Plowshare activists believe is fact: that Christ embodies God; He is the image, as Paul says, of the invisible God. Looking upon Him, listening to Him, following Him, is to be in union with God.

This God is nonviolent to us. He allows His sun to shine upon the wicked and the good; allows the rain to fall upon the just and unjust. He is benign, loving, and compassionate. Never retaliatory, never revengeful. He never punishes us; we punish ourselves. When we sin, are unjust, and exploit one another, we punish ourselves.

It is the will of this God, the God of Jesus Christ, to humanize us to become children of God; we are daughters and sons, sisters and brothers of one another. And that's the biblical basis for nonviolent revolution. That's why we have it, and why it must continue throughout history.

The object is to return to God's order and design. That's the biblical vision. We could call it Eden reasserted, or the New Jerusalem, as does the Book of Revelation; we could call it Thomas More's *Utopia*. It's a very simple concept, and one toward which everyone can work. It means sisterhood and brotherhood. It means a new order of love, justice, and equality. An order where the elderly, children, women, the so-called "weak" members of society are most treasured. It's an order which reductively exists for the children.

These speculations are not illusions or abstractions. They are as concrete and practical as those who are living them. Hundreds of Americans, and many more around the world, realize that it is incumbent upon them to live this vision. They do this in community and through nonviolent resistance. Simply because this is God's will. God determines that the human family will become an order of justice and peace. The Bible is very clear about that; it's mentioned in the beatitudes of Matthew and Luke.

Armies will be disbanded and war outlawed. Cities will decline as people become less dependent on buying and selling. Economics will be revolutionized. Needs, rather than wants, will be paramount. In a capitalist society, economics defines life. In a just society, justice, love, caring, cooperation, will prevail. Politics and religion, the same thing, will strive for the regeneration of the human family.

In this new order, racism and sexism will disappear. Women, become equal partners with men, will no longer be objects of male lust. This vision, and this reality, will embrace community as the only human grouping not subject to domination, power, or violence.

The means for making this vision real is nonviolent direct action; civil disobedience, or divine obedience. Nonviolent direct action carries the truth of justice and love into the marketplace, where it confronts social, political, and economic injustice. It witnesses against the darkness of the way we treat one another.

Civil disobedience diminishes individual narcissism, egotism, and solipsism. It enables us to resist being cogs in the engine of oppression. Our choice is clear: We act to recreate the political order, or we solidify the old order of violence and death.

Civil disobedience unmasks and offers an alternative vision to injustice. For example, throwing blood on the Pentagon identifies those who refuse to shed blood. Likewise, those who scatter ashes at the War Department will never be complicit in designing, deploying, or testing nuclear weapons.

Jesus Christ practiced direct action, as did the Jewish prophets, and other nonviolent militants. Long before our Revolution, Americans resorted to direct action in struggles against injustice. In a capitalist society, there are no other means for representation, redress, or justice. To vote is political window dressing. It makes not the slightest political difference. If it did, the American people would soon lose this "right." The only means for fighting judicial corruption, corporate greed, worker exploitation, police brutality, and militarism is direct action. The Industrial Workers of the World ("Wobblies") were right. You don't vote with the ballot, you vote with your feet and with your life.

To restore God's reign, Christ used two approaches. He taught, and He acted. There was no variance between what he taught, and how He acted. His teaching and actions were subversive and revolutionary. They shook the foundations of the old order of injustice, violence, and death. John's Gospel teaches that Christ did only seven works; the seven works of recreation to match the seven works of creation recorded in the *Book of Genesis*. He showed himself as the lord of life and death.

Gandhi called Jesus the greatest nonviolent resister in history. The church pretends to be to be the church of Jesus Christ. Unfortunately, this is not the case. And that says some rather terrible things about the church; what it has concluded about itself, how it sides with the powers of this world, and how it has emasculated the gospel, reducing it to a painless common denominator.

The Christian who follows Jesus must be a nonviolent resister and revolutionary. There is no avoiding this truth. A Christian must take risks for the Kingdom of God, the New Jerusalem, the new sisterhood and brotherhood. Christians are obligated to resist collusion between church and state, and to fight *nonviolently* against tyranny, injustice, and oppression.

The church has been tainted by imperialism. It has learned to lie relative to the Scripture. The church distorts, suppresses, and refuses to preach the Scripture; the church has learned to lie about its own Scripture.

In the 'sixties, many people embraced violent revolution. I recall one conversation with young radicals who were leaving for the national Democratic convention in Chicago. They were armed with chains, and were preparing for street battles with the "pigs." Revolutionaries, they said, must fight violence with violence. I replied that the means we use to fight for justice *are* the ends. In our struggle for liberation, we must not adopt the oppressor's means; otherwise, we become the oppressor. Using the means of the oppressor is contradictory, counterproductive, and counter-revolutionary.

The Weathermen and women were determined revolutionaries; however, without realizing it, they were simpatico with the United States government. Like the empire they sought to bring down, they believed in violence. They dreamed of creating a better world from the ashes of the old, imperial, structure. They were not successful, nor could they ever be successful in their goal of overthrowing one of the most violent government's in history.

I pointed out to them that violent means never justify noble ends. They laughed at me.

Some years later, I met "Violence is as American as cherry pie" H. Rap Brown. A fiery speaker, SNCC organizer, and leader of the Black Panther Party, Brown spent the 'sixties fighting capitalism exploitation and racism. When we met, the Black Panther Party was in disarray. Some of the Party's leaders were dead, others were in and some had gone into exile.

Brown was trying to drive the drug dealers out of Harlem; telling them, unequivocally, that they had a choice: Stop dealing drugs or die. Concerned about losing the payoffs they received from pushers, the police warned Brown to halt his campaign. When he refused, the cops shot him in the stomach and dragged him down several flights of stairs, nearly killing him.

H. Rap Brown was a courageous man. I respected him, and shared his revolutionary views, but could not accept the means he and others were willing to use to achieve worthy ends.

The American revolution in the 18th century was really just a change in the palace guard. Very quickly, the colonists learned that they had to use measures against the violence of their own government. After the war, Continental army soldiers were given certificates for future redemption, only to discover that they desperately needed cash to pay their debts. In Massachusetts, the new Constitution of 1780 established that only the wealthy could hold public office. The legislature refused to issue paper money. Debt-ridden farmers, many of them war veterans, were hauled into court. Their cattle were sold to settle debts. They were driven from the land.

Armed rebellions broke out, the most famous of which was led by Daniel Shays, a veteran of Lexington, Bunker Hill, and Saratoga. Shays led more than seven hundred armed farmers to Springfield, Massachusetts, where they paraded through town. Samuel Adams, hero of the rebellion against the British, helped draw up a Riot Act, and a resolution suspending habeas corpus. Shays army was defeated, captured rebels put on trial, some of them sentenced to death. Two centuries have passed, but little has changed. The ruling elite still uses violence and intimidation to control the American people. Those who resist the state are vilified, hounded, jailed, and murdered. The FBI, CIA, and other agents of state power wage relentless war against those who resist the evil empire.

Nevertheless, the revolution isn't over.

I see no point in working within an evil system. Christ was never a reformer. He didn't advocate voting for one corrupt politician over another. He never urged people to embrace the state. He told parables about putting a patch on an old garment, which would soon unravel. He preached that we should dismantle, not attempt to patch, the state.

Some years ago, I had a conversation with Parren Mitchell, a black congressman from Baltimore. Mitchell had been a leader of the Black Caucus in the House of Representatives. His district consistently returned him to Congress by an 80 percent plurality. He worked very hard to serve his people, was a person of rare integrity, and was rarely contested when he ran for office.

Mitchell told me that he highly suspected the means he and others practiced in the House. He understood that Congress is an imperial legislative institution, and he refused to vote one nickel for the Pentagon. He was a man of integrity, and could not work within an institution that promoted violence in his own city and throughout the world.

Parren Mitchell's honest efforts were compromised by the violent means he was forced to practice in the House of Representatives. And that's why he left Congress.

I have been asked if I expect to receive the Nobel Peace Prize. On six occasions, friends in the United States and Europe have submitted my name, along with my brother Dan's, to the committee in Oslo, Norway. We have actually been nominated for the prize twice.

I doubt that Dan, Liz, or myself will ever receive the Nobel Peace Prize during our lifetime, or posthumously if it is awarded that way. During the Vietnam War we destroyed selective service records. Later, we symbolically disarmed first-strike weaponry. In other words, we damaged property. Our actions are audacious, starkly clear, and greeted with dread by anyone connected with officialdom, including, one supposes, the peace committee in Norway.

There is always a very slight possibility that we might receive this prize, but personally I'm not sure I could accept it. Despite the money connected with the prize, I don't see the point of being rewarded for doing one's responsible duty. That was Gandhi's view, and it makes perfect sense to me. In fact, I have never accepted a peace prize, and I don't expect that I will.

According to George Bush et al. the United States won the Cold War. History is dead; the New World Order is born. The United States must accept its destiny as *the* superpower, with a God-given obligation to reduce the world to its own Monopoly game, buying and selling countries, bullying governments, building weapons with which to destroy its enemies.

The Cold War may be over, but we cannot cease insisting on the sovereignty of God and the lordship of God over creation. The state is a usurper, attempting to seize sovereignty from God. Dan, Liz, myself, and many others like us, have clung to our Catholicism. In fact, we have arrived at a formula which might serve to define us:

We are Catholics who are trying to be Christians.

I have received many invitations to take an active role in another faith. I cling to my Catholic roots, because the church has given me far more than I've given the church; the sacraments and the scripture. It taught me when I was young, was faithful to me during dimwitted and rather retarded periods in my life. It has stayed with me, and I will stay with the church as long as I live, will be a witness for, and sometimes against, the church.

There's another, rather mysterious, reason for my remaining a Catholic. During the Vietnam War, and later when opposition to the struggle against nuclear weapons was resumed, around 1975, many of those who took risky actions, who suffered heavy punishment, and who stood for basic positions of disarmament, were Catholics.

People have ventured many reasons for this. One enlightened friend ventured that Catholics are more keenly aware of religious and life-giving symbols. Others say that the nuns taught us something about the cross of Jesus Christ, and led us in the stations of the cross, which helped implant a conviction; that we ought to be expending ourselves for the poor, and for those who needlessly suffer.

I've been asked about the archives on the Berrigans at Yale and Cornell Universities, and the many books and articles written about the Berrigan clan and Elizabeth McAlister. How would I like to be remembered? I don't think the question is especially important or critical. Perhaps I would like to be remembered as a Catholic who tried to be a Christian. A person who tried to embody the nonviolence of God, who attempted to stand for those who needlessly suffer; someone who endeavored to welcome and to understand the cross of Jesus Christ.

The 13th chapter of Revelation tells of a Sea Beast, the Beast of Empire. The beast has a number of heads, one of which receives a fatal wound. Empires receive these wounds, but they have incredible recuperative power; at times, they not only recover, but grow stronger than before.

In spite of its ability to recuperate from fatal wounds, the American empire cannot last. One of its near fatal wounds that seemed to heal was the war in Vietnam. Another was the Chinese revolution in the late 'forties. Still another was the military stalemate in Korea. The Vietnam War was the third Asian war the United States lost. And all of these were serious blows to the empire.

Becoming a debtor nation, due to outrageous military expenditures, was yet another blow to the empire. This happened around

1991, when the financial capital of the world shifted from New York to Tokyo. Still another fatal blow, which the empire has by no means acknowledged, is our unwillingness to disarm, our clinging to nuclear weapons. Paradoxically, this is a sign of consummate weakness rather than of strength.

Sooner or later the United States will have to revert from an empire to the status of a nation state. And from that point, it will grow even weaker, before it approaches the status of a just society. In his study of ancient Israeli kings after Saul, David, and Solomon, Jacques Ellul concludes that those who did not invest heavily in a powerful military, and sat on weak thrones, were just rulers.

The United States will become a just society when it loses power; when the empire declines and the consequent nation state weakens.

The greatest impediment to becoming a just society is that, in spite of all efforts, we citizens can not escape the influence of the empire. It directs our thoughts and our behavior; we act out its violence, racism, war-like belligerence, and discrimination against women.

And in this I confess the failures of myself and fellow resisters. We who live in community cannot escape the empire. In may ways we are empire; and resistance hardly transforms us into angels.

According to a University of South Carolina study, violence in America rose 42 percent during the Vietnam War. This is hardly surprising. Our leaders are lawless, so why not we? If the government threatens other countries with the bomb, why not threaten one another with handguns? If our leaders are raping the planet, why not rape our neighbors? Our leaders create a climate of fear and violence. Why do they appear shocked when Americans kill, rob, and maim one another?

When the bomb becomes an article of religious fervor, as it has in America, fundamentalism follows. Anyone who fails to meet the group's standards becomes the enemy. Minorities, immigrants, homosexuals, single parents, welfare mothers, are heretics. They must be denied jobs, refused public assistance, locked up in prisons. They must bow low to Lord Nuke, or face terrible consequences.

The Cold War has ended; yet the United States is secretly rearming; preparing to arm the heavens and build new first-strike weapons; to destroy the world in order to save it.

A nonviolent revolution might save us, but it is hard to be optimistic. Our country has the richest tradition of nonviolence in the world, yet we lack the vision and discipline to initiate a nonviolent revolution.

Why do so so many believe that the United States is a democracy? Why insist that we are the freest, richest, greatest country on earth, when in fact we are insecure, frightened, and desperately angry. Our government is crypto-fascist; the Contract on America is a fascist, not a conservative, document. The war on the poor is orchestrated by fascists. The so-called war on drugs expands police powers, undermines the Bill of Rights, *creates* drug barons, and enables the CIA to befriend traffickers like the Nicaraguan contras.

The bomb is a totalitarian measure, and war is our government's number one business. Unfortunately, most Americans do not realize that, in the guise of national security, their government has declared war on them.

Ronald Reagan laughed at the Constitution, calling it just a "piece of paper," his administration established facilities to imprison dissidents during "national emergencies," Secretary of State George Shultz lobbied for a 'pre-emptive strikes' bill that would enable him to list "known and suspected terrorists" within the United States who could be imprisoned or even killed by government agents.

We cling to the mythology of our glorious past, and reject the reality of our fear-ridden present. But as long as the government clings to the bomb, democracy will be undermined; in time, destroyed. We Americans have an almost obsessive need to embrace the illusion of freedom. We cannot see that the bomb makes all of us prisoners. Nor are we willing to admit that fear and freedom are incompatible. We fail to see the irony in our boast that we are *free* to build bombs, *free* to carry guns, and *free* live in walled-in communities.

The Bible says that hope is closely related to faith. One hopes because one believes. One believes in God's promises, in the ultimate goodness of human beings, in the redemption of Christ, in the advocacy of the holy spirit. One believes; therefore, one hopes. We can't live without hope. We need it as we need water and bread. And so one of the most precious gifts we can give others is to offer hope; to be a hopeful example, standing for life instead of death.

Gandhi said that everyone needs a scripture. We must have a sacred text; it could be Christian, Jewish, Hindu, Buddhist. It could be a philosophy of nonviolence. But everyone needs a text against which to measure life. If we deeply believe in our scripture, hope is generated and offered to others. And we renounce self pity, fear, hatred, or despair.

I'm not trying to simplify human interaction. People come and go at Jonah House. People leave the resistance movement. I've seen it happen many times, and I understand how difficult it is to resist the cultural pressures to give up.

How does one hang on? How does one keep the faith, avoid quitting, joining up, and being conscripted?

We work at hope, together, as a community. Without community, resistance is impossible. We gather from our community hope, strength, commitment, and the courage to continue.

Let me illustrate. One year after Catonsville, a group of anti-war activists—calling themselves the "Milwaukee 14"—were walking to the draft board complex when Jim Harney, a priest from Boston, suddenly lost the use of his legs. Paralyzed, unable to take another step, he called out for help. Harney wrapped his arms around friends' shoulders, and they carried him the six or eight blocks to the draft board. Once there, his paralysis lifted. He helped burn thousands of draft files, and waited to be arrested.

Father Harney understood that the raid was not his alone. He was bound to others by community, and this helped him break through his paralyzing fear.

My critics say that I must "love or leave" America. I have never considered becoming an expatriot. This is my country. I was born and raised here. The United States has fostered and nourished me. And even though the government does not represent the people, this country belongs to us.

People talk about taking the country back from the usurpers, but what does this mean? In the name of liberty and justice, Pat Buchanan and friends want to establish an Old Testament Theocracy. In their ideal world the state will not only be God's representative on earth; the state will *be* God. Persecuting the poor, abolishing Affirmative Action, building more prisons, executing more prisoners, expanding police powers, burning books, denying gay men and women jobs, fanning the fires of bigotry and hate, nourishing the addiction to war; all this will be an expression of God's will.

How anyone can claim to be a Christian and believe these things is beyond comprehension. The God of the so-called Christian Right is a God of hate, not love; revenge, not forgiveness; death, not life. Such a God is bigoted and spiteful, a misogynist who inflicts pain and misery on the human family.

The Christian Right's vision stems neither from the Bible nor the Constitution, but from the dark and frightened recesses of the human psyche.

As for myself, I continue to resist because there is no alternative. I will not join the establishment. That would be deeply repugnant to me. I intend to stay here, witnessing against violence and madness, obsession with property and glorification of privilege.

Plowshare activists go to jail in order to resist the empire. We are innocent, but there is no other way to make our statement. We make it publicly, in court, before the press and anyone who cares to listen. We do not choose to go to prison. That is the government's decision. We violate unjust laws, and take the consequences, whatever they may be. But our submission doesn't mean that we respect the corrupt judicial system. We go to prison for our nonviolent beliefs, not because we accept the empire's rules.

I remember one quotation from the Book of John, where Jesus says something like, "If they hate me, they will hate you also." The implication; if they do not hate you, you are not living the life you profess to live. That is, following me."

Two thousand years have passed, and Caesar reigns. The military occupies our country, a hierarchy of the rich and powerful controls the people's lives, taxing the poor, beating, jailing, killing, those who resist imperial policies.

For over a period of two thousand years, the Bible has been largely ignored or defiled. The life of Christ is not preached by the established church, and it is not lived by many Christians; not to be wondered that so many "Christians" despise the poor and support the military.

St. Paul called evil a "mystery." He used the expression "Mysterium iniquiatus," the mystery of iniquity. We may never understand why people hate, murder, become hyper-patriotic, militarized in their thinking, and addicted to the bomb. We may not understand the mystery, but we can offer a decent, just, and compassionate example.

I have very few regrets. I feel a measure of guilt for not playing a greater part in raising my children. Elizabeth McAlister is competent, capable, and deeply loves all children. She speaks to them on their level, in their language, and with a compassion they know is genuine.

At Atlantic Life Community retreats, bi-annual gatherings of Plowshare activists and their supporters, Liz organizes hikes in the woods, sets up tables where the children draw and paint, rents videos for them to watch, makes sure they have plenty of snacks. The children's laughter echoes through our workshops, sometimes drowning us out. We look up and Liz is playing ring around the rosy with a group of screaming children. When the weekend ends, she hugs and kisses them goodbye.

Liz has been the primary caregiver for our children, and I seldom feel need to contribute more. When Frida and Jerry are home, I study scripture with them, but for the rest, I leave the parenting to Liz.

Some years ago, I was approached by our superior general, who asked if I would be willing to visit Catholic installations, to offer creative ideas regarding the apostolate. I would share what I knew about nonviolence, using my experiences in the antiwar and civil rights movements to inspire Josephite priests.

I had just been released from jail, the Vietnam War was raging. After a little thought I turned the invitation down. My superior general was very decent about my refusal.

I'm not sure how I might respond to such an offer today. On the one hand, I would like a closer affiliation with my Society and with my friends in the Josephites; on the other hand, I'm rather protective of the freedom I have to resist, to go to jail, and to live in community. The church has lifted my excommunication. Nevertheless, I cannot operate officially because I'm a married priest.

Plowshare activists have been accused of being a small band of malcontents, living in scattered pockets of resistance. Of course, like many other critiques, this one is untrue. During the 'eighties, I visited Western Europe eight times. While there, I contacted Swedes, Germans, British, and Dutch activists. Some were planning a plowshare action, most have continued the struggle for disarmament.

We've kept in contact with these people; recently we hosted thirteen Swedes who were planning a plowshares action on their return home.

This is where we stand. For life over death. For peace instead of war. For justice rather than injustice. We continue our witness here in the United States, while others continue abroad.

On January 29, 1996, Jo Wilson, Lotta Kronlid, and Andrea Needham, calling themselves Women Disarming for Life and Justice-Seeds of Hope-East Timor Plowshares, entered the British Aerospace facility in Warton, England. They hammered on the radar cone and control-panel of Hawk 200, called friends and the press, and were arrested.

The disarmed plane was one of 24 aircraft Great Britain plans to sell to Indonesia, which is conducting a genocidal campaign against the people of East Timor. Thus far, Indonesia has killed 200,000 men, women, and children in East Timor.

The "Seeds of Hope" protesters have been charged with criminal damage and burglary, and British Aerospace is demanding 1,000,000 pounds (approximately $1,400,000) in restitution.

Closer to home, Amy Moose, Michele Naar-Obed, and Rich and Erin Sieber acted at the Newport News Shipyard. They hammered and poured blood on four of the vertical launching tubes of the fast-attack submarine, The USS Greenville. They hung pictures of Hiroshima and Nagasaki victims on the ship.

The four were charged with misdemeanor trespass and sentenced to a year in jail. But later the Commonwealth of Virginia dismissed charges against three of the defendants to make room for a federal indictment. In January, 1996, the United States government handed down a five-count indictment: destruction of government property; conspiracy to destroy government property; destruction of national defense material; conspiracy to destroy national defense material; and destruction of the fence at Newport News Shipyard that protects national defense material.

The government hopes to label these nonviolent resisters, as it has attempted to label other resisters in the past, as terrorists. Cumulatively, they face forty-five years in prison.

The Cold War may be over, but the empire shows no interest in pursuing peace. The empire sends its legions to faraway places, hoping to deceive the world, and most of all its own people, into believing its Orwellian fallacy that war is peace. Those who resist this psychotic litany will be marginalized, ridiculed, hauled into court and sentenced to prison.

Yet our voices will not be silenced. We pray that the empire will beat its swords into plowshares; that the God of love will replace Lord Nuke; that the cross will replace the sword.

During the past thirty years, I have been jailed repeatedly, participated in four Plowshare actions, and spent more than seven years in prison. My spirit is alive and well. I do not feel broken. As long as my health allows, I will beat swords into plowshares.

If enough Christians follow the gospel, they can bring any state to its knees. Such Christians are a biblical remnant. In the providence of God, they are the ones who keep the human race from destroying itself. Today, we have only a remnant of those who are deeply convicted of nonviolence, of community, and resistance to a criminal state.

The revolution isn't over. As long as there is poverty, violence, discrimination, militarism, and war, our struggle will continue.

IMPRISONMENT COULD HARDLY BE MORE TO THE POINT
National Catholic Reporter, **February 11, 1994**

I recall an intense discussion 10 years ago. The question in the air went something like this: How do we remain faithful to the gospel in a climate of nuclear terrorism, military interventions and public confusion and indifference? Around the circle, people had their say. Finally, a woman, legendary for her 30 years of antiwar resistance, for numerous demonstrations and jailings, offered this: "We must risk jail without, of course, seeking it. Then we must wonder the value of being there. As far as I can understand, things are that simple."

Our friend was confirming Gandhi's observations that "the truth seeker should go to jail even as a bridegroom enters the bridal chamber"; that "social betterment never comes from parliaments or pulpits, but from direct action in the streets, from the courts, jails and sometimes even the gallows." Or Dorothy Day's statement that "if Christians seek a better life for the poor and relief from the tyranny of nuclear weapons, they must fill up the jails."

Dorothy's "filling up the jails" is her translation of the nonviolent revolution of the gospel. One accepts jail as a consequence of resistance; then the jailed one reaps a paradoxical benefit. As Tom Lewis puts it, "I have to be free enough to go to jail."

"Filling up the jails" also clarifies the struggle, as St. Paul reminds us, not against flesh and blood but against principalities and powers. The struggle is for possession of our own soul and the souls of others. It is a bill of divorcement drawn up against false gods. It offers deliverance to the poor, something quite other than feeding and housing them. It pits the realm of God against the murderous deceits of the technocratic state. Its character, finally, is a quest for liberation. Paul again: "It was for freedom that Christ has set us free."

Christians of every age are confronted by the question of Christ: "And you—who do you say that I am?" Much depends on our answer, much more than we are commonly prepared to admit. And whether our image of Christ is the Suffering Servant, the Man of Sorrows or the one who refused the sword in favor of the cross, the same imperative follows on the answer, whatever form it takes:

"Follow me."

The "following" becomes the fundamental problem. He leads, and we so often renege. We are slow to follow Jesus in living the gospel and building community; slow to follow, resisting, as he resisted, illegitimate power; slow to follow into jail as he was jailed. Slow and then a halt. Follow him in torture and death?

I write this from jail. On Dec. 7, 1993, four of us—Lynn Frederickson, Jesuit Fr. John Dean, Bruce Friedrick and I—disarmed an F-15 fighter-bomber in North Carolina. The F-15 was the winged workhorse of the Iraqi war. It brought death to thousands. More, it is, as the jargon has it, "nuclear-capable."

In consequence of our crime, the government refuses to set bail. According to the judge, we are a "danger to the community." So in all likelihood, we will remain in jail until trial—and undoubtedly afterward.

From the standpoint of most, jail is irksome, boring and absurd. But we have another view. Jail for us is a way of subverting a society that needs more and more jails. Jail is a way of disarming a society that builds nuclear weapons and indulges in perpetual war-making. Jail unites us with the poor, confronting a society that manufactures destitution and homelessness. Jail is subversive of a society that in one way or another manages to shackle the conscience of even its favorites.

Mark declares at the beginning of his gospel that social change comes from "the wilderness." John the Baptizer emerges from that unlikely setting, as did Jesus. Today the "Wilderness" could well be translated as the ghettos and slums of our cities. Out of them emerges an unlikely hope, such spirits as Dorothy Day and the communities that continue to serve the destitute. "Wilderness" also includes the jails and prisons across the land; there resisters appeal to the hearts and minds of others, whether in or out, and testify against the criminality of public authority.

Let me describe briefly our present "housing." The Robeson County Jail is one of the worse ever. Dust thou art. We are lodged in a dustbin where it is all but impossible to obtain a book or change of clothing. Lynn did three weeks in solitary, unable to bear the heavy smoking of the women's cell block. She is now in a smoke-free block. We three men are blessed in being together for Bible reflection and good talk, weirdly isolated as we are from TV, the culture at top volume, at once violent and soporific.

No one of us likes jail. No one in right mind would seek it. But God's word and the strenuous work of community are sufficient for us. We transcend this pit of misery, we shrug, grin and bear it. In measure, we help humanize it.

Meantime, in the so-called real world, the Clinton administration sounds the war tocsin against North Korea. According to this august hypocritical exercise, the vast American nuclear arsenal and the considerable nuclear development of South Korea are equally beside the point.

What then is the point? A perennial worldwide search is on for that all but vanished species, a veritable Loch Ness monster, "the enemy." Purportedly, in some mirage or other, Cuba and Libya together with desolated Iraq have been sighted by the mad clairvoyants.

As for slavish concessions to the Pentagon, President Clinton outpaces former President Bush by a mile—in arms sales, fiscal support, new weapons systems and a belligerent ideology to match. The rich are reassured. The weapons are in place. The great Democratic hope has lately been hailed as the "best Republican in memory."

In this morally polluted atmosphere, we believe that imprisonment could hardly be more to the point. We shudder under the blows of a society permanently mobilized against peace. Duplicity, propaganda, media indifference, institutional betrayal mark our plight. Our people are confused and hopeless.

Let us not give up. Let us continue to nourish one another by consistent and prayerful presence at military installations, in courts and lockups.

Indeed, we need to be free enough to go to jail. We need to fill up the jails.

Nonviolent revolution will come out of the wilderness, as it always has.

And be assured, dear friends, one formidable wilderness today is an American prison.

Philip Berrigan, circa 1995.

Index